DISCARD Civic Center

THE **WHITE GUY** IN THE ROOM

A Political Memoir

THE **WHITE GUY** IN THE ROOM

A Political Memoir

DOUGLAS J. PATTON

Doug J Patton
The Patton Corporation
2120 L St. NW-Suite 305
Washington, D.C. 20006

Thewhiteguyintheroom@gmail.com

www.douglasjpatton.com

Library of Congress Catalog Card Number
ISBN: 978-0-9975284-0-4
Printed in the United States of America
First Edition
$26.95

Book jacket design by Rhonda Saunders, RS Graphx, Inc. and website design by John Allem.

THIS book is dedicated to three African Americans who played a valuable role in my life: Benny, James and Ted.

I met Benny when he was eleven years old; he was the first black kid I came to know personally. I never really knew his last name. He was cocky and sure of himself, but without a formal education. I was most impressed by his independence and confidence.

In my twenties, living on Capitol Hill, I befriended James Stewart, who was probably ten or eleven years old. He was streetwise, full of charm and ambition.

Ted Brown was murdered in 1968 on the streets of Cleveland, Ohio. He provided me tremendous insights into black-white relationships. He taught me to cast aside prejudice because he, somehow, always managed to find goodness in everyone. I think of him often.

From wildly different backgrounds, these three people conveyed to me friendship and understanding. They helped to expand my vision and helped me to achieve important aspects of my life's mission.

ACKNOWLEDGEMENTS

I want to thank Nancy, my wife of thirty-five years, for her patience and understanding during the writing of this book. She knew how important it was for me to share this narrative.

A very special thanks to my late parents, John and Alma; they tolerated, and generally supported my ventures, particularly in the civil rights arena. They felt all Americans should have equal opportunities and should be treated fairly. They also helped provide the foundation for my love affair with politics and the American democratic system of government.

David Rusk and Nick Carbone brought me deeper into the world of politics, especially the mission of empowering people of color.

I cannot count the contributions made by Jonetta Rose Barras; she offered constructive criticism as well as ideas and kept me focused.

I very much appreciate the work of Loran Randles and Joanne Anderson who made very important edits and recommendations. David Osterhout, a close and dear friend of more than 40 years, read my early first draft. I was relying on him to read the final version. Unfortunately, he passed suddenly in early 2014. He always provided encouragement.

My thanks to Colbert I. King, an opinion writer for *The Washington Post*, who offered comments and suggestions. Harry Jaffe, an author and editor with the "Washingtonian" magazine helped me make important connections. Bill Lucy, former Secretary Treasurer of the American Federation of State

County and Municipal Employees (AFSCME), Jerry Fitzgerald, former minority leader of the Iowa State House of Representatives, and Max Berry, my long time friend from Washington, D.C. all provided valuable recollections. Penny George, a neighbor and friend, and Barry Sussman, a former editor at the *Washington Post*, also offered invaluable contributions

A very special thanks to my friend of forty years, former District of Columbia Mayor and Council member Marion Barry, who encouraged me to write this book. Sadly, he did not live to see the final product; he died in 2014.

Many other friends gave me invaluable support and encouragement in undertaking this project; my thanks to all of them.

TABLE OF CONTENTS

INTRODUCTION

THERE always has been a perception in some segments of society that the struggle for black freedom and empowerment in America was a solo venture and that African Americans arrived at their place in the Twenty-first Century without any real assistance from whites. That perception doesn't tell the whole story, but it has helped fuel decades of divisions between blacks and whites. Even now, it underpins continued animosities and tensions. But consider the following facts: Many conductors of the Underground Railroad in the Nineteenth Century were white. The National Association for the Advancement of Colored People (NAACP) was launched in 1910 by a predominantly white group of citizens; only a sprinkling of blacks was there on that first day as founders. Seldom is mention made of the whites, many ordinary citizens, who were involved with the Rev. Martin Luther King, Jr. in the Southern Christian Leadership Conference (SCLC). Its counterpart, the Student Nonviolent Coordinating Council (SNCC), seen as the more militant of the two organizations, also had its share of white supporters. In fact, white women like Mary King, Constance Curry and Casey Hayden were inspired by the ideal of racial equality and played active roles in SNCC. Further, much of the financial backing for civil rights organizations came from concerned whites; they may not have placed their lives on the lines in the battlegrounds of the south, but they certainly opened their wallets.

Then, there were numerous individuals like myself and my friends, including Jerry Fitzgerald, Nick Carbone, Gerald Clark, Chuck Hoffman, Johnny Allem, and Max Berry, who were moved by a desire to make a difference. We directed our skills, talents and energies to help enhance black power, because in the long run, we believed that outcome strengthened America's power. A united country is far better than a fragmented one.

I wrote this book, in part, to commemorate those whites who operated in the background of local and national groups with little or no recognition as they helped African-Americans attain justice and equality in the political arena. While many of them were criticized as members of the population of whites denying or obstructing African American advancement, in reality they were allies of blacks fighting with and in support of their vision of a new America.

Some of those whites, like Andrew Goodman and Michael Schwerner, who were brutally murdered in Mississippi alongside African American James Chaney, are better known. Viola Greg Liuzzo, a housewife from Detroit, shot in 1965 by a Ku Klux Klansman in a passing car in Alabama, may also be a name that readily comes to mind. But how many remember these white contributors: William Lewis Moore, the Rev. Bruce Klunder, the Rev. James Reeb, Jonathan Myrick Daniels, Vernon Ferdinand Dahmer, and Juliette Hampton Morgan? Who remembers that Harold Ickes, who became deputy chief of staff to President William J. Clinton, was one of the many white volunteers who took part in the 1964 Freedom Summer in Mississippi? He was one of eighty individuals beaten by white southern racists. The assault on him resulted in the permanent loss of hearing in one ear.

There are tens of thousand of other whites whose story will never be known but who sacrificed themselves in pursuit of equality for African Americans. This much is true: While many may speak about the racial divide in America, those attempting to close the gap were not all black. Why do we not also speak, then, of the racial coalitions, the racial brotherhood that existed all through slavery, through the civil rights movement and even in today's Twenty-first Century America?

This book is one small segment of that larger narrative about racial coalitions and the contributions of whites to ending discrimination and expanding black empowerment. Perhaps it will reveal some parallels to a small minority of citizens who were fighting elsewhere during the 1930s and 1940s when the Holocaust happened. Recent stories have been reported about citizens in France, Holland, Denmark and even Germany, who were protecting and sheltering Jewish people. It was evident that not all citizens of these countries were enamored with the Nazis. Some of them jeopardized their lives, just as whites in the United States did for African Americans.

I am one of those whites who sought to understand my own involvement. I have experienced a long, wandering journey, not without disappointments, escapes and diversions. Coming from a very rural background in Iowa, including a one-room school house, I assimilated slowly into an African-American environment. I came to better understand the aspirations and hardships of their lives. It was not always easy. Many times, I was the only minority—the only white guy—in the room, which is something most whites have rarely encountered. Even as I and others sought to make our contributions, we were undergoing our own evolution, examining and then eliminating prejudices and biases, of which no one is ever completely free.

The title of this book suggests the role some whites like myself may have played in during the fight for African American empowerment. Many of us were on the battlefields but even more were in the back rooms, and we should be proud of that. We will continue, in my view, to help make the kind of America John F Kennedy, Robert Kennedy and Rev. Martin Luther King persuaded us was possible.

"No man will ever be whole and dignified and free except in the knowledge that the men around him are whole and dignified and free, and that the world itself is free of contempt and misuse."

— Wendell Berry, *The Hidden Wound*

PROLOGUE

I pulled up to the three-story townhouse, which looked as nondescript as all the others in the Southwest section of the District of Columbia. It was 1970, and the area had been ground zero in one of the decades-long battles over urban renewal. For planners and developers, the program, funded by the federal government, had been an opportunity to flaunt talent and make money. But for the people who lived in those communities undergoing the renovation, it seemed more like massive removal. Part of me sympathized with them, but I couldn't get myself too bogged down in those dynamics. If the people living in that section of the city were struggling economically, my circumstance wasn't very different. I thought I was getting a job with the League of Cities, a nonprofit organization that represented the interest of municipalities around the country. Just as I had begun counting the money I believed would be coming my way, I was told someone else had been selected for the job, leaving me with an empty wallet that desperately needed filling. I had come to the townhouse expecting some type of rescue. Little did I know events from that evening would serve to establish me as one of the key architects of black political empowerment in the District of Columbia for the next forty years. I was more focused on basic survival and lacked a crystal ball. I had no idea of the fascinating future that awaited me.

In fact, I didn't know much of anything. I wasn't even sure I had dressed appropriately for the occasion. I wore a simple shirt and slacks. A tie was a feature of my more formal sartorial affair, which was reserved for parties. Jeans and jacket were often my first preference. When an extremely well-dressed guy opened the door, I immediately knew I had under-estimated the evening's attire. I was led to the foyer, decorated with a few photographs on the wall, a well-worn sofa and a small coffee table sans magazines or newspapers, leaving me to wait without any real distractions. I was on my third inventory of the space, when finally, after thirty minutes, Sterling Tucker and three other gentlemen came down the stairs. They were introduced as Carl Holman, Ed Sylvester, and the Rev. Walter Fauntroy.

Tucker had instructed me to show up at the house. I worked for him as a volunteer at the Washington Urban League, where he was the executive director. A nonprofit organization, originally called the National League on Urban Conditions Among Negroes, it was established in 1910 as the result of the merger of two predecessor groups: the Committee for Improvement of Industrial Conditions Among Negroes in New York City and the National League for the Protection of Colored Women. Fortunately, in 1920, the League simplified its name to the National Urban League. By the time I connected with the group's District of Columbia affiliate, Whitney Young was at the national helm and it was considered a powerhouse in the Civil Rights Movement and in black America. Not unlike others associated with the group, I experienced its tough times, including riots following the assassination of the Rev. Martin Luther King, Jr.

Holman, the director of the National Urban Coalition, was new to me, as was Sylvester, who also had been active in the civil-rights movement. The townhouse was his home. Fauntroy was one of its known leaders.

Tucker had found me a job, all right—another political campaign. Fauntroy had decided to run for the new seat in the United States House of Representatives set aside for the District of Columbia. It was a federal territory, and citizens there were allowed only to elect members of the

Board of Education. There wasn't an elected mayor. Instead, a commission, appointed by the president of the United States, managed the city. The nine members of the city council also were appointed by the president. But the District was soon to have a non-voting congressional representative elected by its citizens. That would not just advance the political clout of the District, which was predominantly African American. It also meant greater empowerment for the collective identified as black America.

Initially, I hesitated to accept a job with Fauntroy's campaign, unsure I wanted to carry that responsibility and burden. Then I considered my personal finances. No one had said exactly how much I would be paid, but something was definitely better than nothing. I was told to come the next morning to New Bethel Church in the Shaw neighborhood of the city.

The District of Columbia was then, and remains, a fascinating town, with neighborhoods so diverse tourists or others unfamiliar with it might think they were in multiple cities, instead of just one. Each section has its own unique physicality, personality and history. Shaw, located in the Northwest quadrant of the city, was no different.

The area took its name from a junior high school that eventually closed in the early 2000s. Its moniker was a tribute to Union Colonel Robert Gould Shaw, the commander of the 54th Massachusetts Volunteer Infantry. Most Americans who are not Civil War buffs came to learn of Shaw through the 1989 film "Glory", starring Denzel Washington, Morgan Freeman and Andre Braugher among others. The neighborhood had been a place where freed slaves lived. That may account for the fact that it became, in the late Nineteenth Century and early Twentieth Century, a haven for black intellectuals and artists; the most famous among them was probably Edward "Duke" Ellington. That glorious history suffered after riots broke out there and other parts of the city following the Rev. Martin Luther King Jr.'s murder in 1968.

Fauntroy was pastor of New Bethel Baptist Church, and had been in that role since 1959. After the riots, he and others set about trying to revive Shaw. They had made some improvements, but remnants of the destruction were in plain sight. There was a large room connected to the actual church. When I entered, I was greeted by a nattily dressed young black man.

"I'm John Wilson," he said, adding that he was the campaign manager.

There was an air of confidence and perhaps even bravado to that introduction; it was clear, however, he was glad to see me while still somewhat apprehensive and distrustful. I met others who worked for the campaign and took a quick look around. I realized almost immediately, I was facing a variety of challenges, including the fact that campaign literature was amateurish—although the candidate was impressive.

The fourth of seven children born to Ethel Fauntroy, a homemaker, and William T. Fauntroy, Sr., a clerk in the U.S. Patent Office, young Fauntroy was reared in Shaw. He graduated second in his class in 1951 from the prestigious predominantly African-American Dunbar High School. When he was ready to attend college, his neighbors and members of his church sold dinners to help raise money to pay his tuition. He subsequently graduated from Virginia Union University and earned a degree in divinity from Yale.

At Virginia Union, he met the Rev. Martin Luther King, Jr. They became lifelong friends. Fauntroy married Dorothy Simms and had one child, Marvin; they later adopted Melissa Alice. He also served as the Washington director of the Southern Christian Leadership Conference (SCLC), the group King co-founded following the Montgomery, Alabama bus boycott. Fauntroy also helped organize the March on Washington in 1963. In addition, he helped coordinate the Selma to Montgomery Voting Rights March in 1965, and the James Meredith Mississippi Freedom March in 1966. That same year, President Johnson appointed Fauntroy Vice Chairman of The White House Conference on Civil Rights. A year later, Johnson would make him vice chairman of the D.C. City Council. As Fauntroy mounted his congressional campaign in 1970, he was the executive director of the Model Inner City Community Organization (MICCO), an organization that used federal grants to improve inner city neighborhoods.

While impressive, that personal profile would only take him so far. The other candidates who had entered the race were no slouches. Strong competition meant the basic science of campaigning couldn't be ignored. My question about the statistical breakdown of the voting population was met with only blank stares. Further, working out of a church carried perception and legal problems.

Later that day, I called Tucker, telling him we needed to move into an office, despite the fact during that era churches were a powerful force in the civic and political culture of the city. In other words, there wasn't any separation in the District of Columbia local politics of church and state. That involvement of the clergy and religious organizations in black life dated as far back as slavery. Out of that network blossomed schools, social clubs and charitable groups that ensured the safety and growth of African Americans through the Reconstruction Era and, in some instances, into the Twenty-first Century. That history deserved praise but Tucker understood my reluctance, promising to contact a realtor friend. Within a few days, we had a space at 21st St. NW and P St. NW., in the Dupont Circle neighborhood, a bustling business and social district untouched by the riots and populated mostly by whites.

Meanwhile, I began meeting Fauntroy's supporters, chief among those providing money and political backing was Max Berry, the finance chairman. An international trade lawyer, Berry was Jewish and originally from Oklahoma. He was the lead spokesperson. Others who attended that first session included Polly Shackleton, John Hechinger, whose family at the time owned a leading local hardware company, and David Apter, an advertising guru who was Fauntroy's good friend and public relations professional. All were white and influential. I believe they were glad to see me on board—at least initially.

I moved quickly, laying the foundation and the larger structural arc of the campaign. Al Gollin, a public opinion researcher employed at the Bureau of Social Service Research in Washington, had done extensive work on voting precincts in Washington; he helped with polling data. Wards 1, 2, 5, 7 and 8 were primarily black and blue collar. Ward 4 was mostly middle- and upper-class African Americans, and Ward 3 was predominantly white and far wealthier. The final, Ward 6, was an eclectic economic mix.

The Abramson-Himmelfarb ad agency was my next stop. Knowing I needed concurrence in major strategic decisions, I asked Wilson to accompany me. David Abramson, a slightly aggressive type, but also a very good salesman, led off the meeting. He would continue to be a friend until his death from cancer in 2002. His partner Marvin Himmelfarb, sporting long hair and large tortoise shell glasses, offered a zany appearance. Actually, during the 1970s, most of us cast a strange portrait. Himmelfarb was the idea man with a tremendous creative streak; he eventually left Washington, becoming a successful Hollywood writer. Later, he went to work in New York as a producer for Fox News. The third person at the meeting was an associate at the agency John Burgreen, who eventually handled our account.

Campaigns—successful ones, anyway—do not flourish as pure democracies. I understood that even if no one else did. Thus, I assumed complete control of the operation. One dramatic change I realized had to be made immediately was hiring new workers. The ones that had been employed lacked the requisite skills and expertise. I reached for my rolodex, calling Mary Scheckelhoff, a woman who had worked on the Princeton Seminar in Arlington; it was an effort by certain professors and political activists to encourage college students to participate in elections that would be occurring that fall. I had met Mary while I was consulting there. Many people at the seminar had been involved in either Sen. Eugene McCarthy's or Sen. Robert Kennedy's campaign. About twenty-four years old, Mary also had worked for Democratic candidates in Ohio before coming to Washington. I knew she could hit the ground running. She agreed to come on board immediately; I placed her in charge of moving the headquarters to the P St. NW location. I made a telephone call to Jerry Fitzgerald in Iowa City, asking him to come help organize at the precinct level. He arrived the very next day, driving all night from his home.

After touring the P Street facility, I developed a floor plan to determine telephone locations as well as placement of potential campaign staffers. That layout was sent to the C&P Telephone Company. Early that next morning, I received a call at my apartment notifying me that someone at the headquarters was advising telephone technicians to disregard my instructions. I was incensed. How the hell were we going to win, I wondered to myself, if I have to worry about every little detail? I told the installer to place the phones where he initially had been instructed. David Abramson called later that day, telling me his then-wife Patty wanted to volunteer on the campaign. He described her as very artistic. "Great. Send her over."

"When?" asked Abramson.

"Now." We had no time for niceties. Patty soon took charge of designing campaign stationery.

I determined whose name should be included on the campaign's letterhead. The socio-political reality of the city demanded a racial mix: Berry was white; Dr. Edward Mazique, a well-known black physician, was the campaign treasurer. Also listed were Bishop Smallwood Williams, a black clergyman, Bitsey Folger, a white socialite and civic leader, Joe Sharlitt, a white attorney; Rev. David Eaton, the African-American pastor of All Souls Church who later would become a member of the school board; Polly Shackleton, a white member of the city council; Rev. Ernest Gibson, an African-American clergy; Marion Barry, a black activist and leader of the Student NonViolent Coordinating Council; Ron Linton a white lobbyist; Mary Treadwell, the black director of Pride Inc.; Jerry Wurf, the white president of ASFCME; Clifford Alexander, a black lawyer; and H.R. Crawford, a black realtor who eventually would become assistant secretary of the U.S. Department of Housing and Urban Development.

John Wilson and I soon realized we needed experienced individuals in two important areas: scheduling and press relations. Peter Schott acted as the media representative, but he had relatively little experience. A friend of Berry's suggested I hire two individuals as a package deal for press relations. Both were white; I was not overly impressed. I knew I would have to watch them carefully. I did not believe they were sensitive or comfortable being in the same environment with black people. Getting a scheduler was easier. Bishop Smallwood Williams' daughter, Yvonne, suggested by Tucker and Fauntroy, took on that responsibility. She was among the first black graduates of Barnard College. She took the position out of dedication to Fauntroy.

Meanwhile, Himmelfarb finally had developed the basic message for the campaign: *"He is going to get it all together"*, which Wilson and I liked; the message was that Fauntroy would bring blacks and whites together. The agency also designed a campaign brochure which carried the same message.

With the message set, it was time to drill down. Fitzgerald plunged into the rudiments of a ward-precinct organization. Wilson embraced him; Jerry had the ability to be both very organized and non-threatening.

Berry and Shackleton urged me to meet quickly with the Ward 3 organization, primarily based in Georgetown, Kalorama, and Forest Hills. Fauntroy's support in that community was weak. Channing Phillips, one of his opponents, was much stronger. I had met Phillips in 1968. A pastor and civil rights leader, he made history as the first African American to have his name placed in nomination for the President of the United States during the Democratic Convention in Chicago that same year. He had become the darling of white liberals and certain members of the media. He headed Robert Kennedy's 1968 presidential campaign in the District of Columbia. Handsome and charismatic, I assumed he would be the odds on choice to win the seat. That reality meant we certainly needed to be aggressive shoring up Ward 3 support. Following that agenda, I attended a meeting hosted by Ron and Nancy Linton, who were Fauntroy's ward coordinators. A very respectable group of about fifty people were in attendance, including Frances "Scottie" Smith, the daughter of F. Scott and Zelda Fitzgerald, and Carolyn Agger Fortas, the spouse of Supreme Court Justice Abe Fortas. She smoked small cigars, to which I also became addicted. Her close friend Polly Shackleton also smoked cigars; I occasionally cadged one or two from her during political meetings. Peter and Sally Craig also were in the meeting; like many of the others, their involvement in District of Columbia politics continued for decades.

Using Wilson's contacts and Fitzgerald's vetting, we identified other ward coordinators: Willie Hardy in Ward 8; Nadine Winter in Ward 6; Geraldine Boykin in Ward 7, a Crawford confidant; and Harry and Romaine Thomas in Ward 5. Fitzgerald also recruited Bill Brockenborough in Ward 2 and Anita Bonds, a future chairperson of the D.C. Democratic State Committee and city councilwoman. All of these individuals, who were subsequently trained for political work, would become the core of Washington's local political establishment, competing and winning elective offices in the city after congressional passage of the 1973 Home Rule Act.

The campaign soon received a major break. Wilson informed me that we had to attend a meeting with Fauntroy on 15th St. NW at the offices of the American Federation of State County and Municipal Employees (AFSCME), a national union. I was not really familiar with the group, but it had a local chapter whose members included a considerable number of District residents. Fauntroy went into a closed-door meeting with the President Jerry Wurf and his executive assistant Bill Lucy. We waited patiently outside for at least an hour. Fauntroy emerged even more enthusiastic than usual. Wilson and I were skeptical. The next day proved Fauntroy's excitement had merit. The union endorsed him for office. Then, I was unaware of the organization's role in the Memphis workers sanitation strike that Dr. King had visibly supported, which may have contributed to his assassination in 1968. AFSCME was a union on the rise; its endorsement was a shot in the arm.

That didn't short circuit the hunt for money, however. Every morning, I was caught in its trap. Do we have enough? How do we get more? Our opponents seemed to possess endless supplies of it, Phillips especially. It was as if Fort Knox was located in his backyard and all he needed to do was knock and ask for more. His bounty may have been the result of the fact that Georgetown liberals loved him. The well-known media mogul, Charles Guggenheim, was hired to produce commercials for his campaign, enhancing his allure. Joseph Yeldell, whose family seemed ubiquitous in the city, was another opponent. Unsurprisingly, he had the backing of the old-line black Washingtonians; they were part of the bourgeois. Many of his supporters also were enamored of the presidentially appointed mayor Walter E. Washington.

The challenge facing Fauntroy was not inconsequential. Fortunately, we developed a core of skilled and dedicated volunteers. Most of the black ministers and their congregations were also in our corner. I cannot remember exactly who advanced the idea that we should make a pitch for Fauntroy in the Sunday church services. We were back to that church and state intersection. Some traditions can't be buried. Consequently, the church pitches were made and the offering plates were passed. I received a call from one of the minister coordinators asking if he and others in his group could come by the office that Sunday. He arrived carrying two huge shopping bags, and deposited them on my desk.

"We did not know what to do with them," he said.

The sacks were filled with cash—mostly one-dollar bills, although there were more than a few five, ten and twenty-dollar bills. Almost as soon as they came, the ministers departed, leaving me with the groceries, so to speak. I called in a fellow staffer to help with the counting. Tiring quickly of this task, I dumped both sacks of money in my empty desk drawer and locked it. I went home to my apartment, although I was nervous about leaving the money in a shabbily protected location. The next morning, I placed the money in a large cloth bag and strolled into the Riggs Bank, which was just across the street, and where the campaign had an account.

I hadn't mentioned the money collected to anyone else, including John Wilson. I wasn't even sure how much there was. Figuring it best to leave the details to the tellers, I proceeded to a window where the clerk recognized me and offered a warm greeting. As I deposited the bag on the counter, I mentioned my nervousness; maybe it was all that cash, I quipped.

"I know what you mean Mr. Patton; we just had an armed robbery here about forty-five minutes ago." She wasn't joking. Another teller arrived to help her complete the count of the money I brought in: four thousand dollars was a tidy sum in 1971.

Nevertheless, we still didn't have a major donor base. We needed money for radio spots that had been created by Abramson's advertising agency. On the hunt, some of us, including Wilson, Hechinger, Lucy, and Tucker ventured uptown to Billy Simpson's restaurant on Georgia Ave. NW. A real fixture in the black community, Simpson was a strong Fauntroy supporter. He had invited us there, but warned he didn't want the candidate to be with the entourage. If money was to be exchanged, I agreed, since it was my practice to keep the two separated. After meeting with Simpson, we all sat at the bar. He treated us to drinks; Wilson and I were glad to indulge since we both were always notoriously low on cash. Fifteen minutes into the party, an older African American, probably in his fifties, came into the bar and struck up a conversation with Simpson; the two seemed close. He subsequently handed Simpson an envelope before walking out of the restaurant. Simpson came over to us and placed that same envelope in Tucker's hand; he immediately turned it over to me. I put it in my suit pocket, and we all left.

When I got back to my apartment I examined the contents. There appeared to be more than three thousand dollars, mostly in one hundred dollar bills. The very next morning I again deposited the cash in the Riggs Bank. At the office, Wilson asked how much had been in the envelope, and chuckled when I told him the amount. "So the bookie came through," he said. I was surprised it was book-making money. But I had received it gladly. The underground economy may have saved the campaign.

Things really were coming together nicely: Fauntroy's image and the campaign had undergone a transformation, at least from the public's perspective. The Abramson-Himmelfarb firm had designed a slick brochure featuring Fauntroy in an attractive suit and in various poses with potential voters. We had a bumper sticker, stationery and placards with the same message: *"He is going to get it altogether."*

I insisted Fauntroy wear a beeper so the scheduler or I could remain in touch with him. He almost always ran late for appointments; that device was to mitigate his tardiness. However, even when it worked, moving Fauntroy could be difficult. I believed an advance person could help. A friend of mine from Iowa law school, Bob Rush, had just arrived in town and would soon work at the Justice Department. He had done advance work for me in the Ed Mezvinsky election and also for the Robert Kennedy campaign. I knew he had the experience to do an effective job. I assigned him to Fauntroy for a day to fully assess his skills; we had an especially tight schedule that day. While appointments went well most of the day, at one point, I beeped Fauntroy with no response. He was at a church meeting in the Southeast. I finally reached Rush who had called me, speaking in hushed tones, almost whispering.

"Get him out of there," I said.

Rush replied, almost laughing, "Are you crazy, Doug? Do you think I, as a young white man, am going to go up and pull Fauntroy from the stage in front of all those black people?

I sighed understanding Rush's apprehension. "Okay, do the best you can."

There was an emphasis on targeted precincts. I felt Fauntroy's appearances in Ward 3, which was predominantly white, should be kept to a minimum, and those should be only for fundraisers.

Money, money, money—there was always some one demanding it. Burgreen had become friendly, and was almost in constant contact with me for payments to the firm. He also stressed that money had to be upfront for the radio buys well in advance. I begged Max Berry to organize a finance meeting with top individuals. Hechinger really had not raised sufficient amounts of funds. So, Berry and I decided we should use Hechinger's membership at the City Tavern in Georgetown as a way to insure his presence. We had the meeting with about eight or nine people. I told them all that we had to have cash immediately for radio buys. There was some squirming from the group as I delivered the ultimatum. Marion Barry and the Rev. David Eaton spoke up. They didn't have much, they said, but were willing to borrow five hundred dollars and possibly a thousand from their respective banks. They were the least affluent individuals of the Fauntroy leaders; their offer shamed the others in making pledges. Ultimately, we got roughly five thousand dollars from that little meeting.

Meanwhile, Fitzgerald was very busy recruiting ward and precinct coordinators. Surprisingly, we were getting a substantial number of volunteers coming to our offices, many of them white. That caused me some concern. Both Wilson and I knew we had to keep a balance. I also knew we had to shuttle aside a couple of black workers. Wilson took on that responsibility, but maybe not in such a smooth manner.

I was in the outer office when I noticed a tall bulky bespectacled black man, who appeared to be in his late thirties; I learned his name was Bill

Brockenborough. He seemed irritated, speaking in strong, but not profane, language to our African-American receptionist, who I'll call Sylvia. He started walking out when I called out to him, inviting him back into the office. I was impressed with how he presented himself; it helped that he lived in Ward 2, where we didn't have a coordinator. After about five minutes of conversation, I asked him to see Fitzgerald, who by then had an office across the hall. Brockenborough became our Ward 2 coordinator. In later years, I would come to know that he was an addictive gambler and an embezzler.

Our Ward 7 coordinator was Geraldine Boykin, a friend of H.R. Crawford. Mary Scheckelhoff told me early one morning that Boykin wanted to see me immediately. I said "send her down," even though I was unsure what she wanted. Minutes later, she appeared in my office. Almost six feet tall but soft spoken, she firmly told me that the campaign had not allocated sufficient funds for the Ward 7 political operation. I replied that funds were very tight and we systemically allocated money based on potential voters by ward. She seemed somewhat satisfied; I assured her that we would make all possible efforts to get her more money, if we could raise it. By the time the campaign ended, Boykin and I had become good friends. She told me later that she was angry and upset about the campaign's budget and that she had planned to come to our office that morning to "tell that N____ a thing or two" only to discover the person in charge was not black at all.

The campaign was filled with dedicated workers. It also had its share of characters. A frequent visitor to our offices was a very handsome man, over six feet tall, who was only called "Naked Johnny." He always wore tight fitting black shirts and jeans and a large gold chain around his neck. Frequently, the shirt would be unbuttoned almost to his waist, displaying a well sculptured torso. He could have been a double for Rafer Johnson the Olympic gold medalist. Wilson told me Naked Johnny was occasionally a volunteer for the campaign because he was getting money from Sylvia, who was somewhat overweight and not very attractive. Wilson corrected my observations: "Naked Johnny is basically a pimp—a very smooth one; he knows a meal ticket when he sees one."

One day Sylvia stormed into our office. She spoke directly to Wilson, however. "I need to get paid, and today," she exclaimed. He told her she would get paid when everyone else would, and jokingly told her to leave. Paying no attention to me, she went over where Wilson was sitting behind his desk. She grabbed the cord from a Venetian blind and wrapped it around his neck, jerking him from his swivel chair onto the floor. Even as he was being choked, Wilson laughed.

"Get this bitch off of me," he yelled. I quickly summoned two other workers to restrain Sylvia. Everyone got paid later that day, including Sylvia. Luckily she left the campaign the next day. We were thankful. Naked Johnny was never seen again in our headquarters.

One evening, I noticed a very attractive woman who had volunteered on several occasions. I mentioned her to Wilson. "Doug, stay away," he warned. "She is Nickie's girlfriend." I thought he was speaking about a male person. Wilson smiled, "Nickie is the woman who has been volunteering since last month."

Those with theatrical tendencies weren't just limited to our own internal staff, however. One day, Jim Harris, a stocky African American who could easily find work as a boxer, burst into our 10 x 12 nondescript Dupont Circle office, shouting every known profanity. George Strawn, a white guy with all the markings of a southern redneck—sans their social prejudices—walked along side Harris trying to calm him down.

Without warning, Harris pulled out a .38 pistol and stuck it in my face. I didn't really believe he'd shoot but he was so damn angry and nervous, I worried the gun might go off accidentally.

The salt and pepper duo were operatives of AFSCME, which represented a sizable number of local blue-collar workers in the District government. They had been assigned to work on Fauntroy's campaign.

The night before Harris arrived at the office, I ran into William Lucy, the African American chief of staff to AFSCME's president. Lucy wanted to know how his guys were working out. Not one to bite my tongue, I offered an unflattering critique. I mentioned they had fixated on a couple of bars adjacent to the campaign's headquarters. That next morning, Lucy blasted them. Unsurprisingly, Harris came with his gun and a matching hostile attitude. Eventually, with persuasion by Strawn, he stored both away.

Weapons were constantly being drawn during the campaign: One morning, I asked Ricardo Thomas, the campaign's official photographer, about the keys for one of the two cars AFSCME had provided. Lucy had entrusted them to me exclusively for the campaign's use.

"Rev. Orange took them," Thomas told me. Orange was one of several civil rights activists, including the Rev. Hosea Williams, from the Southern Christian Leadership Conference (SCLC), who had come to lend support—except they weren't always helpful. Wilson was also in the office when I made the inquiry. He heard the exchange.

"Where is Orange?" he asked Ricardo.

"Downstairs at Arby's [restaurant]."

Wilson opened the drawer of his desk, pulled out a .38 pistol and shoved it in his belt. Within minutes he was back with the keys for the car. Without offering any explanation, he threw them on my desk; turned around and returned the gun to the side drawer of his desk. Then, he casually took a telephone call, as if nothing had happened. Later that afternoon, when things had settled a bit, I asked Ricardo what happened.

"John scared me," he said, relaying events frame by frame. "Rev. Orange was going through the line. John told him to give him the car keys."

The Rev. Orange, well over six feet, dwarfed Wilson's five feet eight inches. Given the physical difference it was understandable why Orange delayed his response. But he didn't realize Wilson had a wild streak; we all called him a little crazy—although decades later we would come to know he suffered bi-polar disorder. He grew into a gifted politician but his mental health problems continued; one day he hanged himself in his home. The District government honored him by naming city hall the John A. Wilson Building. But back then, in the 1970s, an unpredictable persona, like his, could be exciting and alluring, casting the person as celebrity before all of that became a marketing tool capable of attracting television producers and million-dollar movie deals.

"John," continued Ricardo, "goes up to the Rev. Orange and sticks the gun in his stomach. He says give me the keys or I'm going to blow your ass away, right now." Even before the sentence was completed, the keys were quickly given up.

How had I, a white boy from Iowa, landed in an office working with a bunch of black people who possessed hair-trigger tempers? That's a good question.

PART ONE

CHAPTER ONE

SOOO-EEE, SOOO-EEE

IOWA was no redneck haven—although it surely was nearly pristine white. Even today, as I write this, only 2.9 percent of the population is African American. I arrived into this white blanket in 1940. For years, my life was all cows, pigs, chicken and way too much manure.

My mother was of German ancestry; she was number five in a family of ten children—six boys and four girls. At five feet one inch tall, she was the shortest, which may have made her more sympathetic toward underdogs. Bright and fit, with a high school education, she loved sports and was particularly fond of cooking, especially dishes unique to Germany. She was born on a one hundred-sixty-acre farm in Dundee, Iowa. A small town with a population of only 300, it was distinguished by a bank, grocery store, hardware store, grain elevator and, of course, two taverns— all lined up on one street. Oddly, she never lived more than twenty miles from those environs for most of her life. Very thrifty—sometimes even miserly—she controlled the family checkbook, unlike most farm wives during that period.

Her father Adolf Becker left Germany when he was ten years old. His fluency in German made him a fount of entertainment. Back in the 1920s, telephones were hand-rung, with party lines. Sometimes as many as twelve farm families could share the same line, which invited lots of eavesdropping. My grandparents had neighbors who were distant cousins of German heritage. Knowing that others likely were listening, the two women frequently spoke in their native tongue. When they went foreign, my grandfather was summoned. He would translate the conversation for my grandmother and the children, who, born in the United States, knew few German words. Invariably, the two cousins would extol the virtues of another Adolf—Adolf Hitler. My grandfather believed, even back in the 1920s, that Hitler was very dangerous and would eventually "sink Germany." He also knew that the German people were resourceful and hard-working but nevertheless they were from a small country that could not survive against the power of the United States.

My father was Scotch-Irish, five feet eleven inches tall, about one hundred seventy-five pounds with a boxer's hands. Most observers described him as ruggedly handsome; he left school after the eighth grade to help save the family farm. "Dad," as we all called him, my mother included, was one of eight children—six sisters and an older brother. His father had immigrated to the states in the 1880's from Ireland; the woman who was to become his wife, my grandmother, came later when she was only eighteen years old; she traveled alone, leaving a troubled family background in Northern Ireland.

Dad and mother were married in 1932 at the height of the Great Depression, which suggested they were very optimistic about their future. He worked road construction, and she was a cook for the crew. Their employer eventually went bankrupt. With no money and checks bouncing, they resorted to draining gasoline from the road grader's tank in the middle of the night to fill their Model T Ford so they could make it back to my grandparents' home. In 1943, with a loan from a state insurance company, they managed to buy a farm near Winthrop, Iowa—ten miles from their rental farm. At a little over three years old, I remember the move in March 1944: With all our possessions packed in a truck, my mother got into the vehicle. I thought she was leaving me because she was trying to get me into someone else's car. I cried hysterically.

After we moved to our new farm, we often went to Independence, which had a population of seventy-five hundred people who were mostly white, with a heritage that matched ours. The seat of Buchanan County, the town was vibrant, and like most others in Iowa of that size, it was dependent on the agrarian economy, which fluctuated from year to year. On Saturday nights, we went grocery shopping there. While my parents picked up items, I'd usually take in a movie at the Iowa Theater, a dingy small place with mice scurrying the floors for leftover popcorn. In 1949, a new Malek theater was built with a very large screen. A person twelve years old or younger only paid ten cents to enter; that eventually was raised to fifteen cents. When I reached thirteen years old, however, the admission had risen to fifty cents. My parents usually gave me that amount, but I had multiple desires for that limited budget. I often wanted to purchase one or two baseball books; I had become a fervent follower of the sport. I knew the first show at the theater was usually at seven o'clock. The second showing of the main movie feature started slightly after nine. The ticket-seller would abandon her window shortly after the second showing began. I would wait until both the seller and ticket taker at the internal door had left and would make my move, entering the theater and quickly stepping inside the bathroom on a lower level. Obviously, I didn't have to use the toilet; that was part of the ruse. After a moment, I went up a gradual ramp to the theater seats, making it appear as if I were a normal theatergoer. That was my routine for nearly a year, executed faithfully with great skill and even greater luck. But then, one evening, just as I settled into my seat, an usher with a small flashlight approached, asking for my ticket stub. I had none, and was truly embarrassed and humbled. He politely escorted me out of the theater. Future Saturdays found me parting with my fifty cents.

Typically after viewing the movie, I joined my parents and their friends at the Red Dot lounge, which was just down the street. When it closed, everyone piled into cars and drove to an after-hours club on the outskirts of Independence called the Silver Slipper. It had a dance floor and a large jukebox that played everything from the Andrews Sisters to Les Paul and Mary Ford. When I grew tired, my mother took me to our 1949 blue Mercury where I could sleep. One sultry summer night, I was awoken by a disturbance. Somewhat frightened, I looked out of the window and saw my father punch out a man, who slid down the automobile opposite our car. My mother came to comfort me, saying the fight was over. My father and his friend Bud Andrews had come outside after learning that five or six men had jumped two of their younger friends from Winthrop. He and Bud interceded, evening the odds. My father's sense of justice was aided by his nimbleness and large hands, ultimately turning the tide.

We lived on a two hundred thirty-five acre farm. I was a member of the 4-H club, which was called the Byron Busy Boys. My family grew corn, oats, soybeans and hay, which was a combination of clover, timothy, alfalfa and native grasses. We had nearly twenty Guernsey dairy cows, Hereford beef cattle, Spotted Poland China and Hampshire hogs, and Leghorn chickens. We were comfortable—not rich but also not poor. It wasn't until 1950 that we finally installed indoor plumbing, eliminating the midnight trips to our outdoor privy; during the winters those outings were mitigated by white porcelain chamber pots placed in each bedroom.

There was work to be done seven days a week. When we weren't harvesting crops or doing chores, there were fences to mend, pigs to castrate, bulls to pinch, cattle horns to cut and other assorted tasks. Once, when I was sixteen years old, my folks were away at a rural electric cooperative convention. I helped deliver pigs at our hog house during a March blizzard. There were multiple sows delivering that night. In one case, the birth canal was blocked. The solution was for me to reach arm-deep inside of the sow to pull out the piglets. Then I placed them in a basket and took them to our house, which was about two hundred feet away from the white two-story hog house that contained straw and grain in the top floor and farrowing pens on the bottom. After reaching our enclosed porch, I used heat lamps and small terry-cloth towels to warm the piglets. Ten or fifteen minutes later, I shuttled them back to their mother. If sows and piglets are separated too long, there's a chance the mother might reject them, believing the offspring belong to someone else. I knew that a litter of more than six piglets meant a profit for our family, so the survival of each was important.

Everyone in our community knew everyone else's business, which could yield bad or good results. When someone had an automobile or machinery breakdown, neighbors were quick to offer rides or assistance. If there was illness in families, folks would bring groceries and help with the chores, including the harvests. My family was the first in our area to have television: a 1953 black and white Zenith, with three channels—ABC and CBS from the two Cedar Rapids stations and NBC from Waterloo. We needed a large antenna on our roof to get a decent reception. Our living room contained a rocking chair and a large burgundy sofa with a matching easy chair; twelve by twenty foot floor was covered with beige carpet remnants that young neighbors like Leon "Windy" Condon usually sat on when they showed up to watch television. No one contested those arrangements, since few had such comforts in their homes. Saturday nights, we watched Jackie Gleason. On Sundays, we were captivated by the Ed Sullivan Show. Many evenings, my mother prepared popcorn from the corn we grew on the farm. A real treat was vanilla ice cream covered with Hershey's chocolate syrup.

August may have been my favorite month. That's when we harvested the oat fields. There would be as many as twelve farmers using a threshing machine. These days, most young Iowa farmers have never heard of such equipment, but it was used to harvest oats and create gigantic straw piles in the farm yards. Karl Quint, a burly farmer, owned these machines. He contracted with individual farmers who pooled their tractors and straw wagons and moved from farm to farm, working collectively. The movie *Witness,* which among other things depicts a barn raising by Amish farmers in Pennsylvania, was reminiscent of our communal system. Quint also allowed me to sit in the driver's seat of the giant Case tractor that pulled the threshing machine. As young boys, we would burrow tunnels into the straw piles, after the stacks had settled for three or four days.

I started driving an Allis Chalmer tractor when I was about eight years-old. My job was to load shocks of oats on the wagons, which was terrific fun under that sun-filled Iowa sky. In the late 1940s, some of the farmers still had teams of Belgian draft horses. They were a beautiful chestnut or roan color. The horses were spectacular beasts with fine dispositions and a great willingness to work. Large and weighing over one ton, they were known as the "Great Horse." Since the turn of the century, they were predominantly used in Iowa. To a youngster, they were intimidating but a joy to observe. Many times, one of our old German-American neighbors, Otto Martin, would hand me the reins for a brief period while we were on the wagon. At noon, we had dinners that could be considered feasts: fried chicken, mashed potatoes and gravy, fresh string beans, homemade biscuits, bread and lots of pies and cakes —all made from scratch.

By 1956, the threshing machine was supplanted by the combine. The harvester or the "combine" was the new farm machine mixing three separate operations of harvesting. First we cut the oats using a simple machine which turned out wrapped bundles tied automatically with twine. Once a field was cut, we had to walk the fields putting roughly ten bundles in a round cluster that looked like a miniature doll house. This allowed a drying process over a few days. Then, we would stack the bundles onto a rack hauled by a tractor to the threshing machine. The thresher would separate the oat kernels from the straw, blowing the straw into large stacks. The oats were hauled to a granary. The combine brought all these elements into one process. No longer was a cooperative effort needed from our neighbors. It was truly a labor saver. It was sad, however, to see communal farming diminished.

Encouraged by my parents, my interest in politics heightened. As Democrats, we were a distinct minority in our rural township. We often discussed state and national events at our kitchen table. In 1952, while only in the sixth grade, I heard a campaign speech by Adali Stevenson, which intensified my attention. Four years later, we watched the 1956 Democratic convention on our Zenith television. A hectic and intense floor battle emerged between Senator Estes Kefauver and Senator Jack Kennedy, after presidential nominee Adlai Stevenson opened up the nomination for vice president. My favorite, Kennedy, lost on the second ballot. I was crushed.

That same year, Herschel Loveless, a Democrat who was my father's age, ran for governor. I was fifteen and a sophomore in high school in 1956 when a teacher urged me to give a campaign speech for Loveless. He won the governorship and was re-elected in 1958. When he ran for reelection, I gave another speech for him before the entire assembly in my senior year; he handily won the straw poll of the roughly one hundred twenty students in my school. My history teacher, Ms. Luella Cook, who I knew to be a Republican, paid me a wonderful back-handed compliment, just after the vote, offering that my fiery oratory had convinced the student body to vote for Loveless, although she said that I was not always factual. Count that as my first lesson in the art and power of political messaging.

CHAPTER TWO

Jack, Jill and Sambo

MY social instruction was provided mostly through the lens of television. It broadened and defined the roles of individuals and groups in the world I inhabited and the larger external environment. As I was growing up in the 1940s and 1950s, blacks were cast mostly as entertainers. Mister Bojangles and others entered our home through the "Ed Sullivan Show." The actors on the "Amos and Andy" show on the radio had no physical image for me until they arrived on television. College sports like football and basketball were not yet televised or were not integrated; we did not get to see standout African-American athletes like basketball forward "Sugar" Cain or football All-American Calvin Jones both of whom played at the University of Iowa in the 1950's. Those were the days of the "Jackie Gleason Show," "Dragnet" and "I Love Lucy." There were dramatic shows like "Studio One" and the "Hallmark Hour." But blacks were absent. Even on "American Bandstand," we never saw them dancing among all the Philadelphia teenagers.

Radio stations were limited and our only daily newspaper was the Dubuque Telegraph Herald, which had very limited national coverage.

Gossip, hearsay and basic stereotyping were the norm. There wasn't anything confusing about it.

Like most grade school students of that era, we were assigned Dick, Jane, and Spot to read, which portrayed the more antiseptic aspects of contemporary white America. There weren't any perplexing questions about that life style. To a large extent, it was my story—very isolated and protected. My one-room schoolhouse, where all class levels were taught by the same teacher, was a mile and a half from our farm, midway between Aurora, Iowa and Winthrop, Iowa. In the winter, with single panes of glass in the windows, it was always drafty. It was heated by an oil burner stove; if you sat too close, you were literally hot on one side of your body and freezing cold on the other side.

The school had a small separate anteroom, called a cloak-room, at the entrance where winter coats and over-shoes were stashed. It had electricity, but was sparsely furnished. Duane Beebe was my only classmate that September 1946. I remember one very cold winter day I was trying to find my galoshes as I prepared to make my way home. I found a pair of older ones; one boot contained human feces. I soon realized that Duane had my overshoes on his feet. Not wanting to venture out to the privy about seventy-five yards from the schoolhouse that blizzard day, he had used one of his own as the toilet. When school ended, he needed clean ones and took mine instead. His caper drew derisive calls from other students, which truly embarrassed Duane. I reclaimed my overshoes and walked home in complete dryness. What Duane did for his feet I never found out.

After that kindergarten year, schools were consolidated. My old schoolhouse was sold. The winning bidder was my father; he had the local Amish, who excelled at moving buildings with the aid of their draft horses, relocate the schoolhouse to our farm, one and one-half miles north. Eventually, it became a hog house; no one I knew ever protested its recycled life.

Negroes or Coloreds, as black people were called back then, operated on the periphery of my world. They were both visible and invisible, baffling me with each encounter, leaving me trying to interpret the experience without the necessary legends or lexicon. "See Dick and Jane" may have been familiar, but "Little Black Sambo," written by Helen Bannerman and first published in 1899, was a different matter. The book was about a young South Indian boy who may have been Tamil—though most people unfamiliar with the book's history, as I was then, believed him Negro, as blacks called themselves then. Decades later, not unlike Negroes, Tamils would fight for their independence. In first grade, I knew nothing of the controversy that surrounded Little Black Sambo—although sixteen years earlier, in the 1930's, the famous African-American poet Langston Hughes described it as a "pickaninny" storybook "which was hurtful to black children."

The story, simply put, was that Sambo had given away his clothing—red coat, blue trousers, purple shoes, and green umbrella—to four tigers in exchange for not being eaten by them. The tigers, all quite vain, began chasing each other around a tree until they were reduced to a pool of melted butter. Sambo recovered his clothes while the butter or former tigers were taken home. There, his mother made mounds of pancakes using that tiger butter. Sambo ate one hundred sixty-nine pancakes.

What was I to think or believe about blacks from such a story? Were they inferior or mythical like Sambo? What about the butter and pancakes? Was his mother the precursor to Aunt Jemima, that black woman with red lips and a red and white bandana wrapped around her head who graced the boxes of pancake mix and bottles of syrup sold in stores?

Both were stereotypical versions of African Americans instilled in rural white Iowans like myself. Neither my teacher nor Duane provided any translation. I received little enlightenment about blacks from my occasional visits to Waterloo, a city about thirty-five miles away.

My Aunt Florence and Uncle Al lived there. They were both union members: She with the Retail Clerks local which had organized workers in Black's Department Store; he was a machinist union steward at a factory called Chamberlins. Waterloo was a small city; the Cedar River divided it into east and west sides: Upper-income whites lived on the west side. The east side was filled with mostly blue-collar workers, including my aunt and uncle, employed at factories like John Deere and Chamberlins, or meat-packing houses like Rath's. Negroes in town also lived on the east side and worked at the same companies as their white counterparts. They were ensconced, however, in "colored" town. I never knew its exact borders, but I remember observing black people on the streets. They were going about their business paying little attention to a young white boy in their midst. One Sunday afternoon, after I took a long walk to downtown, I returned to my relatives' house and was mildly reprimanded for flirting with trouble.

I came to learn that the lines between the races were more starkly drawn in other parts of the country, like Tampa, Florida, for example. Our family traveled there in December 1949 to visit my uncle Maynard Williams and his wife Irene. I was filled with anticipation. My sister Lois had invited her best friend Kay Dey to join us. That was an added bonus because I thought Kay—at five feet four inches tall and blonde hair—

truly beautiful. My father had just purchased a new blue Mercury for twenty-six hundred dollars. It had a wide front bench seat and a very comfortable plush back seat with a spacious trunk. We didn't have a large amount of luggage. Frankly, we didn't own much clothing. We were simple farm folks embarking on a grand adventure. In route, we stopped in Peoria, Illinois, where we stayed overnight with Uncle Art and Aunt Ella, who had a habit of feigning illness, hoping to escape cooking meals. I remember we brought our own staples. My mother packed frozen meat from livestock we had butchered. We also had fresh vegetables and eggs from our leghorn chickens.

We travelled further through southern Illinois into Paducah, Kentucky, and Nashville and Chattanooga, Tennessee, using Route 301. Eventually, we stopped at Lookout Mountain. I was awed by the view from the top. I had seen only flat land in the Midwest. From there, we traveled into northern Georgia on the two-lane highway. Eisenhower's interstate highway system across the United States was still many years away. Soon, we ran out of daylight, and registered at a motel in northern Georgia. The room was drab and dingy with a single, low wattage light sans shade affixed to the ceiling. We were very glad to leave the next morning. Many years later, I reflected on how blacks were not even allowed to stay in such shabby facilities. In contrast to our mostly well-maintained farms in Iowa, the dwellings we passed along the highways were shacks with open doors and windows, and smoking chimneys. Black adults sat on porches as children played in the yards. Those scenes were my first exposure to abject poverty—a kind I had never seen in Iowa—and, there was so much of it.

We arrived in Tampa just before Christmas and stayed through New Year's Day. My Uncle Maynard and Aunt Irene, my father's sister, were pillars of the segregated upper-income strata of their community. He looked and acted like a proper refined banker. In reality, he was one of the top bookmakers in the state. At the time, such gambling was illegal. He used cigar stores as fronts for his operation. In the backrooms, there were lines of tables with only men on the telephones taking bets. It was all fascinating. Since the early 1920s, Florida, especially Tampa, had been a hotbed of "bolita," the illegal but popular numbers game imported from Cuba. Most of the illicit gambling was located in Ybor City. Home to the state's cigar industry, it was known as "Little Chicago." It dawned on me years later that my uncle had to be "connected" in order for him to run his gambling business.

One day, while our family was shopping in one of the large department stores, I wanted to get a drink of water. Near a bank of elevators, I noticed two identical ceramic fountains: One read "white" and the other was marked "colored." I anticipated the colored fountain meant colored water, like Kool-Aid, which I thought would be a treat. I assumed the white fountain meant clear water. I found my father and asked him, in a voice probably louder than a stage whisper 'Which one should I choose?' He quietly told me the one marked for whites. I complied but was noticeably disappointed that I had missed out on the Kool-Aid. Later that day, the reason for the two fountains was explained. I was still perplexed.

The second defining moment in Tampa came on New Year's Eve. My twelve year-old cousin Nancy stayed home while our parents went to a local restaurant. My sister Lois and her friend, Kay, were fixed up with dates by my older cousin Nyda. Our babysitter for the evening was Lillie Mae White, an African American who was the Williams' maid. I found her talkative, interesting, and charming in her own gracious, southern manner. She wanted to move north. She didn't state her specific reasons, but acted as if that relocation meant ultimate liberation. Years later, I learned she never left the south, despite asserting she would have more freedoms— social and economic. Back then, her oppression was illustrated in small ways like the unspoken rules about space on sidewalks. When Negroes approached whites, they were expected to step aside until after the whites had passed. That seemed ludicrous, since there was sufficient public space for everyone. When my sister and I first encountered that dynamic, we were confused and baffled. Tampa was a foreign country to me.

After New Year's Day, we began our trek back home, stopping briefly in Tallahassee. There, my father's sister, Aunt Mary, escorted us to the capital, including the offices of then-Governor Fuller Warren. He had been elected in 1948 on a platform of fighting racism in Florida. After his election, he spoke out against the Ku Klux Klan. Later, it was publicly disclosed that prior to World War II, he had been a member of that secretive and racist organization. He admitted that sin. Interestingly, during his first term, the Kefauver committee, named for its chairman Senator Estes Kefauver, also exposed public officials, including Warren, who were funded by people involved in illegal and criminal activity.

While Warren was governor, an outspoken black man, Harry T. Moore, an ardent activist who had registered more than 100,000 African Americans in Florida, wrote the governor, urging him not to "white wash" the situation of four young black men who had been accused of raping a young married white woman. As the executive director of the Florida NAACP, Moore had organized a campaign against what he had seen as the wrongful conviction of three of the young men. The fourth man had been killed by a police posse while fleeing. With the NAACP's support, a new trial had been ordered. However, on Christmas night, two years after we had been in Florida, Moore and his wife were fatally killed on their twenty-fifth wedding anniversary by a bomb that went off beneath their home. There were eleven other bombings targeting black families in Florida that year. Decades later, in 2006, it was revealed that the bombing was the result of a conspiracy involving four members of the Klan. In that era, the Klan membership was known to include sheriffs, doctors, lawyers, city councilmen and wealthy businessmen.

I didn't focus on much of that during my time in Tallahassee however. Warren, a friend of my Aunt Mary, was not in his office the day we went to visit. I was allowed to sit in his chair, and like any youngster, I imagined myself as governor.

That winter, I went back to my third grade class where Mrs. Elderton was the teacher. I thought she was the neatest, most beautiful person. I guess she reciprocated my admiration since she appointed me class president. No need for an election. Serving in that capacity provided my first experience with running meetings and governing. Initially, southern experiences were fresh in my mind. Over time, they faded, and I found comfort in the homogeneity of my world and the security in the regimen of the farm. I picked up eggs from our Leghorn white chickens, slopped the hogs with the mixture of whey and ground oats, fed the cows every evening with a mixture of ground corn and soybean meal, and assisted my dad when he milked them. Later, I did school work. I also was a devotee of the St. Louis Cardinals baseball team, and regardless of the static on our old Philco radio, summer evenings were spent listening to the game broadcast on KMOX from St. Louis. We never had our own television turned on during the day, except for the World Series. Consequently radio remained our primary news source. Sometimes, I managed to simultaneously watch television, listen to the radio and do my homework.

On Fridays, there was the occasional fish fry at a tavern in Dundee, owned by Aunt Joyce and Uncle "Dutch" Fairchild. My mother and Aunt Ruth assisted by serving as waitresses in the evenings. On winter evenings, they often dressed in Muskrat fur coats. They would sit in the back of the Mercury with me squirreled between them enveloped by the warmth of their coats, as they made me drink from the bottle of soda so they could add whiskey, sips of which chased away any semblance of frosty air. Since my parents were avid Democrats, I was privy to the political discussions over shuffleboard and liquor brought in brown bags. I always found it amusing and hypocritical that there were large signs that read "No Spiking," which meant you weren't to provide additional liquor to your "setups," which were usually club soda or 7-Up. The brands typically favored by my parents and their friends were Four Roses and Seagram's 7. Those Saturday evenings brought large crowds to shop and then usually to party until midnight.

Life was pretty good. One spring day in 1951, when I was in the fourth grade, my friends and I went out for recess to play a pick-up game of baseball. A colored boy was outside, holding his own glove. My buddy Del greeted him immediately, after which we all introduced ourselves. Benny—that was his name—was slight with medium brown complexion. He carried himself erect and possessed a palpable confidence. His clothes were nondescript; mostly he wore jeans and a T-shirt. None of that mattered, really. What drew our attention was that he seemed a very good baseball player, fun, engaging, and a real leader. He also was not passive; he often took charge, telling us how and what positions to play.

Every day at recess, Benny was there; he usually commandeered one of the two baseball diamonds to prevent other classes from getting them. He also took an active interest in the girls in our class, particularly one named Sandra to whom we promptly introduced him. Our class had a field trip one day and we asked our teacher if he could accompany us, although he wasn't student of the school. She agreed. We had another great time.

Benny was a curiosity, however. He was the first black person I would know, albeit for a short period, up close and personal. He defied the expectations I had developed from television. Then, one day in late May, he didn't show up for either of the school's two recesses. He also wasn't there the next morning. Del and I walked downtown—about half a mile—to the railroad tracks looking for him. A month earlier, Benny had showed us the railroad box-car he and his parents called home. His father was probably part of the "section gang" that fixed the rails; they were like migrant workers—except migrants were usually housed in one stationary location. The gangs were constantly on the move in rail cars. Sometimes, local workers in small towns, like Winthrop, were used to supplement the main labor. It was hard work, according to friends of mine whose parents were employed on such gangs.

When we arrived, the box-car wasn't there. Del and I were deeply troubled. Benny was gone. He had left without saying goodbye. Later, it dawned on us that Benny's living conditions meant he likely wasn't in any school. He was part of a vagabond, uneducated group where manual labor came first and public education was a luxury. Still, we missed him.

In the 1950s, as I finished high school, like most youths my age, the center of my world was me—and maybe my friends. It certainly wasn't the plight of black people in Iowa or in America, for that matter.

CHAPTER THREE

A Big Narrow World

WHEN I enrolled in 1959 as a freshman at the University of Iowa, I was already steeped in politics. My parents served as my role models. I also admired Iowa's governor, Herschel Loveless. The state was slowly undergoing a political transformation. Back in the 1940s, in Iowa and in the national Democratic Party, politics were played from the top down. It had always been that way: From Harry Truman through Adali Stevenson, to the Kennedys—John and Bobby—and Lyndon Johnson, the party hierarchy determined who received the nod and therefore approval, access and support. But a shift, almost imperceptible at first, was taking place, giving greater authority to average citizens, commonly called the grassroots. While I did not know it then, that change would help pave the way for my involvement and subsequent influence in not just the local political landscape but also on the national level.

John Kennedy was my hero. His bearing and mystique were unlike any other elected official. His freshness appealed to a new generation of voters, including myself. I wanted to be part of the "New Frontier" destined to change America. But by 1970, the year before I would accept a job with Fauntroy, positioning me to help affect black empowerment in the nation's capital, the change I and others had seen in small, incremental ways became even more significant when Cliff Larson entered the Iowa political arena. Tall and striking, he and his family owned a tavern in Ames, Iowa. In 1968, because of his fervent support for Eugene McCarthy, he and his wife Marlene drew the label of socialists. The name-calling had no effect; he was chairman of the state Democratic Party. He—and his wife— were determined to change the presidential selection process and further diminish the hierarchal model. That push for change didn't stop at the state border, however. The national party began to feel the heat. Senator Harold Hughes, a former governor of Iowa and a family friend, who in 1971 would become my boss when I was a consultant for his presidential campaign, headed the Democratic National Committee's reform commission. It ushered in proportional representation of delegates which configured selection based on the actual percentage of votes a candidate received. That slayed the previous "winner-take-all" policy, which vested power in party bosses to name the delegates to the national convention. Hughes had been a big backer of Senator Robert Kennedy and, prior to the Democratic convention in Chicago, had endorsed Senator Eugene McCarthy, despite efforts by friends and colleagues to keep him neutral.

Later, Iowa would come to hold an elevated role in presidential politics because of its emphasis on grassroots. The first indication of Iowa's import and the new characterization of winners and losers came in redefined Iowa caucuses in 1972; Edmund Muskie, then-Senator from Maine, won. Oddly the public's perception was that Senator George McGovern had done very well—although he won only 23 percent of the caucus. Muskie actually received 36 percent of the delegates. That kind of skewed view accepted by many people became the normal method of analysis.

Blame Johnny Apple, the well-known political reporter for that strange development. Jack Germond of the *Baltimore Sun*, David Broder of *The*

Washington Post, and Apple were political icons and some of the most influential political writers in the media during the 1970s and 1980s. A raconteur, who loved good food and drink, Apple's writings were as colorful as his life. Unsurprisingly, he later became known as a food writer and critic. When he went to the office of the State Iowa Democratic Party asking for an explanation of the caucus results, Richard Bender, a young staffer there and an undercover McGovern supporter, boasted McGovern had exceeded expectations. Bender spun the story Muskie actually "lost"—although he had won. Apple promoted the narrative that McGovern, having exceeded expectations had, therefore, "won." Without knowing it, Bender probably became the first "spinner" of election results. Even today that sort of warped law of expectations drives the caucus analysis.

Muskie was unhappy and angered by Apple and Bender's distorted interpretation. He whined—though not literally. He saved his actual tears for the New Hampshire primary later in the winter. During a press conference there, a paper said something negative about his wife, upsetting him so much that tears welled in his eyes. He later blamed the episode on the cold. Most observers knew better. They perceived it as weakness. Muskie soon became history.

Jimmy Carter followed a similar path in Iowa in 1976, but he exceeded all pre-caucus expectations by actually winning. The peanut farmer from Plains, Georgia may have surprised most pundits—but not the average Iowan. My parents—Johnny and Alma—were enamored of Carter. Deeply involved in their community, the two were fervent Democrats because of Franklin Roosevelt, who, in their estimation, had created an economic opportunity for them to obtain the status they had attained by their hard work. They believed sincerely in helping people rise above their station in life. They knew Carter held that view as well. That philosophy inspired my father in 1964 to run for the Iowa State Senate; he won

8,813 votes or 55 percent of those cast in that election. During his terms, he and my mother were the inseparable legislative couple. He lost his reelection bid in 1968 by roughly four hundred votes. I had managed his first campaign but wasn't there to comfort him during his loss. In 1970, he returned to the legislature, after winning election to the Iowa State House of Representatives; he retired in 1973.

After a chance meeting with him at the Hotel Fort Des Moines in 1975, my parents became caucus supporters in Jimmy Carter's campaign. Built in 1919, the hotel had a somewhat glorious past. Jack Kennedy stayed there in 1960 and Richard Nixon in 1972. Charles Lindbergh also had been a guest. I stayed there for one night in 1968 when I was working for Hubert Humphrey. There also were rumors, reported by a variety of guests, that the hotel was haunted with strange nighttime noises. Carter stayed in a small suite and upon bumping into my parents invited them to join him. There, alone, the trio talked for twenty or thirty minutes—without interruption. His background and experiences as a rural farmer echoed those of my father. In my parents' view, Carter was unpretentious with a humane demeanor that appealed to them. That personality helped him in the 1980 caucus to fend off the challenge from Senator Ted Kennedy. While Kennedy certainly drew the crowds, his eastern aloofness and the perception his heart wasn't really in the race didn't serve him well. Carter eventually would go on to win the presidency, albeit for one term. Afterward, he reflected all the qualities my parents had seen, proving to be one of the greatest humanitarian presidents and politicians.

While no one could have imagined it in 1959, all the machinations and changes, ignited, in part by Cliff Larson more than five decades earlier, made it possible for an African-American Illinois senator to be elected president of the United States in 2008.

Despite my hot romance with politics in my early youth, I never really believed I would evolve into a lifetime agent for the expansion of democracy. In 1959, I was mostly relieved to be out of high school. The last two years had been stressful. In the spring of my junior year, I was kicked off our baseball team by Coach Gordon Halverson after a friend and I, wanting to change from our baseball uniforms into street clothes, found the door to the school locked. We decided to enter through an open window. Halverson went ballistic, accusing us of being disreputable. Adding to that injury, he withheld my letter from baseball from the previous fall of my junior year. The rejection occurred before the entire student body. My parents' intervention only elevated the entire episode.

During that era, school activities essentially were left to teachers and administrators. Consequently, when Dad and Mom stepped up, they received top-level attention: The school superintendent, Marshall Cheever, pledged that "Doug will get his letter." Fulfillment of that promise required a formal vote of approval from the five- member school board, however. I later discovered the actual vote was 3-2. Inexplicably Halverson subsequently left his coaching job at Winthrop and was replaced by two individuals—Tom Heffner and Lloyd Berry. Both were capable and I liked them, but they eventually confessed to me that Halverson and other so-called "respectable" citizens of Winthrop had advised them not to depend on me for basketball and baseball.

I was, naturally, happy to be done with the drama and the back-stabbing. I spent that summer, before entering college, working with my buddy Del Bowden for a small construction company on a bridge project. It was my first full-time job, giving me the feeling of being mature and somewhat macho. The bridges we built were mostly on rural roads at twenty-five to thirty feet in the air; honestly, I was a tad apprehensive since I had a fear of heights, which I never confessed to my co-workers. I was only eighteen years old, and it was tough work; the day began at seven o'clock in the morning and usually ended at six o'clock or later in the evening. I still lived at the farm and used my parents Ford pickup truck to commute to the construction site. Compared to farm chores, construction work was non-stop and a little dangerous, considering equipment we used like jackhammers and dynamite. It was also a different community where many older workers routinely used profanity, some of which I had never heard.

One hot, humid Sunday, I answered a knock on the door and was greeted by Donald Brown from Manchester, Iowa, a town about twenty miles away in neighboring Delaware County. He had just finished his freshman year at the University of Iowa in pre-med. He implored me to go through Rush Week and touted the attributes of his fraternity Phi Delta Theta. Don, I later discovered, had a perfect 4.0 grade point average his first year. He eventually became head of cardiology at the University Hospital. But that day at my home, he provided my first introduction to Greek fraternities; I was indeed flattered he had driven those dirt roads to extend me an invitation.

I followed his advice, which had been the same as my school superintendent in Winthrop, a man I respected. He had advised me to attend Iowa and had also suggested I get into a fraternity. I pledged Phi Delta Theta, joining Brown, who became my pledge father. I was the only one from a real farm; the other twenty-six pledges were from larger towns or cities like Des Moines and Cedar Rapids. I may have also been the only Democrat in the group; most were from better-heeled parents than mine and more inclined to be country club Republicans, whom folks at home commonly stereotyped as snotty and exclusive, often behaving as if regular people were beneath them.

I was quite taken with myself knowing that one of the best fraternities on campus had allowed me into their inner sanctum. I quickly learned about the hazing we would undergo as young pledges from the active members of the fraternity. For example, we had lineups every Monday night at the house, where we were forced to stand at attention, military-style, while being verbally harassed and questioned. If someone failed to answer correctly, that person had to perform an endless number of push ups. Luckily, the physical labor on the farm and bridge construction made me well-suited for such an ordeal. We also were relegated to subservient status in any and all activities while in the fraternity house, forcing us to be at the beck and call of senior members.

Often there were all-night work sessions to clean the fraternity house. One specific occasion could have led to my expulsion from the university. As the pledges were all working, one of my fraternity brothers, Tom Way, asked me to step outside and walk to our lower parking lot. There, I encountered three others drinking beer in my pledge brother Ken Kinsey's brand new Thunderbird. Way and I hopped in; I refused a beer, however, feeling guilty about ditching my fellow pledges. Ken, hearing a suggestion to get something to eat, started the car and headed to downtown Iowa City. He immediately drove through a red light, catching the attention of a police cruiser. He stopped, jumped out of the car and waved at the police officer. Then, as he got back in, he accelerated the speed, traveling at about sixty to seventy miles per hour while beer cans were discarded out the windows. As we approached a sharp right hand turn, the car hit the curb, went over a collection of tall hedges and landed in the front yard of University President Virgil Hancher. We all jumped out, running as if our lives depended on our escape. The police, chasing us, were yelling to halt. There was no way I was going to stop.

In Hancher's backyard, I flipped over a guardrail into a ravine, raced in the dark back to our fraternity house and, once there, dove into bed, shaking from the ordeal. Somehow all five of us eluded the police. Still, I believed my short college career over. The next morning, all the local newspapers carried a photo of the T-Bird on the president's lawn. Incensed, my English teacher held up a copy of one publication for all of us to see and lambasted the culprits; they should be tossed out of school, he argued. Little did he know I was one of those students. That knowledge might have prevented him from giving me an "A." Ken, with a good attorney, was only charged with reckless driving.

That little episode didn't end hazing, however. It continued through "Hell Week." Eighteen of the original twenty-six pledges made the required grade average and became active members. Before our formal acceptance, however, we had to wear burlap bags under our suits to class. Inside the frat house, we wore a raw onion on a string around our necks and were forced to bite into it whenever we failed to respond quickly enough. We also had to eat the classic "white meal: white potatoes, white onions, and oatmeal, washed down with salt water. Just thinking about it now makes me gag. We also managed to survive being enclosed in a small telephone booth while smoking long, cheap cigars. While that may have made me ill, I retain a fondness for a fine cigar.

Looking back now, politics may have been a prime reason for my willingness to pledge Phi Delta Theta. Adlai Stevenson had belonged to that same national fraternity. In my sixth grade civics class in 1952, I gave my first political speech in support of Stevenson, when he was the Democratic presidential nominee. He was a reform governor of Illinois and was considered an intellectual politician. Despite his association, there was a negative side to the fraternity, however: No blacks were allowed in any Iowa fraternity. Most national parent fraternities prohibited the admission of blacks and Jews. A chapter that made the mistake of embracing such individuals would have its charter pulled and denied recognition. There were Jewish fraternities on campus. But they too, weren't welcomed in most Greek clubs. Discrimination or not, I embraced my acceptance. The next year, I found it a little strange that we had at least three Jews who were social affiliates of our Phi Delta fraternity. They took part in all parties and hung out with us. Two of them, Marv Meyer and Gary Lubin became good friends. Truthfully, then, I was too young to fully understand the dynamic between Jews and others in this country. I soon understood the connection between the discrimination they suffered and that of African Americans.

There was a moment in my first semester when I considered leaving the fraternity. My grades were sliding. My pledge father Don Brown talked me out of it. Somehow, I managed to get nearly a three-point average, with an "A" in English. I think the reason I received that grade was an extemporaneous two-minute speech I gave on a subject unique to the farm. Going through an explanation of how one would call pigs, I actually demonstrated the technique at the top of my lungs in our small classroom, which became filled with gales of laughter.

By the next semester, I had become self-assured and confident, spending more time in the student union. Black students were there as well; it was probably the only place they could freely socialize. They seemed accepted and most had girlfriends who were white since few African- American women attended Iowa then. Nevertheless, the roles of blacks in the school were consistent with the narrative that television had presented years earlier. They essentially were entertainers. The football players were like gladiators. I was friendly with many of them—although still mindful that they were never seen at a "Greek" party. Integration was okay, but only up to a point, in liberal Iowa City in 1960.

After a successful freshman year, I resumed my summer bridge construction work which remained difficult and dangerous. I soon walked off the job after a disagreement with my foreman. Three days later, I received an offer from a road construction company, owned by the father of a fraternity brother, to help with repairs to a section of old Highway 20; the work site was a mere six miles from the family farm. It was an adventurous and fun filled summer. Between dating two different girls who lived in opposite directions, and hanging out with a group of guys who went to countless dances in northern-eastern Iowa, I kept myself busy. My father had bought me a used 1955 Ford Fairlane automobile for four hundred dollars. I paid him half out of my summer earnings, giving me the luxury of having my own transportation.

Both Richard M. Nixon and John F. Kennedy were immersed in the 1960 presidential race; the latter eventually won—although he lost Iowa. There was a strong anti-Catholic feeling in the state. It probably cost Herschel Loveless, who was favored to win, a U.S. Senate seat. In addition, Edward McManus, the Catholic Lt. Governor, was defeated in his quest to succeed Loveless. I didn't allow myself to become entangled in those dynamics.

My good grades during my freshman year had earned me a private room at the fraternity house. I tried out for the cheerleading squad at the suggestion of Judy Schnur, a fraternity brother's girlfriend. While the audition was mostly on a dare, I was chosen. I was in great physical shape, which helped, and the obligations were made easy because I was a diehard sports fan. Believe it or not, politics took a back seat to cheerleading.

But once again, my grades began dropping during the first semester of my second year. I decided to move out of the fraternity house to a private, off-campus apartment, hoping to re-establish myself as a serious student. That move expanded my horizons socially and intellectually. No longer relying on Greek life for stimulation; I met new and interesting people including Jews, blacks and a few "artsy" types. I also started working for a Chinese husband/wife team of doctors at the University Hospital, who were examining how disease was transmitted by snails from rice patties to humans. I may have not understood all the intricacies of their study but I began understanding their culture beyond the proper use of chopsticks; at $1.40 per hour, the pay was good.

That summer, my parents introduced me to an insurance salesman; he handled group hospitalization coverage for farmers who were members of a rural electric cooperative. It was a huge blessing. I had grown tired of construction work, so I took the state insurance test and passed. With my Ford and plenty of time, I sold insurance all summer. I not only made instant money, the policies I sold would pay me financial annuities well into my first year of law school, providing me a measure of stability.

As summer's end neared, I wasn't enthusiastic about returning to the University of Iowa. I contemplated transferring to the University of Colorado or the University of California in Los Angeles. At Colorado my application was too late. I reconsidered U.C.L.A., determining it was too far away for my 1955 Ford to journey.

I talked over my options with the McDevitts, who I considered a second family. They lived in a large house in Winthrop. The father was my dentist. He had four sons; the youngest, Joe, and I became close friends from the time we were ten years old. Devout Irish Catholics, they were always caring and attentive to me. They also introduced me to a life beyond Winthrop and the farm. They all were avid readers and subscribed to the *Wall Street Journal*, the *Chicago Tribune* and intellectual magazines like Harpers. I stayed overnight many times at their home when I was a teenager. That close relationship led me to value their opinions. They urged me to apply to Marquette University in Milwaukee. I did, and was accepted.

The McDevitts also introduced me to the Wolkomir family in Milwaukee, who wanted a live-in boarder to babysit their fourteen year-old son, Michael. The previous year, he had been stalked by a mentally disturbed woman, who even broke into their house. The Wolkomirs were Jewish, and through them I became immersed in their culture and traditions. I compared the experience with a graduate-level course. Maurice Wolkomir, or Mory as he liked to be called, wore wire-framed glasses, was slight of build and fairly intense. During WWII he had been a member of the Office of Strategic Service (OSS), the forerunner of the present CIA. Once, while he was away on business, his wife, Josephine, narrated the story about an incident that took place during her time as a WAVE (Woman Accepted for Volunteer Emergency Service).

Established in July 1942 as a division of the U.S. Navy, it consisted entirely of women. One evening, Josephine had come back to her dormitory room where she lived with the other WAVEs at the training center at Hunter College in New York City; she discovered a large swastika painted in red lipstick on her bathroom mirror. Tears came to her eyes, as she recounted the experience. She asked that I sit still in the living room while she went upstairs. She returned shortly, holding a small tin box. From it she pulled photographs of naked corpses of Jews; others stood around wearing minimal clothing. She said Mory took the pictures while being an undercover OSS agent in the concentration camp. They were priceless and unforgettable. I still vividly recall a couple that revealed bodies piled like cordwood in stacks at least six feet high. In another, a prisoner pushed a wheelbarrow filled with three bodies; their limbs dangled over the sides. Josephine told me that Mory didn't completely trust the United States government. He kept copies of photographs to prove the activities of the Nazis and the breadth of the Holocaust. I was moved by what I saw as well as by Josephine's stories. They raised a larger question: If discrimination still continued in the United States against Jews and blacks, what was the war about?

PART TWO

WAITING ROOM
FOR COLORED ONLY.

BY ORDER
POLICE DEPT.

CHAPTER FOUR

Skipping the South, Shipping Out

BY February 1962, I had transferred from Marquette back to the University of Iowa. My cousin Nikki Patton approached me about accompanying her that summer to Mississippi. I was entering my senior year in college and was pondering my next move. But other young people around the country were going to the aid of African Americans in their fight for civil rights. Nikki wanted to volunteer with the Student Non-Violence Coordinating Committee (SNCC). The group was affiliated with the Southern Christian Leadership Conference, begun by the Rev. Martin Luther King, Jr., the Rev. Ralph Abernathy and the Rev. Joseph Lowery. The prime leaders of the southern Civil Rights Movement, they had inspired thousands of people to fight against centuries old oppression and discrimination. SNCC, with an army of college students, intended to converge on several southern states, including Mississippi and Alabama, determined to register thousands of blacks to vote. A pert redhead, Nikki fit the stereotype of a sorority girl. Still, she was determined to play a role in the movement. She and I existed in different worlds, however. She was from a comfortable suburban Wilmette, Illinois family with considerably more independence than myself. Equally important, my view of the world, at that time, wasn't necessarily black versus white. It was rich versus poor, or some equivalent.

Entertaining Nikki's proposal was impossible. I couldn't escape the reality of my need for money, particularly since my faithful green and white Ford Fairlane was holding on for dear life. The tires were getting bad and the transmission was starting to fail. Overall its body was definitely becoming atrophied. Without me, Nikki eventually opted not to make the trip down south.

As my graduation day in 1963 approached, my friend Terrance Ferry pointed a way to the future, though in hindsight it may have been more an escape. Late one day, as we walked to Donnelley's Irish Pub for a few drafts, he told me he was going to Europe that summer. Ferry was a halfback for the Iowa Hawkeyes, prone to troublesome injuries, but he had been an all-state high school football player from Boone, Iowa. He wasn't your average jock, however. He was very independent and irreverent. Some even described him as "a bit of a hippy" or avant-garde. He also possessed a rugged handsomeness that many compared to Robert Redford. Ferry suggested I come along for the adventure abroad. Intrigued by the idea and unsure of my post graduate possibilities, I decided to check with my insurance manager Dick Burrell to decide whether I could get an advance on my annuity payment, which usually ranged from one hundred dollars to one hundred twenty dollars monthly. I was fantasizing about Europe when, in fact, I was totally broke and would probably have to sell group insurance that summer. That reality didn't constrain me, however. I considered how much money I would need, probably six hundred dollars. Today, that sum would be equivalent to over four thousand six hundred dollars, adjusted for inflation. Dick told me National Travelers had agreed to the "loan" of six hundred dollars. I was elated. Not only was it enough to bring a dream to life, it allowed me to delay a decision about my career choices. The ship on which Ferry and I were to travel was scheduled to leave Montreal before the graduation ceremony, which meant there wouldn't be the usual college closure.

We hitched a ride to Montreal with one of his fraternity brothers. When we arrived, I looked up McGill University and discovered there was a Phi Delta Theta fraternity on campus, so we just showed up at the door. It was nearly June and not many people were left in the house. They welcomed us cordially. That evening we slept under the stars on their rooftop. The next morning we went on board the "Arkadia," a Greek ship bound for London. The ship was old and filled with many nationalities and classes. Most passengers were from Canada and the British Isles. There were a few Americans, but in 1963 traveling to Europe was still expensive, a treat reserved primarily for the upper-income strata—not poor college students like Ferry and myself.

The voyage turned out to be one of the best ten days of my life. It was a new frontier with many new relationships: an elderly Scottish couple, an African-American graduate student studying abroad for a year, and a couple from Iowa, accompanied by their daughter-in-law, an attractive blonde with her 5-year-old son. I began a ten-day affair with a Canadian girl from Ottawa, who was three or four years older than I. Ferry also met someone, which forced me, at times, to find alternative sleeping arrangements. Over the course of the trip about twenty of us hung together as a group. We spent our time in the sun, drinking Heineken beers at ten cents per bottle. We also put on a play, a spoof about traveling on a ship. The other passengers and crew served as the audience.

Every day we had lunch and dinner at the same table, covered with white linen tablecloths, our food was served on fine china. On the fourth day, our African-American table mate was summoned to the captain's headquarters. He returned fifteen minutes later, his face ashen and filled with an expression of shock. His good friend Medgar Evers, the field secretary for the NAACP working and living in Mississippi, had been assassinated outside his home with his wife and children in the house. Ferry and I were speechless. It was the first time I knew anyone who had direct association with someone brutally affected by southern racism. After the ship docked, I read details about the murder. But candidly, while the story made a distinctly negative impression on me, it was soon forgotten within the rhythms of my youthful adventures.

Our ship made a short stop in Cobh, Ireland, before traveling on to London, where Ferry and I stayed for several nights. We said goodbye to our Canadian shipmates and headed to Dover, England, hitchhiking separately. I was picked up by a milkman, which forced me to accompany him at each home stop, including many in the outskirts of London. Hitchhiking then was relatively easy and safe, even if the rides sometimes were unusual.

Despite the inconvenience, I made it to Dover, connecting with Ferry, who had met a young British guy with a car headed to Paris. We gladly accepted his offer of a ride, first traveling on the ferry into Calais. At one point, the Brit grew tired so I took over driving, which was a little scary. The two-lane road was narrow and there was a light rain. Nevertheless, we arrived at our destination in the great city of Paris. We checked into a low-rent hotel on the Left Bank. We soon hooked up with a young French couple who in their very nice Citroen car, took us on a tour—from Montmartre to the Eiffel Tower to the French bistros. A few days later, I met two female students from Columbia University in New York. Ferry had fallen ill and was confined to his room, leaving me on my own. One evening, I took the girls back to our room, but Ferry's illness had worsened and he had no interest in meeting anyone—not even new girls, which underscored the seriousness of his condition. They left and I persuaded him that a walk would do him good. After a block, he was leaning against a building unable to go further. A hospital was near and he checked in. I suspected he had eaten something that didn't agree with him. It turned out that he had a bad case of dysentery. I went back to the hospital room the next day and told him I intended to hitchhike to Cologne. I would find accommodations, and leave a message for him at the local American Express office. Before cell phones and e-mails, that was a primary way of communicating.

My plan experienced a slight obstacle, although I easily found a ride with a young French man, who dropped me in Cologne's central district about eight that evening. When I tried registering at several hotels, even ones out of my price range, I could not find any available. Seeing a young couple, whom I thought to be German, I sought their help. The man, who spoke English fairly well, told me to follow them. I was traveling light with only one small suitcase; still, I was exhausted. After checking two or three more hotels, he reported that a major convention in Cologne had consumed all the rooms. He asked me to wait while he spoke with his lady friend, whom I later discovered was his wife. Surprisingly, Klaus and Christina Brodbeck offered me space in their home. Their generosity was no simple act: They had a one year-old son and were crowded in one of the bedrooms in Klaus's mother's two-bedroom apartment. I was embarrassed to displace them. But they later decided to stay with Christina's parents. I expected Ferry to arrive soon. They told me not to worry, that he also would be welcomed.

The next morning, I met Klaus's mother, a truly gracious and personable German woman in her early fifties. She had reared Klaus and his younger brother Hans through World War II. Her husband, a railroad executive, had been killed when his train was bombed about two weeks before Allied forces ended the battle. Ferry and I could thank President Kennedy for the Brodbecks' embrace of us. He had just given his "Ich bein eine Berliner" speech a few days earlier. The Germans thought him courageous, particularly because of the continuous Russian threat at the height of the Cold War. Interestingly, the United States had almost come full circle. His father, Joseph Kennedy, had been a fervent opponent of the U.S.'s involvement with Great Britain in WWII. He thought the British were trying to draw the United States into the war and believed Germany would easily overwhelm them. That position, which he publicly expressed, cost him his ambassadorship to the Court of St. James; President Franklin D. Roosevelt had him recalled, essentially firing him. Roughly twenty-five years later, another Kennedy had come to the aid of the Germans. The Brodbecks told me they wanted to reciprocate. So, they gave us the warmth and hospitality of their home.

Ferry arrived two days later. Not only did the Brodbecks house and feed us home-cooked meals, Klaus assisted us in finding a vehicle to continue our travels. It was truly a rudimentary vehicle with unsynchronized gearing and manual pop-up turn signals. Nevertheless, we purchased the 1949 blue Volkswagen, paying only four hundred German marks or one hundred twenty-five U.S. dollars. We knew we were lucky to have made the friendships of the Brodbecks. The next day, after profusely thanking them, we were on our way to Copenhagen, Denmark.

Two sights I remember well: First, we toured the Carlsburg Brewery and drank too much. Second, we went to Tivoli Gardens. From there, we went to Hamburg, spending one night in the red-light "Reeperbahn" section of the St. Pauli district, where the Beatles got their start. It was a popular spot for tourists and locals. Prostitutes were in abundance; most were on display in department store-like windows. It was fascinating but seedy. People in the crowds were representative of many countries. Ferry and I walked into a pub and sat at the bar, having a local Hamburg Pilsner beer. Then, the music started and a "woman," clad in a large yellow chiffon dress and spike heels, walked the wooden plank right in front of us. I whispered to Ferry that I was certain she wasn't a "she." Chicago, Minneapolis and New Orleans, La., were filled with such entertainers who seemed to defy reality. French singer Charles Aznavour asked in a song "What makes a man a man?" The dancer that night asked the opposite of that question. Sensing perhaps I was dubious, she began undressing directly in front of me. I ignored her as best I could until the finale when she threw the yellow chiffon dress over my head along with the blonde wig, bringing laughter from the patrons who knew the secret: he was merely a female impersonator.

"Let's get out of here" I told Ferry, exclaiming "I told you!" along the way as he chuckled at my expense.

While traveling, we stayed abreast of events back home by reading the *International Herald Tribune*. President Kennedy was having issues with his legislative program, since Congress was still basically controlled by southern Democrats like Senator Richard Russell in the Senate and Howard W. Smith from Virginia, chairman of the U. S. House of Representatives Rules Committee. I sent my parents postcards almost weekly, providing them details of my trip. There were not a great number of young American tourists who looked like us. So, we found ourselves usually embraced by the local population. I should have felt a tinge of guilt, perhaps. After all, there were people back home registering black southerners to vote and losing their lives in the process. I, on the other hand, was having one long party.

The next day, after our rather unique night out, we headed for Berlin. Highway access was very limited. We decided to enter East Germany at Helmstedt. At this access, named Checkpoint Bravo, we came to an abrupt stop. There was a long line of cars waiting to enter the autobahn that went to the garrison city of West Berlin. Since the end of World War II, East Germany, with the backing of Russia, permitted only one main road into West Berlin; that made the journey into the city very difficult. Further, once on the autobahn, there wasn't an opportunity to exit until fully in West Berlin. Aside from the considerable wait, we had to pay a toll fee. At Checkpoint Bravo, there were plenty of armed soldiers. Most were East Germans, but there were also a few Russians, who seemed to be in control. Despite those conditions, West Berlin had become a Mecca for American and other Western tourists. Still, its isolation from other parts of Germany and the difficulty entering it, helped create the feeling of a city living on borrowed time.

We were not discouraged, however. We presented our passports to the East German administrative personnel for processing. As he examined them intently, we noticed a young man about our age in black motorcycle garb. He engaged us in a rather loud conversation about the absurdity and ridiculousness of the process. We remained quiet, concerned about drawing any undue attention to ourselves and creating any type of disturbance. Finally, with our papers stamped, we were on our way. We saw the same cyclist outside who, walking up to the tall Russian at the door, told him "Boy, you think you are pretty dapper and important don't you? Well, I am not as impressed as you are."

Ferry and I quickly walked past, making sure no one thought us associated with the brash upstart. As we made our way to our car, however, he caught up with us and introduced himself as Myron Bylich. His cycle, a black BMW R60, was absolutely beautiful. Ferry and I took an immediate liking to him. He was a graduate of Boston College. We decided to travel together as well as room together in West Berlin, and went through Check-Point Charlie together to reach East Berlin. The contrast between the divided cities was enormous. The West was lively, filled with neon lights and plenty of American military personnel. East Berlin was drab and oppressive. The trip between the two was like going from Times Square to Independence, Iowa.

We stayed in West Berlin about four nights before heading south to Switzerland. Ferry had heard Lucerne was a wonderful city, with a beautiful lake and surrounding mountains. From there we drove to Innsbruck, Austria, on the way to Brenner Pass. In Innsbruck, we met a somewhat older, black-American couple and approached them for directions. We soon found ourselves in a long conversation about their experiences. They were from the Midwest, and stated emphatically that they were being very well treated in Europe. The paucity of African Americans may have made them a curiosity. Later, I would learn more about the history of blacks in Europe. Most migrated to the continent to avoid the oppressive discrimination that marked their lives in the United States. Paul Robeson and Josephine Baker were early travelers but others, including James Baldwin and Nina Simone, came and made places like France and London home, until their deaths.

Ferry and I took turns driving through the Alps. While one of us drove, the other rode with Myron on his BMW cycle. Just outside Lucerne, I was on the bike when he rolled into a steep curve. I was tossed off, leaving much of the skin on my left leg on the highway. Fortunately, neither Bylich nor the bike was injured. By happenstance, a Red Cross ambulance came along, and stopped to help us. The two men quickly bandaged my leg; before long we were off to Italy. As we crossed the border, Bylich decided to leave us, heading to Turkey to visit relatives in the country of his ancestors. It was sad to see him leave; in a short time he had become a good friend. Ferry and I continued with our sojourn, traveling through Florence, then to Rome, stopping in Pisa to see the leaning tower.

One evening, it began to rain fairly hard and we didn't have a place to sleep. We located a small covered bridge near the city center and parked. We placed our sleeping bags under the bridge. Out of harm's way, we settled in and slept soundly. We both awoke about six in the morning to find that we had unofficial sleeping partners. Italians down on their luck also were there under the bridge—except they only had newspapers on the ground and over them to keep them warm and dry. We immediately rolled up our bags and left. On another night, after heavy drinking, we planted ourselves in pasture we thought was safe to sleep in. We awoke early in the morning to the pounding hooves. We had not only slept next to a horse-racing track, we also had deposited ourselves on a lively anthill. We beat a hasty retreat.

We arrived in Monaco wanting to see Monte Carlo, since we were fervent James Bond devotees. The next day we drove to Aix-En-Provence and to our final destination, Barcelona. We stayed only one night in one of the pensions. They were very popular in the fifties and early sixties. They are now commonly referred to as hostels, appealing to younger and less well-off tourists. We stayed only one night in one of the pensions, which were small, usually inexpensive, hotels that offered shared rooms. They were very popular in the fifties and early sixties. They are now commonly referred to as hostels, appealing to younger and less well-off tourists. We decided to go to Masnou, a lovely beachfront city outside of Barcelona. It was much cheaper and we had the option of sleeping on the beach. Almost immediately we met a group of young college girls from South Africa and Germany who were all either related or friends from their respective universities in Munich.

After four days of sun and sand, Ferry knew he had to get back to the university to begin fall football practice. He left to go home via Portugal. I stayed for another four or five days on the beach. A local restaurant allowed me to clean up and shave in the restroom in the mornings. In the evenings, I slept under an overturned wooden boat with mosquito netting over my face. One evening, as I was dozing off, two uniformed soldiers with light machine guns were patrolling the beach. Sleeping on the beach was forbidden. I simply ignored the ordinance. Franco, the dictator head of Spain, was paranoid about invasion from the seas and had Policia Armada, or Grises, patrolling the beaches. The Grises or "greys" (due to the color of their uniforms) were a constant reminder of the existing dictatorship. I feigned sleep. One of the soldiers kicked sand on my face and body. I didn't stir. They eventually moved on, believing me harmless or drunk. I breathed easier and fell back to sleep. The next day, however, thinking I had worn out my beach welcome, I left for Frankfurt, Germany. I said a hasty goodbye to the German girl from the college group with whom I had become quite close; then I started up the VW and got on the road, again.

CHAPTER FIVE

Beyond Heineken

I decided to stay and work in Europe, preferably in Germany. I wanted to experience my parents' and grandparents' native land, connecting with a piece of their history and, thus, my own. Grandfather Adolf had been right when he warned about Hitler and how he might ultimately destroy Germany. I wanted to better understand how my grandfather had made his assessment. Equally important, I wanted that exploration to be deeper than what would come from being a mere tourist. Consequently, upon arriving in Frankfurt, I headed to the US Army post; I had heard civilians sometimes were hired there. At about five o'clock in the afternoon I found myself outside the gate in front of a large brick enclosure that was the size of a fort. Where could I find accommodations, I asked a soldier with MP on his arm badge. Come back later that evening, he told me, and he would help me get a room in one of the barracks in the compound. I left to purchase a meal at a local pub, and returned as he advised at about ten o'clock but he wasn't there. I hung around the entrance a few minutes until another officer noticed my presence. I explained my situation, recounting my previous conversation. He asked me to wait, and within fifteen minutes he returned, directing me to a building about five hundred feet away. Grab a bunk on the second floor, he told me. All the beds were without sheets or blankets. Some soldiers were already asleep. I climbed on the top bunk, where there was already a blanket and an uncovered pillow I fell fast asleep. I was awakened suddenly around two in the morning by agitated voices and giggling young women. I thought I was dreaming. The overhead lights came on and three or four MP's bellowed orders to some of the uniformed soldiers, who had smuggled in German prostitutes, and were attempting to hide them in their uniform lockers, which is nearly impossible by any standard.

One of the MP's glanced up at me. He may have thought it a little strange that someone was sleeping with only one blanket and no sheets. I worried I'd be evicted in the middle of the night. He hesitated a second, then continued herding the prostitutes out of the barracks. I breathed a huge sigh of relief, considering myself lucky. Early the next morning, as I was shaving in the bathroom, a soldier at an adjacent sink struck up a conversation.

"Did you get in with the 101st?" I nodded yes, not really knowing about any such unit or being able to communicate in military lingo. He seemed content with the answer. I quickly jumped in the hot shower—enjoying a luxury that had escaped me for days.

Just outside the barracks, I met a recently discharged young soldier in civilian clothes who introduced himself as Luis Espinosa. He intended to hitchhike north to Dusseldorf to get a job where he had friends at the American military base. We struck a deal: If he paid the major portion of the gas, he could ride with me. We stopped in Cologne and stayed one night with my German friends, who accommodated us but were a little apprehensive about Espinosa, a Hispanic from the Western United States. He had been in the US Army for several years. He was unpolished, however, and lacked a formal education.

The next morning, we arrived in Dusseldorf. We stayed in an apartment and slept on the floor with his Army buddies. Back home I had lived a comfortable life. My situation in a foreign country was providing me with a practical understanding of how economic limits can sometimes force one to lower one's standards and adopt to the situation. Further, as I observed Espinosa and his friends, and much later, as I lived in the country for a few weeks, I came to appreciate the fact that blacks weren't the only people discriminated against. On some days, I imagined I could have been in some segregated southern town. But I am getting a little ahead of the story.

Espinosa's friends told me about possible job opportunities at the British commissionaire, which was the equivalent of the U.S. Army PX. I went there the next day but found myself in a Catch 22: The British official there relayed that to acquire a job in post-war Germany, a work permit was needed. At the permit office, I learned I had to be employed before such a document would be issued. The promise of a job was insufficient. They needed written proof. So, I drove back to the British commissionaire, and after much discussion, the manager took pity on me and stamped the necessary form confirming I had a job. He warned I had to get the permit that day. I hopped in the VW and drove back to the municipal office, barely arriving before closing time. After the numerous ink stamps by the German bureaucrats going through at least four levels, I received the required permit. I suddenly understood how the Nazis had indicted themselves with regard to the atrocities of World War II. They had maintained a perfect paper trail, keeping records for years and years— even after the war. It was obviously an obsession.

 The commissionaire, where I worked for the British as a stock boy, was located in a huge building, with four stories and a basement that consumed an entire city block. Only about a quarter of it was usable because of limited electricity and plumbing, however. In reality, it was a series of dark or nearly dark rooms and hallways. During its heyday in the 1930s and 1940s, it may have been used by the Nazis as a communal space for youth, males and females, as they built the "super race" in Germany. I was given a room upstairs with a bed and shared the showers with others in the building, although I was the only occupant in that section. I counted myself very fortunate, since by then I was completely broke. We were fed lunch through the British kitchen on the second floor. I became friends with the other workers, who lived on the top floor and were an interesting bunch, to say the least. There was David, who was a tall, lonely, single, good looking guy from somewhere in England; Charlie, a Cockney from London, was married to a German woman who was in England where she preferred to live. Another Brit was married to a delightful German woman; and a Dutch man had a British roommate who was half- Asian; I suspected they were gay. There was a middle-easterner also called Charlie, who wasn't well liked. Two younger boys—one Maltese and the other British—were about sixteen, or the minimum working age. Things went splendidly for two weeks. David and I became good friends. He was dating a German girl and I met several of his friends. The Cockney Charlie thought of me as a son he never had; we occasionally went to the local pubs where he would treat me to fine German beer.

Then, the mood shifted one day. At about one o'clock in the morning, Cockney Charlie awakened me; someone had broken into the building. We had to help the British military police find the culprit. A platoon of soldiers could have hidden out in that vast complex without discovery. After two or three fruitless hours, we gave up the search. A few days later, I had my worst experience. Charlie, the middle-easterner, periodically sexually harassed female workers. I also caught him attempting to molest the young males, particularly the Maltese teenager who had adopted me as his protector. I stepped in, telling Charlie to back off. He did. But I

THE **WHITE GUY** IN THE ROOM: *A Political Memoir*

wasn't satisfied. Five minutes later, he was dozing on a dolly while the rest of us were working. I snatched it from under him and threw him up against a concrete wall in the hallway. Then, I retrieved the dolly, turned and walked down the hallway toward the delivery truck. I heard Adrian, the Maltese youngster, screaming: "He is coming for you, Doug!" Charlie had a meat cleaver he had gotten from the butcher shop. Without my own weapon, I dropped the dolly car and raced to the office of the British manager, Mr. Culbertson, whose first name we never bothered to learn. I excitedly told him Charlie was chasing me and was mentally unstable.

"Doug, do you really believe that Charlie would cause physical harm?" he asked, brushing off my concerns.

"Yes I do Mr. Culbertson." I left his office determined to avoid the basement.

Within thirty minutes, the drama of the morning was exacerbated. A friend ran up to me asking whether I had any food or items from the store. He told me to go to my room immediately and discard them. An SIS officer was in the building since Culbertson had reported the meat cleaver incident. The SIS, often known as MI-6, was very similar to our FBI and was in charge of criminal incidents at the British posts. I ignored David's advice—although he told me that to save his own skin, Charlie had told the SIS agent that every employee was stealing. It was essentially true. When I started, I had attempted to purchase some food items and toiletries such as razor blades. But I had been told the store could only sell to British citizens. Without sufficient funds for gas to drive to downtown Dusseldorf, and feeling desperate, I made a cardinal mistake. I took a few items—crackers and cookies and toiletries—from the store. Other workers, particularly the Germans, also pilfered merchandise. I was summoned to Culbertson's office by the SIS agent that day, and confessed my offense.

They already knew because they had searched my room and discovered the princely sum of $5.05 in merchandise. I was dismissed. They also fired four other employees including Charlie. I was told to leave the next day. I felt dejected.

I had intended to stay at least through the winter. I had a job I liked, room and board, and I enjoyed the people with whom I worked. What I had done was stupid—and illegal. The next morning David, Cockney Charlie, and the other Brits came to me. They told me they had gone to the SIS and Culbertson and pleaded that I be retained. They agreed to keep me but said I couldn't stay in the building. It was a noble gesture by my co-workers. Without room and board, the pay was insufficient to cover my expenses. I learned a valuable lesson at twenty-two: Don't take something that isn't yours.

I drove over to Espinosa's place of work. He was ready to move on, but wanted to go back to Southern Germany, preferably the Munich area. We teamed up again—truly a pair of strange bedfellows. We drove the next day all the way to an Army post near Schleissheim, close to the infamous Dachau concentration camp of World War II. Schleissheim was the army airfield site where Espinosa used to be stationed. That evening, we somehow gained entrance to the non-commissioned officers club. Espinosa had several buddies still there. I felt somewhat uneasy. Alcohol— and a lot of it—seemed to be the main binding ingredient for these men. Espinosa asked them if there was a place for us to sleep. They directed us to a barracks room. I still had my sleeping bag and grabbed space on the floor. About three or four in the morning, the overhead lights came on over our prostrate bodies. A large sergeant-type ordered us out. He was an old enemy of Espinosa's. We went back to the VW where we dozed until daylight.

Later that day, I found a place to stay with a middle-aged German couple, who had two unheated small rooms. After the wife became comfortable with me, she confided that she had had a son born out of wedlock to an American soldier; she placed the child for adoption. Now, however, she and her husband had no children, just a beautiful German shepherd they adored. I took to them, and was thankful for shelter over our heads. We obtained jobs on a German water pipeline construction crew. Within ten days, Espinosa had had enough, however. He obtained a civilian job at the Army base and moved out of the house.

I soon realized I needed to renew my work permit at the local municipal office in Munich. During that process, I spotted two attractive women who also were acquiring permits. They were South Africans. I was particularly enamored with one, Inga Klugkist. Unfortunately I had to get back to my construction job and didn't have time to get her full dossier. I liked her personality, composure, and great looks. The next night, I was determined to find her. Inga and I developed a relationship. We went out for cheap dinners and, as a rule, shared the cost since neither of us had many marks. As we got to know each other, she talked about her upbringing in Apartheid South Africa, which was more extreme than the water fountain experience I had confronted in Tampa. I didn't really challenge her. It was more questioning her perspectives, which also provided me opportunity to examine my own opinion. I subsequently learned her stepfather was a finance minister there. Her real father may have been a Fascist. He died in prison during WWII after being captured by the British. She was starting to question things, albeit slowly, about the Apartheid policies of South Africa.

Meanwhile, my blue VW began suffering mechanical problems, forcing me to park it on an incline to facilitate jump starting. One evening after dinner, I left the car running on a street. Inga always had to be back at her dorm by eleven o'clock. I didn't want to risk the car not starting. When we finished our meal and made it back to where we had left the car, it wasn't there. A passerby told us the police had taken it to the station three blocks away. The VW was parked in front; the engine was off. I asked Inga to wait while I went inside. A tall Nordic-looking man, speaking in German, asked for the registration papers. I had them but I knew they had already expired, which would place me in a great deal of legal difficulty. So, I acted as if I didn't understand any German. No one in the station understood English; they became increasingly frustrated. After a few minutes, Inga walked in. The perfect actress, she pretended we had never met. She was inquiring about her work permit, which was a great cover. The young officer, undoubtedly taken with her looks, asked her if she spoke any English. "Yes," she told him. In German, he told her to ask me about the papers to the car. I continued my charade while Inga posed the question in English. I lit up, pretending to just now understand. They are at the boarding house in Schleissheim, I told her in English. After back and forth, and given his mounting frustration, the officer finally gave me the key to the car. Inga left. Within two minutes, I also left and got into the car, which somehow I got started. I drove around the block and picked her up.

A week later, during one of our evening visits, I suggested we move to London via Cologne. I could ask the Brodbecks to dispose of the VW; we could take a train to London, obtain work permits and employment, and live together. She said yes. I told her I would be back the next evening. That morning I told my German employers it was my last day. They paid me and we departed without any bad feelings. I also notified my landlords, who were genuinely sad to see me go. That Monday evening, I drove to Inga's dormitory intent on finalizing the details for our move to London. At dinner I noticed she was rather pensive.

"Did you give your employers notice?" I asked.

She paused and then told me she had decided against going with me. I was crestfallen. She had inquired about whether I could be hired by her employer, because she wanted me to stay. She believed they would hire me. However, only women were given dormitory privileges; men had to find their own quarters. I knew the salary was not nearly enough without the free living quarters. Still, I was ready to make the trip with her to London. I pleaded, but she had made up her mind. She tried to entice me to stay, saying we could ski that winter in the nearby Alps, staying with her relatives. I declined. Months later, in a letter I received after I was back in Iowa, she told me that she feared I would leave her in London thinking I would be overcome by homesickness. Her instincts were probably correct.

Reluctantly, I got in my VW and drove straight back to Cologne. The roughly three hundred sixty miles were not without incident. On a tight budget, I was not about to limit my resources while taking care of my needs. Fortunately, I had met a young GI through Espinosa who had told me he could obtain gas. I contacted him; he gave me a time and location to meet him. When I arrived, he was holding a drab olive-green five-gallon can of petrol. I think he worked at the Army motor pool and simply stole it. I wasn't about to protest. I quickly placed it in the front trunk of the VW, and left early afternoon, driving slowly so as to not arouse notice from the German police on the autobahn. As I was getting tired, I stopped at a rest area and used up the last of the five gallon can. But, the car stopped abruptly. It was dark and I may have been about one hundred miles from Cologne. Another vehicle was in the rest area. In my broken German, I explained my circumstance. The individual obliged by pushing my VW with his vehicle. To my relief, it started up again. I made it to the Brodbecks' home by about eleven that evening. Luckily, Klaus was there, and I was thankful to be with his family once again.

CHAPTER SIX

Candles in the Windows

MY European trip and the trajectory of my life would be altered by the events of the next evening, November 22, 1963. They would push me into politics while forming the nexus between me and African Americans, although at the time I had no indication such dramatic alterations awaited me. Things began very innocently and with pleasure. The Brodbecks and I were having a very satisfying dinner, when the telephone rang around seven o'clock. Hans, the younger of the brothers who was enrolled in medical school, excused himself and went to the kitchen to answer the call. The conversation, in German, was muted. So, I really couldn't discern what was being said. When he returned, speaking in broken English, he asked Klaus and myself about the word "assassination." I thought for some reason a leader, probably France's Charles de Gaulle had been killed or an attempt had been made on his life. Hans shook his head negatively. "No, no." he said. "Kennedy."

Disbelieving him, I got up and turned the radio to the BBC. Kennedy had been shot; his condition uncertain. I was in shock, as were the Brodbecks. Ten minutes later, as we all sat waiting for more details, the announcer said he had been declared dead. Dinner immediately ended. There I was in a foreign country completely powerless to do anything about what was happening across the ocean in my native land. I listened to the BBC for hours before finally forcing myself to turn off the radio and go to bed. The next morning, after breakfast, I went for a long walk through the streets of Cologne. Dejected and depressed, I thought it might help. It didn't.

At the Brodbecks I listened intermittently to BBC reports. After an early dinner, I walked to the famous Cologne cathedral. Only twenty-two, I did not have any friends or my parents around to share my grief. I needed comforting. When I entered the beautiful and crowded church, many Germans were kneeling in prayer. I took a place in a pew, bent down, and offered prayers for Kennedy, the American people, and my own loneliness. I believed the German people were equally despondent. It was quite dark when I left the church. Walking back to the Brodbecks, I saw a sight I have never forgotten. There were lighted candles in the windows of all the houses and apartment buildings, casting a distinct glow throughout the entire city. I was truly grateful and felt humbled by what I perceived as an outpouring of sympathy for Kennedy—a man I considered a hero. When I entered the Brodbecks apartment, only Klaus's mother was still awake, sitting in a corner of the living room, which contained the light of a single lamp. Small in stature, she reminded me of my own mother. She had been crying, and told me she was extremely sorry for Kennedy's death. I said thanks but was unsure what else I could offer, particularly since she sincerely felt as if she had lost a "close friend."

During the next few days, I prepared for my trip back to the states. My European odyssey had come to a very abrupt end. Then, I, and undoubtedly the rest of the world, was shocked again to hear someone named Jack Ruby had shot Lee Harvey Oswald, Kennedy's alleged assassin. What was going on in my country? Life was in turmoil. I knew I had to get back to the states and to Iowa.

At breakfast, I asked Klaus if he knew someone who would take the VW off of my hands. I eventually received one hundred forty marks—about thirty-five American dollars—and said goodbye to my beloved blue VW. I went to a travel agency, hoping to find a freighter that took passengers. One was leaving Rotterdam about the fifth of December headed for Newport News, Virginia. The fare was one hundred thirty-five dollars, which I did not have. I reached out to my parents, which wasn't easy for me—or them. They had to travel to a bank in Oelwein, Iowa, about fifteen miles from their farm. I'd asked for one hundred fifty dollars. The money came by wire two days before the freighter was to depart. I got a ride by car to Rotterdam from Cologne, a distance of roughly one hundred sixty miles. When I saw the ship, the H. M.S. Henning Oldendorff, it was impressive. One of the crew asked me in German if I was English, meaning British. In his broken English, he asked if I would assist him in carrying on some luggage. Sure, I told him. He took one of my small bags; I had shipped most of my clothing back to my parent's farm, keeping only bare essentials plus an overcoat, hat, and gloves. I soon discovered it wasn't luggage he needed my help with, but a case of German beer for crew members. He wanted me to carry it on since they were only allowed a daily maximum of two beers. I lugged the crate up the gangplank, deposited it below, and then found the way to my cabin. It was roomy but very Spartan. Kevin Ramsey from Nashville, Tennessee, a college dropout who had been in Europe for over a year, was my roommate. We had a double bunk; boarding after him, I was relegated to the top.

The freighter had a total of twelve passengers, including two college-age Dutch girls, a discharged American soldier and his German wife, two Swedish gentlemen probably both in their mid-thirties, and a delightful American couple in their sixties. The husband, Walter Phillips, was born and raised in Germany and was an artist well-known for his paintings depicting clowns. His wife was demure. He was more outgoing. They lived in Winter Park, Florida. But, for years, he had been a waiter in a number of Broadway restaurants in New York, including the famous Sardi's. Walter was truly a character: He had made it through two depressions in Germany before immigrating to New York in the late 1930s. While on board, he taught me chess, which with he, the American GI, and Ramsey, Walter and myself played non-stop.

The ship's captain was a true conservative German; I imagine he had been a card carrying Nazi during the war. His first officer, also German, wore a monocle reminiscent of those old 1940s movies. There were usually two tables in the Captain's dining room; Ramsey and I avoided sitting there. Since we were both twenty-two years old, we had healthy appetites, but, all the passengers noticed meal portions were small. One day, I mentioned the size of the meals to the crew member for whom I had lugged the beer. He was puzzled and surprised, saying there was plenty of food in the galley. He promised to bring us more after the Captain and first officer left the dining room. He did, and that evening we gorged ourselves. The next evening, as we were eating food brought by the crew, the Captain barged in with one of his officers and began clearing the table. He threatened to throw Ramsey and me in the brig, essentially putting us under what would have been considered house arrest. I was frightened. The next day, we were back to meager meals, but the crew sent us a message to come below to their quarters. When we arrived, one table was piled with sandwiches and other items. We were somewhat nervous about sneaking food but that did not deter us. We thought we had fooled the Captain, so the next two or three nights found us in the crew members' cabins. The hunt for food went on like that for most of the remaining days.

A constant theme for the discussion among passengers was Kennedy's assassination and the aftermath. Both Phillips and my bunkmate were

Kennedy admirers. We missed the funeral procession, including little John-John's salute as his father's hearse passed, as well as the unbridled outpouring of grief by African Americans, many of whom saw the president as their champion. Initially reluctant, Kennedy had embraced the 1963 March on Washington while Terry Ferry and I traipsed across Europe. Certainly the Rev. Martin Luther King, Jr., bringing together more than 200,000 citizens of diverse ethnicity and economic background should have made African Americans an immovable force. Nevertheless, they still relied on the largess of federal elected officials. Consequently, Kennedy's death brought understandable consternation about whether their progress would be halted. Much of this news I gleaned from old newspapers. On the freighter, there wasn't any radio to be commandeered. The German captain and his subordinates were unfazed by the sufferings and sorrow of the passengers.

Being in the North Atlantic in December meant we had to strap ourselves into our bunk beds while sleeping. One belt went across our ankles and the other over our chest. There were times when the ship seemed in an endless pitch and roll pattern, causing it to be at a forty-five-degree angle. I was, of course, relieved when we finally arrived in Norfolk on a fairly peaceful day. Walter had asked me if I would carry some of his unsold paintings from the ship upon landing. Thinking that we would simply disembark by way of a gangplank onto a dock I readily agreed. To my rude surprise, we would leave the ship by a rope ladder into a tugboat in the middle of the harbor. There was I carrying four large paintings on a narrow rope ladder with wooden steps down the side of the ship. I thought that any minute, I would fall into the water. I made it into the tugboat. Fortunately, one of the crew members had carried my small suitcase. Safely aboard, we motored into the main dock. I said goodbye to all my fellow passengers, realizing how much I would really miss Walter. He was humorous, worldly, and had become a dear friend in the ten days we had been on the ship.

I had about twenty-five dollars in my pocket. My small travel bag included toiletries, one shirt, underwear, and a bottle of French cognac, which I believed would be a great present for my parents. With my heavy overcoat, gloves, and a hat, I was prepared to hitchhike all the way to Iowa. A bittersweet feeling came over me. I was happy to be back on the shores of the United States, but what had fueled my return weighed heavily. As I walked from the dock, it dawned on me that this was the first time I had been in the South since the winter of 1949 and 1950, when we went to Tampa, and I discovered white and colored fountains, a maid longing to be up north, and gambling rooms. A melancholy swept over me, but I was soon comforted by the sight of the golden arches—McDonald's. I went in and ordered a simple hamburger with French fries. I felt lucky to be back on American soil. Although miles from home, I breathed a sigh of relief.

I must have been a sight for sore eyes. On the ship I had begun growing a beard. My hair was long. I was wearing pretty meager clothing. Generally, my appearance certainly didn't invite charity. If I was to get home, I would need a lot of luck and generosity.

I soon found Highway 60, for which I had been searching. I trudged through Norfolk, focused on Lexington, Virginia, which meant going through the Blue Ridge Mountains. As night approached, the cold arrived. I managed one short ride with a trucker, who told me there would be minimal traffic since it was a two-lane highway that was very dark and went through the mountains. He was right. Fortunately, two young men stopped. They were driving to Lexington and both were graduates of Washington and Lee University. Aware that Lexington was a university town, I asked if there was a Phi Delta Theta chapter house. They told me there was, and promised to drop me there, although I was certain they likely were mystified that a person of my appearance would be a member of any fraternity.

Despite my tattered and road-weary look, I walked into the frat house as if I belonged there. It was close to midnight; still four or five members were talking in the living room. I told them who I was and blurted out that I was an Iowa Beta, which was the designation of our chapter at the University of Iowa. They nodded in acknowledgement but may have been skeptical about the veracity of my statement, especially since they were all clean-shaven, dressed in coats and ties. I told them I had just returned from Europe, was headed to Iowa and needed a place to sleep. They pointed me to the long couch in the basement, where I immediately fell asleep. When I awoke, probably around seven in the morning, I wanted to resume my travels, and quickly went to the small bathroom to brush my teeth and shave. The door suddenly opened; an elderly black janitor or house boy, as they called him, entered with his broom. Seeing me in my state of disarray, he dropped his broom and fled. He may have thought me a vagrant. I ran after him trying to assure him that I was not some thief. Visibly shaken, he eventually calmed down.

Getting back on the road, luck, once again, was on my side. I caught a short ride out of Lexington; my goal was Cincinnati, Ohio. A gentleman in an older automobile, which looked to be a 1955 Chevrolet, stopped for me. He was going all the way to my destination. That satisfaction was short lived, however. He was from the south—Kentucky, I believe—and he was going north to find work. He constantly used the N-word and asked if my parents were wealthy since I was coming from Europe. I lied a little, telling him that I was broke, had no college education and, like him, I was going back to Iowa to find work. I guess he bought it. As we drove through the night, he mentioned he needed to sleep a couple of hours in the car. So, he stopped and bought a half-pint of whiskey to help him relax. I climbed in the back seat but, somewhat nervous about him, I never really closed my eyes. Early the next morning, he dropped me on Highway 460 just south of Chicago. I was thankful for the long ride, but also very glad to be rid of him. It was getting bitterly cold and I had lost one of my gloves, making hitchhiking even more difficult. Then, a single driver pulled over in a very new 1963 Chevrolet, asking my destination. Iowa City I said, hoping to make it by nightfall. "Get in." He was headed to Muscatine, Iowa, about an hour's drive from there. As we drove along, I noticed that he had a Masonic ring on his left hand. My father is a Mason, I told him. That made him relax and quickly open up, talking about how he had been in Kentucky caring for his ailing mother and was headed back home. He had been away for two weeks and was eager to see his wife and two teenage daughters. He owned and operated three service stations in Muscatine. We pulled up to his residence at about six that evening. It was a fairly large, modern house in an upper-income neighborhood. "Follow me" he said, as he went to the main entrance. I agreed, knowing that with my beard and unkempt appearance, he didn't want to scare his family. When we entered the house, the family was shocked to see me behind him. He explained in a rush of words that I had hitchhiked from the East Coast, was the son of a fellow Mason and was on my way to Iowa City. After a few minutes, calm came over the household; the family was content that I was not some derelict intent on robbing them. They insisted I stay for dinner and offered me a room for the night.

I did eat some food, but I was eager to get home. I asked to use the telephone and called a close friend and fraternity brother Jeff Lowe, a senior at the university. He lived in Iowa City. When I got him on the line, he told me another frat brother Jeff Gallager had a car and they would come and pick me up. They arrived in Muscatine two hours later with young coeds in tow. I squeezed into the back seat.

The drive took only about fifty minutes and we pulled up to an apartment house in Coralville, just outside Iowa City. It was my long time fraternity brother Ken Kinsey's apartment; a party was in progress. I walked in, self-conscious of my appearance and odor, and then heard very familiar loud music coming from the hi-fi. "I Want to Hold Your Hand" by the Beatles was blaring; I actually thought they were only a European attraction. But they had a growing fan base in the United States. Things and events had changed quickly and radically for me in just six months. I felt a distinct contrast between myself and the fraternity group and their dates. It was as if I were having an out-of-body experience, looking on those gathered but not being a part of them. I had matured dramatically, and felt we no longer had the same things in common.

I called my parents in the morning and by eleven o'clock, they had arrived. I was, of course, elated to see them. I piled into their 1962 Mercury and we headed for the farm. As we passed the drab, snow-covered countryside, I was relieved, tired, but rather melancholy that my trip had ended. After about ninety minutes, we pulled into the farmyard; I saw that the new farm home they had started in 1962 was completely finished. As I sat down in their living room, I poured a glass of the cognac I had brought from Europe. I looked at my parents and offered them a drink. We sat back. They seemed to be observing me to discern any noticeable changes. I was conducting my own examination of them, of the surroundings, luxuriously soaking in the comfort of familiarity.

"I am home," I thought to myself. "But where do I go from here?"

PART THREE

CHAPTER SEVEN

Which Way From Here?

WINTERS in the Iowa countryside can be somewhat depressing. The fact that I found myself in my parents' house, with no job or income and a little uncertain about my next move, exacerbated my low mood. My twenty-third birthday was only a couple of days away, and Christmas wasn't far behind. The absence of American newspapers and magazines other than the *International Herald Tribune* while abroad had created in me a voracious appetite for such publications. The United States had changed figuratively and literally. Kennedy was gone; Lyndon B. Johnson had taken the reins of the presidency; and racial unrest had heightened, particularly after the 1963 March on Washington. In my mind, I kept replaying Kennedy's inaugural comments: "Ask not what your country can do for you, but what you can do for your country." What I could do, I wondered, to make things better. I could contribute to politics, since that remained close to my heart. But before any of that, I needed a job. I wasn't going to depend on my parents. Further, if I intended to act on the idea of my attending law school at the University of Iowa, I certainly had to earn money. I learned Collins Radio in Cedar Rapids was hiring. Founded in 1933 as a producer of radio equipment for the military and scientific communities, it was the largest employer in that city. In 1973, Collins radio became the current Rockwell Collins. I applied for work and was hired as a distributor supervisor. I didn't have any transportation, so I wasn't certain how I would get to the job. Fortunately, my father had a good relationship with the local Ford dealer, Bob Jensen. With my father co-signing, I was able to purchase a new 1964 Falcon. My monthly annuity payments from my insurance company were enough for me to meet car payments. During one of the trips to Cedar Rapids prior to my employment, a fraternity brother, who was a staunch Republican, mentioned that a young man named John Culver had come back to Iowa to run for Congress. Culver had Kennedy connections. I was intrigued. Republicans in the congressional district were concerned that Culver had broad appeal and the ability to raise sufficient campaign funds. The congressional district was fairly divided between Republicans and Democrats. I definitely was interested in helping a close ally of the Kennedy family in his possible entry into politics.

A former Marine, Culver also had been an outstanding football player, drafted by the NFL's Chicago Cardinals. He wasn't all brawn, however. He had gone to Harvard and roomed with Edward Kennedy. Culver also had been involved in Kennedy's 1962 U.S. Senate race in Massachusetts; later, after Kennedy was elected, Culver served as his legislative assistant. My parents said a newspaper article mentioned Culver's name in association with Professor Richard "Dick" Clark, a teacher at Upper Iowa University located in Fayette, Iowa, about forty-five miles north of our farm.

Clark was originally from Lamont, Iowa, the town nearest to where my parents lived earlier. They knew him and his parents, and were excited that with Culver, they might have a very formidable candidate in the 1964 election. Democrats had been starved for a credible challenger to James Bromwell, the Republican incumbent. Elected in 1960 over a Democrat

Len Wolf, Bromwell had been re-elected in 1962. Now Democrats, including my parents, thought they had a great chance to regain that seat.

When I returned to Cedar Rapids for my interview at Collins Radio, I decided to call the Bradley law firm that Culver had joined. Cell phones weren't even a figment in anyone's imagination back then. Public telephones dotted the landscape. I spotted one and dialed the firm, telling the secretary I was just passing through. I wondered whether Culver could perhaps meet me. After waiting about a minute, I was totally surprised when he picked up the phone. Stop by now, he told me.

Well over six feet tall and two hundred pounds, Culver was physically and intellectually impressive. A few minutes into our conversation, another gentleman walked in introducing himself as Dick Clark. Slightly overweight, he was very personable with a good sense of humor and a ready smile. He was the more relaxed of the two. Culver had a definite intensity about him. Months later, I would discover he also had a temper. Both men wanted me to come aboard as a volunteer; I was flattered. That meeting was my introduction to elective campaigns. Culver and Clark would subsequently teach me the mechanics that served as the foundation for a career spanning more than four decades, and that helped shape black leadership in several urban centers.

Voter targeting in the entire 2nd Congressional District was my first assignment. I researched every precinct, beginning as far back as 1946 and continuing through the 1962 election. That work was tedious and required meticulous attention to detail. Without computers or even a typewriter, it took me twelve weeks to compile the statistics and, once finished, I was very proud, particularly since I simultaneously worked split shifts at Collins radio. The compiled data established the specific outlines for the campaign, providing a historical perspective on the District. While identifying potential voters, I discovered that over the years, the 2nd District was becoming more Democratic, enhancing the opportunity for a win. I color-coded maps of the areas where Culver should spend his time and effort. Interestingly, even then, blue was for Democratic leaning precincts; red was more Republican.

Bromwell was into his second term and would be Culver's general election opponent. But first, Culver had to win the Democratic primary. Dr. James Feld, a dentist and a Catholic, would be his competition. Then, the core of the Iowa Democratic Party was Irish and German Catholics. They viewed Culver, who wasn't Catholic, as a carpetbagger. It didn't matter that he had worked for the first family of Irish Catholics. Further, Frank Less, an Irish Catholic, had run against Bromwell in 1962; some people thought he deserved another run. That characterization and their opposition proved insignificant.

Aided in no small measure by my parents, our other relatives and friends in the District, Culver won the primary handily. During that campaign, I learned the art of advance work for political candidates, organizing counties and straw polls. Those were lessons that define a campaign and, if properly handled, help predict success. Mastering them came through trial and error, however. One weekend, the campaign asked Brian, another volunteer, to drive with me to Lansing, Iowa, which was in the northeastern part of our congressional district located in Allamakee County. The van we traveled in was white with a large "Culver for Congress" image painted on each side. The trip was taken principally to introduce our campaign to the "Lansing Fish Day," where residents cooked up their best seafood and held other activities to celebrate their river culture. When we arrived around noon, we ventured into the first tavern we saw, carrying our Culver brochures. There was a miniature copper bust of President John F. Kennedy behind the bar; I immediately felt relieved. An Irish owner, Verlin, greeted us warmly and we stayed for a light lunch. The rest of the day, Brian and I went from that establishment to nearby houses, promoting Culver. As night drew, we decided to go back to the bar. The crowd was huge and raucous. Someone in a booth hollered for us to sit with them. Without warning two middle-aged men suddenly became involved in fisticuffs. As I watched it develop, the Irish owner Verlin vaulted over his bar, trying to separate the two men to throw them out while shouting profanities. His wife grabbed him by the neck, but being slight of build she flew like a ragdoll through the air, unable to stop him while pleading he cease the use of profanity: "For God sakes Verlin, your mother is here." It was a spectacle. The local police finally arrived, arresting the two instigators. Nobody seemed to be seriously hurt. I was impressed with Verlin's physical ability.

Later that evening, Brian and I made the long journey back to Cedar Rapids. We thought proudly that we had more than sufficiently circulated Culver's name in Lansing. Campaigning required that we always be alert but relaxed, and not too "pushy." We had to ensure that the candidate's name was out there while presenting ourselves as neutral in appearance and manner. I also learned two simple but necessary campaign techniques— how to affix bumper stickers, and how to affect straw polls.

The All-Iowa Fair, held every year in Cedar Rapids at Hawkeye Downs, was the second largest such event in Iowa. I had recruited six teenagers, male and female, to help Culver. As the cars were pulling into the large parking lot, I came up with the idea to assign three different teams of two each to approach them, asking whether the green and white Culver for Congress sticker could be affixed to the rear bumper. I was confident that we had established a sure-fire system, and I walked to the main fair grounds trying to find Culver to tell him of our success and to determine whether he needed any other assistance. Before I could ask him what more he wanted, he rebuked me, asking me why I was not back in the parking lot. "Who do you think you are, too good to be applying stickers," he asked while looking at me harshly. I was dumbfounded. Instead of being patted on the head, I was basically kicked in the butt. Having lost my proud demeanor, I learned a good lesson: don't ever expect any thanks in political organizing. Frankly, it also could have been that Culver was telling me that I was not above my team, and that he was the leader.

That fair also provided my first experience with so-called "straw polls." The local paper, *The Cedar Rapids Gazette,* operated a booth where it was taking a poll. I always assumed those surveys were a true indication of voter sentiments. Wrong. The next day, results indicated Culver was behind. He called, telling me to establish a quick phone bank of volunteers to call Democrats urging them to go to the fair and to vote for him. Soon, we had an effective daisy chain of callers. We also suggested they vote more than once because we were convinced the Republicans were doing the same. Thus, I became personally involved with "stuffing the ballot box." By the third day of the fair, the *Gazette* reported that Culver had sprung into the lead over Republican nominee, James Bromwell. Surprise. Surprise.

There were other lessons learned that political summer. One day, I was driving Culver around Cedar Rapids when we passed a barber shop. Turn around, he told me, suddenly realizing he needed a haircut. Stepping out of the car, he asked if I had any cash. I readily handed him a ten dollar bill. That was the last I saw of that money. From that day, I always made sure I did not have any cash—even when I did. I found out later that elected officials, or those campaigning to be elected, rarely had any cash on them.

At Collins Radio where I continued to work, things were quietly heating up. All three shifts were comprised of white-collar computer operators. We felt we were being used and abused by management; we endured meager pay and uncomfortable working conditions. Moreover, top managers had a very patronizing attitude. The dissension grew quickly and our group of about one hundred sixty employees began having meetings off site to explore solutions. We decided to organize a union. I was nominated to research the local 238 Teamsters union. The Culver campaign had allowed me to meet the local representative Keith "Moose" Johnson. He was amiable but very tough. Local 238 was a very strong and active union, headed at the time by Harry Wilford. Our six-member executive committee drove one day to the Teamsters headquarters in southwest Cedar Rapid. With Wilford seated behind his desk and Moose in a side chair, we talked of unionization. Five minutes into that conversation, one of the individuals in our group and a friend of mine, Keith "Casey" Clough, decided to become more forceful. Pointing to the large oil portrait of the national president of the Teamsters, Jimmy Hoffa, hanging behind Wilford's desk on the wall, Casey said, "Everyone knows that that guy is a crook. But we still want to work with you." Wilford swallowed hard. I knew he was not going to become enraged at the remark because he wanted to gain a foothold in Collins Radio; it was, after all, the largest employer in Cedar Rapids. We left the meeting feeling good about our chances. After we had secured the required number of signatures, an election was to be held that summer.

Leading up to that vote, we constantly worked the operators to make sure we would win. One individual wasn't certain he wanted to join. During a break, I approached him at the computer he monitored. He quickly became defensive, arguing that he had a spouse and family to worry about, while I, on the other hand, had neither wife nor children. Other operators were in situations similar to his, I said, adding that no one was going to appreciate his selfishness. My actions could have been perceived as intimidation, especially since I reminded him he had to walk to his car at night after his shift and I could not guarantee his safety. Visibly upset, he urged me to tell our colleagues that he was all for the union and was going to vote affirmatively. Whether he did or not, I was never certain. But we won the election a few days later.

The Culver campaign didn't suffer from my juggling a variety of issues. Coming off his primary victory, I had another idea: expand my family's involvement in politics. My father had been encouraged by many Democrats to run for the State Senate from Buchanan County. K.P. "Red" Harrington was the incumbent in the state legislature and also wanted to move up in the ranks, running for the senate. In strong language, he sought to dampen my father's ambition, telling him he should vie for a seat in the state legislature—his seat. In possession of historical election data, however, I knew my Dad had a better shot. Sure, he was a Mason of Irish Protestant background, but he had many long time Irish Catholic friends in Delaware County. He also favored aid to parochial schools—a serious issue during the 1960s. Catholics were trying to preserve their schools and religious teachings. I urged my father to stake out the senate seat. He informed Red of his decision, and Red immediately asked to meet with me. So, one Saturday afternoon, I met with him in Independence at the Shamrock Tavern, an establishment I often tried to avoid. It was unpleasant: dark and musty, rife with the smell of stale beer and heavy cigarette smoke. There were only two small windows facing the street, which allowed little sunlight. I suggested the location, not wanting to meet in one of Red's establishments, which would have given him the psychological edge. I told my father not to come. Red and I hunkered down in a booth; he argued he was owed the senate seat, given the time he had served in the state legislature. I listened politely but countered he wasn't entitled to anything. I sternly told him he would face my father in a primary. Get ready. I boasted further that we would raise a bunch of money for the race. At twenty-three, I had never raised a dime for anyone. Red seemed perplexed and a little agitated. After twenty minutes, we both left. Two weeks later, he filed to run for re-election in the State Legislature. My father was the sole candidate for the senate seat in the Democratic primary. We had won the bluff. That summer, our family also perfected the art of retail politics, going door-to-door to meet voters. I recruited a young woman named Ellen O'Conner and her friend to help my father with door-knocking in Manchester where he was not as well-known. On a pleasant Sunday, we divided the streets, speaking with voters on his behalf. In that 1964 fall election both Red and my father were victorious.

Parallel to our local political activity in Iowa, the national scene was getting more intense. The Republicans held their convention at the Cow Palace in San Francisco from July 13 through July 16, 1964. They nominated U.S. Senator Barry Goldwater of Arizona whose famous remark "extremism in the defense of liberty is no vice" received nationwide coverage mostly to negative reaction. Most Democrats in Iowa were encouraged by the choice; Goldwater had pushed aside many moderate Republicans like Pennsylvania Governor Bill Scranton, who could have posed a bigger problem in the general election for Democrats. Goldwater's hard stand was because he was trying to appeal to white voters in the South, who resented Washington directives.

The 1964 Democratic convention was held in Atlantic City from August 24 through August 27. Unsurprisingly, Lyndon Johnson and his vice presidential nominee Hubert Humphrey became the team. I watched the convention with interest when Robert Kennedy introduced a film tribute to his late brother and received a twelve-minute standing ovation. Tears came to my eyes. I realized it had been less than a year since I had been in Cologne, and learned of the assassination.

Truthfully, the Republicans may have had their issues with racial discrimination and how best to handle African Americans, but the Democrats were not exempt, considering the controversy over seating delegates. For example, the composition of the official Mississippi State Delegation at the convention made clear the party was engaged in a form of segregation, denying blacks equal voting rights and full participation in the political process. A compromise supposedly had been reached between the Democratic National Committee and The Mississippi Freedom Democratic Party which was an integrated body rather than the all-white group. But the Mississippi Freedom Democratic Party, led by African-American civil rights activist Fannie Lou Hamer, rejected the compromise and walked out, which would have given African Americans only two seats in the delegation. Hamer had been arrested in 1963, along with other activists on false charges and was almost beaten to death in a Mississippi jail. She never deviated from her goal of equality for blacks. When Vice President Humphrey and others appeared at the Democratic Convention that year to persuade her to accept the compromise, she refused. She was probably exhausted by this time by all the barriers thrown in her path. In her statement there, which eventually was placed on her headstone, she declared "I am sick and tired of being sick and tired."

While I was organizing for the Teamsters and Culver, there was the brutal murder of the three young civil rights workers in Neshoba County in Mississippi on June 26. I shuddered, realizing the seriousness of white hatred. I was both outraged and frightened by it. It had been only two years earlier that my cousin Nikki and I had contemplated going to Mississippi.

I looked at my work and was well aware of the contrasts between the politics and the day-to-day rigors at Collins. There wasn't much difference in what was happening there and the unspoken discrimination on the job. All the computer operators I was helping organize into a union were white males; there wasn't even a white woman in the unit. We had only a very few blacks in our congressional district—most were in Cedar Rapids. For instance, Dr. Percy Harris, a big supporter of Culver's, was the first African American to complete his hospital residency in Cedar Rapids. Still, he had to overcome virulent racist attitudes when he moved into an almost all white neighborhood in Cedar Rapids.

That September, I left Collins and started law school in Iowa City. Going to law school had been a longstanding goal. I came to realize through observation and research that lawyers frequently were at the forefront of important public policy changes that often set the country on a positive social and economic course. I imagined myself a member of that movement. I continued working for Culver, helping my father, and commuting from Cedar Rapids to law school early in the mornings, however. We were rewarded in the November elections. Johnson won in a landslide, Culver won, and my father won his state senate seat handily. I was elated; 1964 had been a good year. I considered my next step: perhaps Washington, DC., the epicenter of national politics. I thought Culver might be my ticket.

CHAPTER EIGHT

Big Game Hunting

AFTER the exhilaration of the 1964 November election victories, I immersed myself in the rigors of my freshman year in law school. Soon, however, I would come to realize the imperfections of politics and come to understand the dirty little secret of what happens when someone tries to play the game by different rules.

Despite the country's forced realization of its racially discriminatory past, it was as if Iowa was not paying attention. It may not have been operating somewhere around the time of the suffragette movement, but my class at law school was predominately white and male. There may have been four females and two African Americans. I noticed the imbalance, but was not driven to do anything about it. Instead, I focused on me, me, me.

I managed to find a new two-bedroom apartment on the outskirts of Iowa City, which I rented with two other students. With the money I had saved working at Collins Radio and my monthly annuity from my summer insurance sales, I had enough to get through that first year. I learned that my friend Bill Perkins, an Iowa football player, and another African-American on the team, Chet Williams, were also renting in the same apartment complex. I would have to rely on them during the coming winter.

With my father having won, my parents had to obtain housing in Des Moines for the legislative session. The Democratic sweep in Iowa, as well as at the federal level, brought an air of excitement and anticipation that great things were going to be accomplished. Governor Harold Hughes was a reformer; I knew my family would be part of the coming change. My prediction would be mostly accurate. Progressive legislation in Iowa became the norm. A bill passed, for example, that created community colleges that would allow lower income students to attend them while living at home. My father was a proud co-sponsor. The legislature also voted to open up their committee meetings to the public, to lower the voting age from twenty-one years old to 18 years old and to provide for judges to be appointed rather than elected. It enacted the Iowa Civil Rights Act of 1965. Unlike in today's political atmosphere, many legislators' attitude was that they did not care about being re-elected so they did what they thought was right and beneficial to their constituents. That attitude and their actions resulted in many of them not being returned in 1966. Unfortunately, there were times when constituents didn't act in their own best interest.

I visited my parents in Des Moines two or three times. I greatly admired them. They had come a long way since the1930s depression era. During the session, they went everywhere together, not only to political events, but to all social occasions. As one of my father's fellow legislators told me, "They were inseparable." My father was also a sure solid vote for Governor Hughes's legislative initiatives. The year was fairly uneventful except for one occurrence which could have caused me physical harm and extreme embarrassment.

 I had met a woman about my age the previous summer in Cedar Rapids. She was working at a local dry cleaner where I took my laundry. She was friendly, and from was Cedar Falls, where she had been a high school classmate of a fraternity brother. I asked her out, discovering later that she was divorced and had a young son who was three or four years old. She lived on the east side of downtown in a third story walk-up apartment. We dated for about six weeks. One evening, we went out to dinner and came back to her apartment. I parked my car in the rear parking lot. Suddenly, there was a loud knock on her downstairs door. She went to a window and told the person below to leave her alone. She had company, she said, prompting the beating to become more incessant. I sensed there was a group intent on physical harm. Call the police, I told her, believing I didn't have minutes to spare. I went to one of the bedrooms, threw open a window and went out onto a basically flat roof on an adjacent property. I was still three stories from the ground. I flipped over the lip of the roof and dropped one story to an overhanging fabric awning. Then, I pushed out from the side of the building, falling to the concrete sidewalk and onto a major thoroughfare. Somehow I made it to a pay telephone to call the police. I was informed the police were on site, everything was all right and I could retrieve my car. I came across several officers who had one of the individuals in handcuffs; he was shouting obscenities at me, vowing to kill me when he had the opportunity. I casually asked one of the officers if they had searched him; they had not. One of the officers took me aside telling me it was good that I had vacated the apartment quickly since the individuals were the infamous Rodriguez Brothers, notorious in Cedar Rapids. I quickly left the three of them and the police. I got into my Ford Falcon and drove off heading back to Iowa City.

Driving the approximately twenty-five miles home, I realized the woman I was dating was leading a double life: one with a law student with a respectable background, another with a known thug. I was certain the Rodriguez Brothers had my license plate number. What should I do, I wondered, to protect myself?

When I reached my apartment, I immediately called my friend Bill Perkins, who had two other football players as roommates. I relayed to him the events of the evening; he said he was coming over. As I look back now, I had cast the black football players in the role they had played on television, as tough guys, gladiators, able to fight any and all manner of beast. Then, however, I needed brawn; Perkins and his friends possessed plenty of it.

"Do you have a piece?" Perkins asked when he arrived. "You should have one." He said he always kept a pistol in his car glove compartment. I was somewhat taken aback. Perhaps I was a little naive. I should have recognized that he may have needed a piece. It was 1965, after all. He was African-American in nearly pristine white rural Iowa. Fortunately, I never had any fallout from the Cedar Rapids incident. Twenty-five years later, I learned at least one of the Rodriguez Brothers was in the Iowa state prison, having been sentenced for murder.

Word of my encounter with them that night in Cedar Rapids slowly spread throughout law school. Most students were not quite sure what the specifics entailed but they knew some Hispanics or Puerto Ricans were involved. In the late spring, at an annual dinner banquet, I was presented with an old pair of worn out tennis sneakers. The third-year law student Chris Green, who also had been an undergraduate fraternity pledge brother, was master of ceremonies and declared the honorary award was given to me in the "speedy furtherance of U.S./Puerto Rico relations." It received many laughs, except from the faculty members, who had no knowledge of what had actually occurred.

As May raced by and finals loomed in June, I figured it was time to reach out to John Culver. I called Dick Clark, by now his chief of staff, and spoke about coming to Washington, D.C. for the summer, hopefully to work. I also found myself broke again; I had exhausted most of my savings during the first year at law school. He urged me to come anyway, but was vague about whether a job would be waiting. The uneasy feeling of not having something concrete was offset by my enthusiasm. I decided to gamble and left for the District of Columbia on an early June morning in my Ford Falcon. I placed a few suits and other clothing in a trunk. My mother packed a light lunch and gave me thirty-five dollars. She also uttered a typical saying from her conservative financial background: "Try to make it last." Even in 1965, that amount of money was not a princely sum. Still, I appreciated it. I drove straight through, occasionally stopping on the side of the highway for two or three naps.

On a late weekday morning, I arrived in Washington by way of New York Ave. NW. I will never forget my first sighting of the U.S Capitol from afar. I was overwhelmed. When I finally reached the building, I found a parking space and went to Culver's office, immediately meeting my old friend and fraternity brother, Mike McDermott. He already had graduated from the law school at Iowa and had volunteered for Culver in 1964. He had been hired as his legislative assistant. Mike and his wife, Sue, also a University of Iowa graduate, had come to Washington in January. She successfully landed a position as a dental hygienist. The two generously offered me their living room couch until I could obtain employment and find a place to stay. I didn't think it would take long for me to land a summer job and permanent housing. But Washington was not as easy as I thought. After two or three nights at the McDermott's, Dick Clark and his wife Jean offered a basement bedroom at their house in Silver Spring, about a thirty-minute drive from the Capitol. I accepted their offer. After the move, I decided to take a few days to tour some of the Smithsonian Museums along Independence Ave. NW. At one point, I found a park bench to take a rest, and soon struck up a conversation with a woman who may have been in her early thirties and was very attractive.

She was a tourist from upstate New York. We agreed to make the round of museums and other sights together. Later, I learned she was Puerto Rican and a professor. We spent the next four days together, continuing our tour and having lunch or dinner. During our sojourn, she talked about life in New York State and the discrimination she had experienced. Perhaps those were the first candid conversations I had with a minority in the United States. As we parted, I received notice from Culver's office that I was accepted as a paid summer intern at the United States Agency for International Development (USAID); I was the seventy-sixth intern hired that summer. Based on its budget, there were only supposed to be seventy-five. But Culver, a member of the House Foreign Relations Committee, undoubtedly eased the way for me.

The next day I proceeded to the state department building, a behemoth of a structure located in Foggy Bottom, where I was processed in and told I would have a top secret security clearance, which was already in progress. That same day, I received a telephone call from my mother. She had been visited earlier in the week by two people from the F.B.I. They were fine gentlemen, she told me, adding that she and my Dad invited them for lunch. "They knew more about you than I ever did," she said with a chuckle.

Simultaneously, I met Michael Fitzgerald, who was from Cleveland and intended to enroll that fall at American University to get his doctorate. John Wise, another intern was from Lubbock, Texas, the birthplace of Buddy Holly; Wise agreed to share an apartment with Fitzgerald and me for the summer. With housing decisions out of the way, we headed to Georgetown for food and drinks. After ordering beers and sitting at a small table, John needed to make a telephone call from a payphone in the bar, and took his drink with him. That was prohibited, we learned. The waitress immediately came over. She and Wise became involved in an animated conversation which was out of earshot. When he returned to the group, he sat down shaking his head and relaying that he had been told he had to sit down while drinking. We were all stunned that in the District of Columbia, the nation's capital, blue laws were in effect. That surely was a carryover from the old South where it was held that if men were drinking and standing, they could harass women sitting down in restaurants. What a foolish belief. .

I wasn't the only person who received an internship through political connections. Fitzgerald's father, a lobbyist in Ohio, was close friends with Charles Vanik, the Cleveland Congressman on the Ways and Means Committee. Wise's godfather was George Mahon of Texas, chairman of the House Appropriations Committee. The family of Mary Mackleman, another intern, lived next door to Richard Daley, Chicago's mayor. Irv Gubman, soon to become a close friend, who was attending the University of Chicago law school, had worked for Donald Fraser, a member of the House Foreign Relations Committee. Jim Guest had worked for Senator Edward Kennedy.

Fitzgerald, Wise and I found a small shuttered row house on New Hampshire Ave. NW in Foggy Bottom for rent at three hundred thirty-two dollars. It was a short walk to the state department. We bought a few pieces of used furniture and moved in. Everything was new and exciting. However, we would learn that the summer of 1965 was filled with contrasts and contradictions.

There was a preponderance of blacks on many of the streets in Washington, D.C. I should have used that reality as an opportunity, perhaps, to delve into the cultural and racial differences that had been on the periphery of my life since I was a child. Now there were enough blacks for me to observe and to learn more than what I had seen on television, or heard from the maid in Tampa, or from the football players in undergraduate school. But, truthfully, I was in no hurry to jump into a world that I felt ill-suited to join. And so, I looked the other way. I plunged myself into the whiter side of the city, and perhaps even the more elite section of it, although that may seem laughable considering that my roommates and I didn't even have enough money to buy an air conditioner, prompting us to stay out late cooling off, which morphed into non-stop partying.

Fitzgerald had a girlfriend who shared a house at Rehoboth Beach, Delaware with a group of female friends. Many weekends were spent driving the two and a half hours to romp in the sun. Many of the friends I have today, I met that summer. Taking the partying to new levels, he obtained a list of all the foreign countries Independence Day events. Most were at embassies, of course. We made our way through the receiving line, meeting ambassadors and their wives while giving our names and announcing our U.S.A.I.D. affiliations, which served as passports. U.S. A.I.D was the primary agency for disbursing loans and grants to many of the countries whose embassies we visited. Our hosts may have believed we could be useful. Consequently, we were provided fine liquor and delectable food. No one ever challenged us.

At the Embassy of Jamaica's party in the middle of July, I noticed a good looking black woman, who was receiving much attention. Somehow an introduction was made and we eventually became friendly. I learned she had been Miss Jamaica, but now lived in New York City. She invited me to visit; I accepted the offer. I had never been to the city. I went by train arriving at Penn Station one Friday afternoon. At her apartment, I announced I was taking her to Greenwich Village to a bar called Maria's Crisis. My fraternity brother Chris Green and his wife Nancy were to meet us. Chris had recently joined the law firm of Mudge Nixon; after losing the 1960 presidential race, Richard Nixon had become the principal partner. I had not told the Greens anything about my date other than that she lived in the city. When I walked in with Valerie, I was certain that some of the bar patrons were a little confused even in liberal New York. Chris never forgot it, saying that "Patton was always full of surprises." It was my first interracial dating experience and a notable one.

Making that choice certainly seemed odd, since I had made little effort to engage the black community in the District of Columbia. Perhaps I simply wanted to determine whether there was any difference. Perhaps I simply wanted to shock my friends by showing them I had come into a new environment much different from my Iowa background.

The period at the U.S.A.I.D. was serious, however. I found out the agency was reputed to be a cover for Central Intelligence Agency operatives in many countries and perhaps even in the District of Columbia where it was headquartered. There were seventy-six interns in A.I.D. and seventy-five in the state department. As was customary, the A.I.D. interns selected certain representatives from their group to be their leaders. I was chosen to be the Speaker Chairman. The state department interns chose an African-American first- year-law student from Harvard to serve in a similar role. He may have been the only black in both groups. Together we were responsible for scheduling speakers to address our combined group of interns. We had some highly respected and well known speakers, including Averill Harriman, Llewellyn Thompson, Charles Bohlen, Walt Rostow, William Bundy and Ellsworth Bunker—all of whom were titans of American foreign policy. They relished the opportunity to speak to our august group.

The Viet Nam War was beginning to heat up and the speakers were basically supportive of the war and then-president President Lyndon B. Johnson. One of the last speakers we had heard from who was considered a rare catch, was McGeorge Bundy, National Security Advisor to Johnson. When he started talking in the State Department amphitheater that morning before the assembled group of approximately two hundred people, he was rather low-key. We had allowed other employees from State and A.I.D. to attend since Bundy was at the pinnacle of American foreign policy. After his ten-minute presentation, the question and answer session began with an innocent inquiry about our involvement in Viet Nam. Bundy nodded and then said tartly "Thank you, next question."

Someone else asked yet another Viet Nam question. Once again, Bundy refused to even acknowledge it, moving to the next person with a raised hand. The audience was becoming uncomfortable with his lack of respect and apparent arrogance. Hissing started. This group was part of the political establishment—not a bunch of anti-Viet Nam protestors. We thought the questions fair and certainly did not involve any confidential or top-secret issues. As the hissing and booing became more audible, Bundy simply folded his notebook and strode out of the amphitheater. We were all angry.

I was a little confused about how to respond. On one hand I was the beneficiary of the political process. After all, I had landed a coveted internship that was seen as an initiation into the establishment. I was really put off by the establishment leaders, including Bundy and the other hawks, like him, who were arrogant and evasive. Didn't we deserve a little respect as being part of the team?

Many of the summer interns told me and the state department chairman that they wanted a speaker who represented the other side of the Viet Nam issue. It was clear Bundy was favorably invested in the war. The most outspoken person who could be considered dovish was Senator Wayne Morse of Oregon. With support from the interns' leadership, I contacted Morse's office and immediately got through to his personal secretary, who was very pleasant I extended an invitation to the senator to be a guest lecturer. She thought he would be interested but said she needed to get back to me. I became a tad self-assured and cocky about securing the senator to be our speaker. All of that bravado was short-lived however.

I received a call at my office the following morning from the U.S. A.I.D. congressional liaison, asking me to come immediately to the office in the State Department building. As I entered, I was ushered into Director William Gibbon's office. Three other men, including Sherwin Markman, a prominent lawyer from Des Moines, Iowa, were also in the room. He led off the conversation, reminding me how I had become an intern. He also noted they were aware I had contacted Senator Morse. I affirmed their information, although I was quite puzzled about how they had found out so quickly and why that would be a problem. I realized that "bugging" or "tapping" telephones was probably how they knew about my actions. I was asked to withdraw the invitation. They argued that his appearance would be an embarrassment to the president. Initially, I tried dodging their request. The room grew tense. Markman then basically ordered me to withdraw the invitation that day. I was left to determine the nature of the excuse I would use. I was also told A.I.D. leadership wasn't to be implicated. I understood the message clearly.

Humbled, I called Morse's office yet again, reaching his personal secretary. She told me he was not available on the date I initially had offered and wondered if there were any alternative times. I was relieved, of course, and promised to call her back after consulting with intern leadership. I called Markman's direct line and told him of the rescission. "Good job," he said, thanking me for what I had done. I realized, if my phones had been tapped, he already knew the outcome of the call.

During the 1960s, telephone surveillance was rampant; I didn't really know how rampant. Certainly, as the country would learn later, many African-Americans were victims of government spying and counterintelligence aimed at undermining the civil rights movement and corrupting its leadership.

That summer of 1965, at twenty-four years old, my political naiveté certainly was fading. Interestingly, within a few months, Markman had become a special assistant to the President at the White House.

I began considering my next step. I had briefly spoken with Ed Irons, an older black professional, at A.I.D. I ran into him a few blocks from the State Department as I was headed back to the office one day; he invited me to share his taxicab. He asked me, as the trip was ending, if I was satisfied with my present position in life.

"No. Not really," I replied.

"That's good, Doug. Never become satisfied," he advised, explaining that once enthusiasm left one's life, you become boring and uninteresting. It has proven very good advice.

I had decided to return to Iowa for law school. Then, I reversed myself, choosing, instead, to remain in Washington. It was too late to apply to George Washington law school; I made it just under the wire and was admitted to American University. Mike Fitzgerald, then at American University, was getting his doctorate. We were still sharing the row house in Foggy Bottom, although John Wise had returned to the University of Texas law school. Almost immediately, I realized I didn't like going to law school at night. In January, while still in night law school, unemployed and with only one can of tuna in my kitchen cupboard and seven cents in my pocket, I had decided I had to quickly change my circumstance. I called two of my friends—George Hamilton and Jim McFalls, both aspiring physicians—and asked for short-term loans. They came through for me.

The lack of money didn't infringe on the good times, however. That winter, before Christmas, Fitzgerald and I were invited to a party at the 8 and I Sts. SE. Marine Corps Barracks. It was the home of the elite honor guard of the Marines that had duty at the White House. Through Charles Robb, Peter McCarthy and other Marines we had met during the summer at Rehoboth, we received a coveted invitation. The party was spectacular with the young, white elite in attendance. The White House Marines partied very hard because many of them could be shipped out to Viet Nam at any time. Many young lieutenants never came back. Given the growing sentiments against America's military and the draft, which captured so many young men, security at the Marine Barracks was very tight. Weeks earlier, the first major anti-Vietnam march had taken place on the Mall. I had gone down with a friend to observe. Participants were mostly political leftists. Mainstream America was essentially ignoring the story; not enough of its community had been affected. I became aware of the extremes on the issue, and frankly a little unsure of my own feelings. When I was nineteen, severe migraines, poor vision and asthma combined to get me a military classification of 4-F. That meant I didn't need to worry about being sent abroad.

I continued my pursuit of employment. Perusing the want ads, I found that Red Top Cab Company of Arlington, Virginia was looking for experienced drivers. I also contacted a downtown employment agency, hoping to locate a longer term job. My semester at law school was over; I elected not to continue. I chose not to go home to my parents for Christmas; 1966 and the serious changes it would bring were staring me in the face.

In the interim, however, I started driving for Red Top cab. It was a perfect part-time job for me. I essentially drove in the evening while I interviewed for full-time employment during the day. Unsurprisingly, all the Red Top drivers were white. I asked a supervisor, or maybe it was even the owner, why no persons of color were employed. If he hired blacks, he said, his regular passengers would be intolerant and that could cost him money. Remember, he said, this is still a southern city. I kept driving anyway.

Then, one evening around nine o'clock, I received a radio call for a passenger in North Arlington. When I arrived at the pick up point in front of a bar/restaurant, there was a very tall white man probably in his early forties. He said he had to go to Vienna, but first he wanted to stop a few blocks away to pick up a trench coat. While waiting, I actually considered leaving. He was very strange. I usually carried a wooden two-foot club under my car seat. That evening, however, I had forgotten it. I also had a date with a girl who was supposed to meet me at our row house. This was my last fare and Vienna was a long distance away. Still, I waited. The man came back to my cab and proceeded to get in the front seat, announcing as he entered, "You do not mind if I ride in front."

Now, I was more than a little nervous. As we drove towards Vienna, the road became more deserted and dark. He also said he knew how to wrestle, although he was not a good boxer. He went on to say that he didn't want any trouble out of me, which I thought odd. It occurred to me, he was on something other than liquor. Suddenly, he pulled out a stiletto-like knife, muttering he had a "new type of pen" with a real sharp point. He flipped it open, revealing a ten-inch blade while saying, "I think you should pull over and have a good look at it."

As I came around a darkened curve all at once there was a Chevron gas station lit up like a baseball field. I was never so relieved and lucky in my short life. I turned abruptly into the station, telling my passenger "I have to call my wife." I sprung from the car while he, befuddled, remained in his seat. I passed the attendant telling him quietly "Do not go near my cab." I immediately called my dispatcher, using the panic key code number. He told me to stay on the telephone while he called the police.

Meanwhile, my passenger had gotten out of the car, clearly confused as to what he should do. In short order, three police squad cars pulled into the Chevron station. I motioned them to the passenger. They threw him up against the cab, simultaneously disarming and handcuffing him. After I answered a few questions, they drove away with him.

I had no fare, but I had my life and was mad at myself for getting into such a predicament. I drove the cab back to the Arlington headquarters, got my Ford Falcon and headed for the sanctity of our row house. My date was already there; Fitzgerald had let her in before he left. I told her I was not really interested in going out to eat, so we had snacks. I also needed a drink and poured myself a martini. After about two hours of listening to my harrowing experience, she excused herself. I went to bed, but read for about thirty minutes, trying to relax as I pondered my luck. The following Sunday morning, she called me about nine o'clock, asking if I was all right. I was, of course. She said she was concerned because I had at least seven martinis while we were together.

Hearing the story about the man with the knife, nearly all my white friends invariably asked "Was he black?" When I said he was white, they became silent.

I suppose I should not have been surprised by the question and the prejudice, offered sotto voce. Nor should I have been shocked when my answer yielded no reaction, not even an admission that many of my friends believed blacks, particularly the men, capable of only violence.

CHAPTER NINE

Selling Pills and Traveling Two Paths

I moved on the margins of African-American life in the nation's capital, and I began to see, if not understand, the duality of American society. There clearly was one world for whites and another for blacks. Even the most liberal whites seemed to accept that fact, despite the passage in 1964 of the Civil Rights Act and, the next year, of the Voting Rights Act. These laws were expected, somehow, to knit blacks more tightly into mainstream society. They had not done that job, however. Many blacks still lacked real power or influence.

The District of Columbia, the land beyond the federal enclave where I worked and where most of my social contacts lived, was predominantly African American. Yet the local political and economic decisions were being made by whites—mostly white men. The city, managed by a three-member commission appointed by the president, was treated more like a federal agency than an actual municipality. There seemed to be a movement to alter the form of governance, but quite frankly, it lacked the political muscle to effect change. It would be another decade before the predominantly black city would be given the opportunity to partially govern itself.

The reality of D.C.'s quasi-colonial status registered with me, with remote objectivity, the way it might a social scientist. It did not affect my life, either the breadth or richness of my experiences-although, except for my influential set of friends, the contours of my life were not that much different than ordinary District residents. Leaving the cab-driving job underscored that fact. I was faced with the need, once again, to find employment fairly quickly.

Eaton Laboratories, a prescription drug division of Norwich Pharmacal, based in Norwich, New York, was looking for a local salesperson. I applied for the position, and was hired. It meant I could basically stay put. My job at Eaton, which began May 1966, required that I call on physicians in D.C. and places as far away as Fredericksburg, Virginia.

White physicians in D.C. concentrated around I St. NW while black doctors were mostly found on either Georgia Ave. NW or Florida Ave. NW. My supervisor at Eaton, a conservative who lived in Virginia, was almost apologetic when he told me my sales territory included black physicians. Later, he mentioned the company was relieved to hire a white salesman who had no misgivings or reluctance to sell their products to African-American physicians. That meant, he said, they didn't have to hire a black salesman, which, even in 1966, would have been a first. Eaton wasn't much different than many other American corporations.

Not unlike other southern urban centers, there had been extensive white flight from the District to the surrounding suburbs after the 1954 Brown v Board of Education Supreme Court ruling, which was the result of five well-crafted and deliberate challenges filed by lawyers with the National

Association for the Advancement of Colored People (NAACP). The organization had sought to end the segregation of public schools. The "separate but equal doctrine" that perpetuated that system evolved after Supreme Court in the Plessy v Ferguson case issued its ruling in 1896 that essentially upheld the rights of states to keep blacks and whites apart, as long as the accommodations were equal. The five NAACP cases included one surrounding the District of Columbia—Bolling v Sharpe. It was filed by James Nabrit who took over after Special Counsel Charles Hamilton Houston became ill. Ultimately, the Justices slapped down the Plessy v Ferguson ruling, requiring states to bring black and white children together. Many whites in the nation's capital objected to the order. Rather than attend schools with black children, they fled the city.

Still, there existed white bastions in the city's downtown central business district as well as the upper northwest residential neighborhoods. Many of those areas, such as fashionable Spring Valley, had covenants that prohibited selling property not just to blacks but also Jews and southern Europeans like Greeks and Italians. I ignored the discriminatory nature of such practices, however. Instead, Fitzgerald and I moved into one of those exclusive white enclaves along MacArthur Blvd in what was known as the Palisades, taking us one rung up the economic ladder. That status was enhanced when my employer provided a new 1966 Chevrolet Impala for my use, allowing me to discard my old Ford Falcon.

Before long, I began calling on black physicians in my territory including those at Freedmen's and Children's Hospitals. The former had been established in 1862 to care for freed, disabled and elderly African Americans. After the Civil War, it became the facility used by Howard University Medical School to provide practical experience for its students. It was still under the control of the federal government, however. Then, in 1909, a new building was constructed on the university's campus at 6th St.

NW and Bryant St. NW. In 1967, Howard gained control of the hospital; around the same time I was introduced to the hospital and its doctors. Eight years later, Howard would build a more modern facility, which bore its name. Freedmen's became the site for the university's School of Communications. But a permanent museum was also created inside the building, celebrating the hospital's history and its role in the health and welfare of African Americans.

Until my work with Eaton, I had not encountered such a large cadre of black professionals. Some of my white friends constantly asked "Aren't you scared?" I shrugged, never articulating whether I believed the myth of blacks as demons, perpetrators of all America's ills. I certainly was careful about where I parked the Impala. Whatever fear I may have possessed went undetected by blacks on my sales route, however, as evidenced by the fact that one African-American nurse told me, "You don't seem to be too concerned being around us [black people]." I couldn't afford to be frightened. I needed the job and the money it brought to finance my lifestyle, including paying my tuition, if I ever decided to return to law school.

I was growing more comfortable with African Americans. I even asked Darlene Briscoe, a black woman with whom I had worked at the State Department, to join me for dinner. She accepted my offer, although I had not considered where to take her. I may have been able to walk into a club up North with Miss Jamaica on my arm, but sliding into a restaurant in the nation's capital with a black woman was an entirely different story. I chose the Astor restaurant, located on M St. NW between 19th St. and 18th St. NW. A Greek restaurant with good food, it was unpretentious and catered to a middle-class, primarily white crowd. But I also knew from one of my friends who gambled that the top floor hosted almost non-stop nightly poker games with professional players. Consequently, I suspected, to avoid imperiling their nefarious activities, they would be compelled to avoid any potential incidents in the restaurant. So, I made a reservation and showed up with Briscoe.

Other than some patrons' sidelong glances, we had a pleasant dinner. Then, I realized I had to take her home. She lived with her parents in far northeast, a predominantly black, working-class community. As a young white man, driving through far northeast in a white Impala with a black woman, I should have been a tad nervous. But I wasn't. I dated Briscoe sporadically over the next year, meeting her parents and other relatives without controversy.

Meanwhile, I began to develop an interest in jazz and joined the Left Bank Jazzy Society. For a small fee, it allowed members to enjoy jazz greats who principally performed in clubs in the black sections of town. Everyone was friendly and I felt accepted or at least tolerated. W.E.B.DuBois, a co-founder of the NAACP, had once talked about the duality of black life. I certainly wasn't African American, but somehow I had begun leading two distinctly different lives—one white and affluent; the other more integrated with tentacles among blacks and the middle-class. In a few years, the mastering of that duality would serve me well.

Often, I found myself in Rehoboth Beach, Delaware, enjoying the company of my white friends. One hot July Saturday while there, I met someone who affected my life for the next two years. I found him inside the circle of a large group of young sun-bathers from which music emanated. He sat on a canvas stool, playing a guitar and singing ballads. . Who was this African-American man and how did he get here, I wondered? As the afternoon wore on and the sun began to set, the crowd slowly dispersed. Always one to enjoy staying on the beach late into the evening, I struck up a conversation with Ted Brown, who had a magnetic personality and it wasn't surprising to me that he and I bonded. Besides, it was hard to turn away from his music. A native of Cleveland, Ohio, and a Roman Catholic, he was married with two children. He was probably six feet tall and about one hundred ninety pounds with fairly dark skin; his facial features resembled Louis "Satchmo" Armstrong.

Ted had been on the Mike Douglas show in Cleveland, had made two albums, performed at the Purple Onion in San Francisco and had come to the Washington area to find singing gigs. I was never sure how he got to Rehoboth. After spending a great bit of time with him that weekend, Mike Fitzgerald and I extended an invitation for Brown to stay free at our townhouse in D.C. We had an extra cot in our half-furnished basement with a bathroom. He accepted and eventually began working in several nightspots, including the Market Inn, a favorite watering hole for elected officials and their staffs, lobbyists and tourists. Inside, there was an alarm system that alerted congressmen and their staff when a vote was about to take place. That kind of association with the Capitol gave it the patina of a prestigious and classy place. One evening I joined Brown at the Inn for a meal before he performed. As we sat in the outer foyer, which had a few booths adjacent to the bar, he told me not to be alarmed but a giant rat was scurrying around behind me. Turning slowly, I saw it darting between newly arrived customers' legs; they were oblivious to its presence. I never ate a meal there again. He was always a draw whenever he played, although invariably most of the patrons were white. He loved to cook and confessed to me that he wanted to have his own restaurant where he could also entertain. Intrigued by the concept, I said I would help. I had spotted an empty restaurant in Georgetown at the corner of Wisconsin Ave. NW and K St. NW. I discovered it had been leased to a former Washington Redskins football player who was forced to close it because of financial reasons. I set up a meeting with the owner/agent, who seemed of Greek heritage. Ted and I walked in together. My attention was immediately focused on the interior. The place had been closed for at least three years, and although it needed a few touches, it looked as if it could open within a day or two. All the dining room tables had white linen along with red napkins neatly folded. The silverware was perfectly aligned. In the kitchen, every pot and pan was hanging overhead and all the platters and knives, were perfect in appearance. In later years, I remembered it as being eerily like the hotel in the Jack Nicholson classic movie "The Shining." The owner/agent was asking some outlandish rent, however. Brown seemed strangely quiet throughout the meeting. After we left and were in my car, he said that while the man had shaken my hand in greeting, he had not extended the same courtesy to him. I had not recognized the snub, but became incensed, realizing the owner would never lease to us, even if we had the money. He tried to calm me. It wasn't the first time he said he had had such an unpleasant experience. We did search unsuccessfully for other locations. Over the following months, we frequently talked about race and its implications on his life. He wasn't angry, however. He accepted the discrimination as a fact of his life.

He introduced to me to the after-hours club scenes in Washington. There was an infamous place on Swann St. NW to which we went to around two o'clock in the morning. It made me nervous; the owners or managers seemed racist. I suspected they didn't want Brown in their establishment. But we enjoyed him immensely. He stayed with Fitzgerald and me at our row house for much of the winter and through the early spring the following year. That St. Patrick's Day, we decided to throw a party—a rather fancy party—at our house. I put on my tuxedo; I had to alter the pants since I had severely sprained my ankle playing outdoor basketball. Back then, doctors placed heavy casts on sprains. Brown made his famous bean soup. He was in the kitchen when three beefy male party crashers showed up at our front door. Standing at the door, I politely informed them it was a private affair. One of the individuals took off his green Irish party hat and slammed it in my face. Instinctively, I punched him in the face with my right fist, knocking him through the screen door. The blood spurted from his cut face, showering my brand new white tux shirt. The taller one then punched me from the side in my right eye. I came up under him with my cast leg in his groin, knocking him to the floor. After punching him, my friends pulled me off. But, the men still refused to leave. Hearing the commotion, Brown came from the kitchen and took effective action. Those guys, obviously mistaking him for a bouncer, immediately exited the party. I was becoming even more of a social animal. Through friends I was invited to join Bachelors and Spinsters (B&S), a club that held three social events a year, mostly at the Sulgrave Club on Dupont Circle, where black tie was mandatory. Earlier, I had purchased my first tuxedo. In college, I always rented or borrowed one from friends. But I had hit the big time. The B&S carried prestige, and since I loved to dance, I was elated to be invited to join. The group featured live orchestras like the one led by Peter Duchin, the son of the legendary Eddy Duchin, the New York socialite on whom a popular movie had been based. I thought I had arrived, socially at least.

By the early summer of 1967, I decided that I needed my own apartment. Group living had run its course. The least expensive apartments were on Capitol Hill. I found a top floor unit of a row house in the nine hundred block of Pennsylvania Ave. SE. Unknowingly, I was integrating the area and soon met yet another person who would change my life.

James Stewart, an African American, was all of eleven years old. He lived around the corner at 10th and Pennsylvania Ave. SE in a run-down row-house. He had numerous brothers and sisters. After I completed my sales for the day, James would appear at my apartment, desperately needing attention and approval from an adult mentor, I concluded. I guess I filled that position. He wore an assortment of nicknames like "Boo" or "Bug eye," although he did not have extraordinarily large eyes. After one or two days when he did not appear at my doorstep, I went to his house looking for him. The door to his house was opened briskly by a very large black woman, who I assumed was his mother. She obviously knew me at least by reputation. I asked if James was around, she turned and yelled through a gaping hole in the ceiling of the foyer "Boo, your friend is here!" James peered through that same hole, before scampering down the stairs to greet me. I was dismayed at his living conditions, but off we went.

My friendship with James and the other neighborhood youths had another benefit. Their older brothers were a rough looking group, but they never bothered me or my car, which was always parked on the street. While I lived in the predominantly black neighborhood and was making friends there, I continued to socialize in an all-white world, going to the beach in Delaware, attending black tie events, dating and going to Georgetown bars and restaurants. I was nevertheless broadening my vision. And soon, the parallel worlds in which I had existed would intersect, taking me deeper into African American culture and causing me to morph into a kind of warrior against racism.

That role began, perhaps, when I met David Rusk, captain of the Washington rugby team that I had sought out to join. Interestingly, he was son of Dean Rusk, the Secretary of State. I learned that David was also the deputy director of the Washington Urban League, which had been one of the big six organizations that staged the March on Washington. He persuaded me to volunteer with the organization, and subsequently introduced me to its president, Sterling Tucker—the man who eventually would bring me to that southwest townhouse. I also began to meet more professionals in the black middle-class, many from upper Sixteenth Street NW—the area commonly known then and now as the "Gold Coast." The neighborhood had once been white, but as blacks became more expert at getting around land covenants, they were able to purchase homes in upscale communities.

Meanwhile, my dual paths had brought me into friendships with whites such as Charles Robb. His engagement had been announced to Lynda Bird Johnson, the daughter of the President Lyndon Baines Johnson. Two of Robb's friends, J. Edgar Nichols and Todd Owen, had decided to throw a large black tie party for Chuck and Lynda at the exclusive Madison Hotel in Washington D.C., I was fortunate enough to be invited, and it was a spectacular affair with around one hundred twenty guests and a live band. There was not a black person at the party. That all seemed a little odd to me, given the fact that President Johnson had pushed through both major pieces of civil rights legislation, altering the course of history for millions of African Americans.

The president's contradiction was my own. Despite my volunteer work and growing understanding of the issues affecting blacks, I did not alter my trajectory. Rather, I became more rooted in white Washington. A friend persuaded me to move from my Capitol Hill apartment to Rosslyn, Virginia, which was directly across Key Bridge from Georgetown. It was roomier, had a fireplace, and was less expensive. James Stewart, my young friend, still visited me, however, and I continued my Urban League activities. I also took a black physician, who I called on, Dr. Sanders, as my guest to a Washington Redskins game. What was a surprise to me was the small number of black fans at the games. I observed, though, that the famed flanker back Bobby Mitchell had been the first African American to play for the team, only five years before in 1962.

Late that summer I started dating a girl from North Carolina on a regular basis. She had accompanied me to the black tie affair at the Madison

Hotel as well as numerous other social functions. One bright Saturday fall day in mid-October, we were planning to attend, with another friend, Fred Fearing and his date, the Middleburg Hunt, which essentially was the fall horse-racing season. We also played touch football on the mall in an organized league. We had a very good team, which, ironically, was the Young Republicans. I played tight end with Fred at the quarterback position. On the day of the Hunt, we decided to play a game. Late in the action, I went up in the air to catch a touchdown pass. As I caught it, I got hit from behind in the back and landed awkwardly on my left ankle. I heard something snap and I limped off the field. I was determined not to go to the hospital, however, since I wanted to go to the hunt in Virginia.

Fred, his date and I drove home. We picked up my friend, creating a foursome, driving to Middleburg with a bottle of Jack Daniels; the whiskey helped dull the pain at least for the time being. When I got out of the car, however, I was having trouble walking. A smallish African- American male noticed my predicament and offered to carry me piggyback up to the top of a small hill. I learned that he was a jockey. That must have been quite a sight with a black person maybe weighing one hundred twenty pounds carrying a one hundred seventy pound white man. I was truly thankful. He may have been the only black person in the entire crowd.

As Christmas approached, I decided to go home to spend the holiday with my parents. I invited my friend from North Carolina to come. She agreed, saying she could fly in on Christmas day. I flew solo and my parents picked me up that evening from the Cedar Rapids airport. Arriving at their farmhouse around ten, my father went straight to bed. My mother made a sandwich for me, which I enjoyed with a bottle of beer. Sitting in their living room, I buried myself in local newspapers. After a few minutes, my mother, sitting on the couch directly across from my chair, asked about my girlfriend's appearance. She had almost no association with people from the South. Plus she was aware of my budding civil rights activity in Washington. I slowly lowered the newspaper and in a very serious tone informed her that my friend was black. She uttered a little gasp, laughed nervously and said, "You are kidding me, aren't you?" I replied sternly, "No," and raised the newspaper back up covering the smile on my face. After two minutes of silence, my mother asked again whether I was serious. Lowering the paper, I said again that my friend was black, and, if my mother objected to her presence, I would have her cancel her flight to Iowa. "Oh no," she replied; I covered my face, hiding my smirks. After another two minutes, mother said, "Doug, she's pretty light-colored isn't she?" With that question, I laughed nearly non-stop. Mother by now realized that I had been teasing her. She was angry with me, but also relieved that my friend was not black—although I think, even if she had been, my mother would have been accepting. She had come a little way herself in terms of racial issues. My friend came for Christmas. As the year ended, I kept recalling that song by Bob Dylan "The times, they are-a-changin…"

CHAPTER TEN

Jaguars and Riot Patrol

THE year had started innocently enough. But 1968 proved one of the most tumultuous years in contemporary America. Before it would end, it would refocus me more intently on the mission I had outlined after my European sojourn. I had promised then to do my part to help repair the tear in our society evidenced by the 1963 assassination of a beloved president. Even as I worked to focus on that self-appointed assignment, I maintained a satisfying social life, although my friend from North Carolina had discontinued our relationship. I began a friendship with a woman, Stephanie de Sibour, while auditioning in December for roles in the Washington, D.C.-based Hexagon Club's performance. Established in 1955, the club consisted mostly of whites, many of whom were amateurs. I was selected for the company; our productions were comprised of a whole series of comedy numbers, songs and dances, which essentially were spoofs of the Washington political scene. One number I will always remember was about President Johnson and his wife known as "Lady Bird." But instead of the real life characters, another actor and I were cast as Bonnie and Clyde from the movie popular at that time. The stock phrase from the film, "We rob banks," was substituted with "We rob governments." The skit brought the house down.

Since de Sibour also had an interest in civil rights, we recruited white friends to volunteer with the Urban League and other organizations, including D. C. Build Black, which promoted African American empowerment and self esteem, to sensitize them to racial issues within the inner city. I continued working for Eaton Laboratories. After almost two years, I was getting edgy about my future, however. I decided to reapply for law school at the University of Iowa, hoping to begin that fall. I would have to modify those plans.

Senator Robert Kennedy announced for the Democratic presidential nomination on March 16, 1968, in the Caucus Room of the Old Senate Office Building. Senator Eugene McCarthy had already entered the race. Further, it was assumed Johnson was going to run, but he had not announced. His presidency was deeply embroiled in the Viet Nam War. The conflict was taking a daily toll on him and the public's perception of him, although he had inherited that war. McCarthy had thrown a large scare into the Johnson presidency by winning a substantial vote in the New Hampshire primary, polling at 42 percent of the vote compared with Johnson's 59, who, as the incumbent, was expected to show in the 70s or 80s.

Knowing several of Kennedy's immediate staff, I decided to attend his announcement, bringing a small camera and hoping to capture the moment for posterity; as he was leaving with his wife Ethel, descending the congressional office building stairs, I said in a loud voice "Senator Kennedy;" he looked up, and I snapped the picture.

Then, two weeks later, on the night of March 31, 1968, I received a bigger surprise. My good friend David Lambert and I, with our respective dates, were at a party at Carl Arnold's in suburban Virginia. He was a close friend and confidant of Congressman Wilbur Mills, chairman of the powerful House Ways and Means Committee. President Johnson was to give a television address. The party was at full throttle when he came on CBS. Someone may have turned down the volume, as we were becoming jaundiced from experiencing one too many presidential speeches. Consequently, we only learned of Johnson's announcement after Walter Cronkite, in closing comments, repeated that the president would not seek re-election. The entire party ended, with everyone rushing out to their home telephones. We were shocked.

Things were shaking up Washington. It wouldn't help that the Rev. Martin Luther King, Jr., announced his intention, during a November meeting in Frogmore, South Carolina, to launch in 1968 a campaign to push for a federal, thirty billion-dollar anti-poverty package. A major aspect of his efforts would be Resurrection City, an encampment of poor people and leaders on the National Mall. The National Park Service had granted a six-week permit, allowing three thousand citizens to take up residence in makeshift housing. The Poor People's Campaign, as it came to be identified, was an unofficial acknowledgement that Johnson's so-called War on Poverty was a failure. That effort had been derailed by the Viet Nam War.

Five years after the 1963 March on Washington, King had become an outspoken opponent of the war. His opposition wasn't just rooted in the fact that as a disciple of Mahatma Gandhi, King was a pacifist, uncomfortable with any kind of violence. He had become even more entrenched in the demand for economic justice—not just for African Americans, but for poor whites and others. As designed, the Poor People's Campaign would include three components: Resurrection City on the Mall, a push to change select federal policies, and lastly a march that would bear the name of the initiative, which would culminate with a message from King. The Washington Urban League was to play a pivotal role in the execution of the campaign. Since I volunteered with the organization, I was pulled in, touring the proposed site and agreeing to provide support. It would not go off as planned.

The evening of April 4, 1968, I was home watching television when the newscaster announced that the Rev. King had been assassinated in Memphis. He had gone there at the urging of AFSCME, the union representing the city's sanitation workers, who were primarily African American. Jerry Wurf, along with his executive assistant William Lucy, had requested King's appearance. Both men later became close friends of mine.

King's murder dominated local and national news. While I had been developing inroads into black America, I remained somewhat disconnected. Naively, I prepared to make my morning sales visits, although I debated whether I should proceed with business as usual, especially since there was nothing usual about the assassination of a man who had won the Nobel Prize for Peace and had become a worldwide role model for disenfranchised people. Looking out of my window in Rosslyn, I saw smoke billowing from a section north of the District of Columbia's downtown. A telephone call interrupted my thoughts. It was Carol Randles, a chief assistant to Sterling Tucker at the Urban League. Originally from Iowa, Carol had come to the city a year earlier seeking employment. Tucker scooped her up. She wanted me to come to the League's temporary headquarters at 6th St. NW and K Street NW., where a Rumor Control Center had been set on the second floor. Almost as soon as I hung up my phone, ending the conversation with Carol, my close friend Bill Oldaker called, telling me he wanted to help and would pick me up. He arrived in his blue Jaguar sports car. Neither of us considered the madness of using such a vehicle, until much later. So, we went on our way to the League's office. As we drove down K St. NW, we realized the extent of the turmoil sweeping through the city. Approaching 7th St. NW, we saw flames spurting from a liquor store on our left. Several cars were overturned, including a Mercedes Benz. A traffic light at the intersection of 7th St. and K St was red; Bill slowed, attempting to follow the law. With my left foot I stepped on his accelerator, causing us to speed through the red light. Gangs of black youths were streaming onto the streets. Don't stop for anything, I told Bill. We safely reached the Urban League office; we parked the car, noticing that some automobiles were outfitted with orange placards. We passed through security, which was composed of a few volunteers, and made out way to the second floor. All the windows in the building wore the same orange signs I had seen on the cars; they basically informed the police and later the National Guard troops that we were trying to assist law enforcement, thus "safe."

The Rumor Control Center was staffed by Urban League employees and other volunteers; its purpose was to communicate about Resurrection City and the upcoming march as well as to dispel any false rumors about the Poor Peoples Campaign. A bank of telephones sat on long tables, each one was manned by an individual well versed in the program and events of the day, which would get worse as the hours proceeded.

The whole situation was eerily reminiscent of a 1959 movie I had seen when I was a freshman at the University of Iowa called "On the Beach." It starred Gregory Peck as the commander of a submarine which travels to San Diego to investigate a mysterious sound after the whole world has been polluted with nuclear fallout, killing all life. The Urban League building seemed like the submarine where we were observing the whole of Washington D.C. under siege. We could see fires in various places and hear the incessant police and fire sirens. We were on the telephones almost non-stop, answering calls from all over the Washington-Metropolitan region. Many were suburbanites nervous about whether black mobs soon would be marching on their white enclaves.

Bill had been assigned an interesting, but dangerous task. With an African American beside him and a large orange placard in the windshield, he was to patrol the city and report back observations. After an exhaustive night, he approached me around four in the morning, asking if I could accompany him in his car. Now we were two white guys were in a Jaguar with only a large orange placard in the windshield, labeling us as "good guys" to the police and National Guard soldiers. We proceeded up 14th St. NW, determined to check on the destruction. The streets and sidewalks were littered with refuse, including mannequins from stores that had been looted. Fires were burning everywhere. We rode up to Columbia Heights where the infamous Manhattan Auto dealership was located. Manhattan had a history of being an unsavory business that had victimized its customers both black and white. When we arrived at its location, we saw that not only was the main building ransacked and burning, but every car in the lot had been burned. Revenge was being meted out. To tell the truth, driving through a riot as we did, was a prime indicator of our absolute ignorance. Maybe subconsciously we reasoned that because of who we were we were not in danger.

I was more nervous about the many National Guardsmen, who were young and inexperienced; I worried they might inadvertently shoot first and ask questions later, without regard for color or class. President Johnson had activated 13,600 soldiers to assist the outmanned D.C. Metropolitan Police Department. After driving a block past Manhattan Auto, I told Bill to make a U-turn and head back to the Urban League. Several blocks ahead, there was a mob of youths sprinting across 14th St. NW, although a curfew was in effect. Our orange placard may have been a pass to drive around the city. At night, however, it was nothing more than a paper shield.

By the time the anger of African Americans over King's assassination had been satiated and things had quieted that Sunday, twelve people had been killed, 1,200 buildings had been burned, including over 900 retail and convenience stores. Prime business corridors frequented by blacks, like the 14th St. NW corridor, H Street N.E., and U St. NW., had been severely damaged. Later, many other businesses soon fled the city. The affected areas did not recover until decades later in the 2000s.

Clearly I had become somewhat entrenched in parts of black Washington. I paid attention when, on April 27, Vice-President Humphrey announced his candidacy for president of the United States. Democrats now had a three-way contest for the nomination. I liked Humphrey, but I wasn't anti-Kennedy or anti-McCarthy. I had friends in all three camps. My work at the Urban League shifted my focus more to the civil rights struggles, causing me to bypass national politics, particularly the Viet Nam War. Passions about the war were heated on all sides, but civil rights transcended petty political differences. The "Black Power Movement," instigated in part by Stokely Carmichael, H. Rap Brown, and others, such as the Black Panther Party, was creating deeper divisions in the African-American community. Many blacks had followed a more moderate path in their fight against racial discrimination. They believed in integration, having fought many battles, including winning Brown v Board of Education and the 1965 laws prohibiting racial segregation. Embracing the Carmichael agenda, they believed might imperil these gains. Tension also had seeped into King's Southern Christian Leadership Conference. In some respects, at the core of the divisions was a battle over who would claim the leadership mantle, becoming the official voice of black America. African Americans weren't the only ones at odds.

I continued to assist the Urban League with preparations for the Solidarity Day, which had been renamed the Poor Peoples March, and would be the apex of King's campaign. Prior to his murder, the event was set for May 30, but was moved to June19, 1968. Director Bayard Rustin suspended activities until campaign organizers clarified the goals to avoid incidents of violence. A split over control of the organization may have also prompted the delay. Some people were critical of King's successor Ralph Abernathy, asserting that he lacked the intellectual muscle and charisma of his predecessor. Before the revised date for the Solidarity Day March, Rustin resigned, which was an enormous loss. After all, he had been the chief strategist for the successful 1963 March on Washington. If there was anyone who could bring disparate groups together with one unifying message, he was that person. So there was concern about the future of the effort. But Abernathy didn't miss a beat. He appointed Sterling Tucker to replace Rustin. That's when I got really busy.

Tucker and David Rusk asked if I could lend even more support. I still had Eaton responsibilities, but I promised to be at their headquarters every day. Soon I found myself as the unofficial volunteer coordinator, manning telephones almost nonstop.

Then, on June 5, Sen. Robert F. Kennedy was assassinated. I wanted 1968 to end, post haste. There was far too much trauma. Could the country recover?

When, a few days later I had switched on the television in my apartment, I simply wanted to relax. The station was showing replays of John F. Kennedy's funeral, which I had missed because I had been away in Europe. All those emotions stored away from that year came tumbling out. I burst into uncontrollable tears.

In five years, the nation had gone through major tragedies: The assassinations of President John F. Kennedy, Malcolm X, the Rev. Martin Luther King, Jr and now Robert Kennedy. He had been in the middle of his campaign, gaining momentum with such speed and certainty, many were preparing for a second Kennedy in the White House. He was shot, shortly after completing a powerful speech in Los Angeles. The scene was as chaotic as it had been when his brother was shot in the convertible as his motorcade made its way through downtown Dallas, just as it passed the School Book Depository. Fortunately, Robert Kennedy's supporters had managed to capture the shooter, Sirhan Sirhan.

I was overwhelmed. Harry Belafonte would later pen his song *Abraham, Martin and John,* bringing the younger Kennedy into the fold: *"Has anybody here//Seen my old friend Bobby//Can you tell me, where he's gone...."*

Robert Kennedy's political philosophy mirrored King's; the two believed it was important to bring together blue-collar whites and African Americans. Whites did not engage in violent protests, but certainly felt a rage similar to what had been expressed by blacks after King's murder. A second Kennedy's death rocked a deep part of my soul. There would be a huge vacuum, not just on the political scene but in the nation's humanity. A man who engendered hope and the potential of America, as his brother had, was lost to all of us—forever. No one like him, or any of the others we had lost, would ever arrive on the national stage again. What followed, I thought at the time, would be mostly imposters.

Still, we could not abandon everything, fold up our tents, and forget the Poor People's March. Many individuals who had signed up to volunteer for Kennedy's presidential campaign gravitated to our effort, increasing to 400 the number of volunteers. I was aided by people like Joanne Manning and Anne Fitzpatrick who worked exceedingly hard. By June 17, I was working eighteen to twenty-hour days. There were five other individuals, a mixture of blacks and whites, who were largely responsible for the March's logistics: Charles "Chuck" Hoffman, David Rusk, Chip Wood, Leonard McCantz and Horace Morris. By June 19, we had our meetings with officials from the National Park Service, who were not always the most cooperative. At four that morning, Hoffman and I toured the site from the Lincoln Memorial to the Washington Monument to ensure everything was in place. Starting from the Jefferson monument and moving east toward the Washington Monument; all logistics and operations had to be in place. Hoffman, a white guy, right out of Hollywood casting, was a perfect overall coordinator. He was anal, had a great sense of humor, wore a handle-bar mustache, and dealt with both whites and blacks effortlessly. With the large lights and the volunteer activity of organizers, plus the police presence, the March had the overall aura of a giant movie production.

Hoffman gave me responsibility for the large tent located near the Washington Monument, which housed over fifty telephones, dozens of placards, and the assignments for the volunteers. By seven o'clock that morning, I was on the move: Entertainers, notably Eartha Kitt, Bill Cosby, Peter and Mary of Peter, Paul and Mary, Marlon Brando and several others, started arriving around ten o'clock. Ossie Davis, an outstanding actor who served as the master of ceremonies, had recruited many of the celebrities. He and I hit it off immediately and stayed in touch for a few years after the event. Volunteers were assigned a specific celebrity. Anne Fitzpatrick assisted Bill Cosby, who was not well known but had a clean reputation. By 2014, he had become an object of scorn rising from numerous allegations of sexual misconduct. Dozens of women accused him of drugging them and taking physical advantage of them. At the March, he gave what he called his "Robin Hood" speech about making sure that poor people could live in dignity with sufficient resources to address their needs. Things went well, although at one point, when the crowd swelled inside our tent, the force was so great it nearly toppled the structure. Sensing imminent danger, I grabbed three or four marshals who quickly moved people back.

The Park Service, notorious for low estimates, placed crowd numbers between 50,000 to 100,000. I observed David Rusk arguing with the head of the agency that the figure was closer to 100,000. The Park Service was only following orders from the administration, I believe, to minimize the importance of that day. Vice-President Humphrey spoke, but was booed. Senator Eugene McCarthy, Coretta Scott King and Reverend Ralph Abernathy got a better reception. Sterling Tucker gave a short speech, which received the loudest applause because he, with assistance, had performed a minor miracle with the March. There was no reported violence or unpleasant incidents. We were all elated that the event was such a success.

As the March activities subsided around five thirty that evening, fatigue overtook me, and I fell asleep under a nearby tree. One of my volunteers woke me; it was almost eight o'clock. As I reached over for my small leather briefcase, which had been adjacent to my legs, I realized it was gone. It contained my notes and papers, including the names, addresses, and telephone numbers of the volunteers. I became almost physically ill. Someone had been brazen enough to steal the briefcase while I slept. It was my fault: I should have entrusted it to one of my assistants. At large events like that, there are always thieves and scam artists lurking in the crowd waiting for the first opportunity to do damage. The next morning, I also learned our telephones in the tent had been stolen, despite the security stationed at the site. I was never sure, however, that my briefcase had just been taken by a thief. The FBI and U.S. Park Service police had plenty of observers around the March. The information in the briefcase would have been very valuable to them.

Years later, the public learned that through COINTELPRO (Counter Intelligence Program), a series of covert, and at times illegal, projects had been conducted by the FBI. About 85 percent of COINTELPRO resources had been used to target groups like King's organization, the SCLC, the NAACP, and CORE (the Congress of Racial Equality). This was during the era when J. Edgar Hoover was the director of the FBI. He seemed to have bugged everyone. Eventually, Congress passed legislation that allowed individuals to request information about themselves that may have been contained in FBI files. Ironically, Robert Kennedy also had been a target of FBI surveillance. He had been attorney general with oversight of the FBI. . Years later, after filing a Freedom of Information Act request, I received documents about myself; much of it had been redacted. The report concluded, however, that I was not a threat to the U.S. government.

What a relief!

CHAPTER ELEVEN

A Necessary Detour

SOON after Resurrection City closed on June 23, I received a telephone call from Stephanie de Sibour, the woman I had met auditioning for the Hexagon Show; she wanted me to meet with her boss, James Cuff O'Brien, the political director for the United Steelworkers, a very strong union within the AFL-CIO. Interestingly, she actually was working for the Humphrey campaign. Saying yes to her request would take me away from the civil rights work in which I was becoming intimately involved. While I had arrived on that path mostly by happenstance, it was satisfying. Nevertheless, I subsequently met O'Brien, who was in his early forties, sophisticated, urbane with a fine Irish sense of humor. I also found out later he had a master's degree in labor economics. He was very unlike most of the major labor leaders I had encountered. We had a lively conversation and I believed we became instant friends.

He called later, asking me if I was interested in performing advance work for Humphrey. I went to the candidate's headquarters on 17th St. NW, meeting Tom Hart, the Midwest coordinator, who asked if I was engaged in another assignment that might conflict with my involvement. Tom was a human dynamo; he would become a close friend for the next forty years. The next afternoon, I was on a plane headed to Des Moines, where I met other individuals on the advance team, including Ardon Judd from Dallas, and John Elliott and Don Joel, both of whom were from Philadelphia; the latter was in charge of media. Advance work for political candidates can be very complex, particularly when dealing with someone like Vice-President Humphrey who was already in office. It was a fine dance between having a candidate who could wade into interesting and sometimes controversial issues and one who had to measure every word he spoke for fear he might bring down a world of trouble on his colleagues back home in Washington.

Humphrey was to deliver a major address at Veterans Auditorium in Des Moines. The Iowa Democratic Party was holding its statutory convention there. I was given a quick course by Elliot on Humphrey's personal peccadilloes, including his choice of beverage, the time constraints, and the main thing "never touch Humphrey," even during an attempt to get him moving. He didn't like being touched by advance men. Maybe he didn't like the appearance it gave of him not being in control or being led around like a dog on a leash. That evening, I also met the three secret service agents assigned to him. The lead agent was a short, sandy haired individual, probably in his mid-thirties. Then, I called my parents, knowing they were in the delegation, and told them I likely would have the good fortune to see them.

That morning, Humphrey arrived with Tom Hart; the two were busy courting delegates. At the hotel, I met Humphrey's assistant Ofield Dukes, an African American with whom I later developed a decades-long friendship. From my vantage, it seemed all presidential candidates had their lone black assistant. Kennedy, for example, had Rafer Johnson, the 1960 Olympic gold medalist, who, with former National Football League player Rosy Grier, had tackled Sirhan Sirhan at the assassination site in Los

Angeles. Sometimes those African American defenders were bodyguards, other times they were like Dukes, the bridge to black America. They were translators ensuring white candidates didn't commit an unforgivable faux pas, and could speak more coherently about cultural issues and aspirations of African Americans. After meeting Dukes, I went to the auditorium and walked through my responsibilities, timing everything Humphrey was to do in a few hours.

He arrived at the side entrance in a black limousine. As he got out of the car, accompanied by a secret service agent, I waited patiently about four feet from his side. As we walked toward the door several teenage girls stopped him, asking for his autograph. He gladly obliged. I did not notice, but an Associated Press photographer snapped a picture, with me in the frame. It would run the following day in several major newspapers. I led Humphrey into the auditorium, where he mounted the stage to deliver his address. The campaign correctly anticipated a large contingent of anti-war protestors in the balconies. At the conclusion, Humphrey addressed the whole convention hall when he stated, "One cannot just boo for peace." It drew a standing ovation from the delegates on the floor. As I moved along with the secret service agent to lead Humphrey out the side door to the waiting car, we realized that a huge crowd, along with the media, had created a major obstacle to our exit. I sensed that the secret service constantly worried about a stationary vice president being hemmed in, especially after the experiences of Kennedy's assassination and King's murder. I instantly locked arms with the agent who was short but in great physical shape. We knew we had to keep Humphrey moving so we acted as a battering ram to clear a path for him. Fans and photographers were sent in every direction as we busted through. But we had no choice. As he got in the car, the agent turned to me thanking me profusely, saying, "Quick thinking Doug, thanks." I was grateful for the comment, but I also realized that was part of my job.

I had told my parents to meet me at the hotel in Des Moines where a private reception with Humphrey was being held for delegates and other influential Democrats. When I arrived my mother and Dad were waiting outside the reception room, unsure about when I would appear. I quickly asked them if they had gone through the receiving line. Don Joel had set up one where attendees could have their picture taken with Humphrey. I waved at Joel, asking him whether they could enter the line. He said they couldn't, since Humphrey had cut off the photographs. I quickly escorted my parents into the private reception area telling them to go to the front of the room by a lectern where Humphrey was supposed to enter from the adjacent room, to deliver a short speech. As they proceeded reluctantly to greet Humphrey as he entered, I turned to a photographer next to me who had overheard our conversation. I asked him to take a picture of Humphrey and my parents. "Don't worry, I got it," he said. I handed him my father's State Senate business card. I quickly left the room saying a speedy good-bye to my parents; I had other unfinished business in the hotel. What's more, I had to catch a flight back to Washington D.C.

Later that next day, I had another pleasant surprise. My mother called and told me that my Dad and she had received calls from relatives and friends in California, Florida, Colorado and other states. The individual who I had asked to take their photograph was also an Associated Press photographer, and, not unlike what happened to me, the picture of my parents and Humphrey and had appeared all across the United States in major newspapers.

James Cuff O'Brien called, asking if I would come by his office. He told me during our meeting that Humphrey and top campaign staffers were elated about the great trip and reception in Iowa. O'Brien then offered me the chance to work for Humphrey either in Iowa or northern California. I thought it over for a day and then decided to take the position in Iowa.

I was planning to return there for law school in the fall, so I knew the transition would be simpler. It wasn't, however, although I had thought the chance of having a major role in a national campaign would be advantageous. I gave notice to Eaton Laboratories of my intention to leave, and my main supervisors Phil Read and John Schultz were very supportive and understanding about my resignation. I called my parents in Iowa telling them, and they said they would drive out to Washington to bring my furniture and other possessions back to Iowa. I no longer had a car at my disposal. But I was fortunate in joining the Humphrey campaign because 60 percent to 70 percent of my salary would be paid by the Steelworkers union. O'Brien told me his good friend Dick McQuire, treasurer of the Democratic National Committee (D.N.C.) assured O'Brien that he would pay the difference. They would match the salary I had had with the pharmaceutical company. Many Humphrey staffers, I found out later, did not have paid positions. I was lucky. Once my parents arrived in Washington, we loaded up a small U-Haul and headed back to Iowa. Somehow I managed to convince the Teamsters in Des Moines to lend me a car. Once in the state, I was basically on my own.

Making the decision to join the Humphrey team full time was the serious detour I had anticipated when I got that call from de Sibour. Signing on with that campaign meant I was closing the door on the work I started of trying to end poverty and empower African Americans. I did not know whether there would be a re-entry into the civil rights arena. I took solace in the fact that I might be able to do more on the national stage. With Kennedy's death, I thought Humphrey could achieve major accomplishments while permitting him to come from under the bad reputation he garnered in 1964 when, following Johnson's instigation, he prevented Fannie Lou Hammer and the Freedom Democratic Party from being seated as delegates to the national convention. Consequently, I gave my full attention to the campaign, embracing every aspect of the assignment. That determination was solidified when I considered the condition of the Iowa organization. It definitely was lacking. There was strong support in the state for McCarthy. In addition, many Kennedy supporters couldn't come to grips with the loss of their leader; consequently, there existed a tremendous vacuum.

I managed to find a suitable campaign headquarters downtown paying the first month's rent of five hundred dollars out of my pocket. Then, I tried to do two things: energize the Humphrey image in the state so at least we had the perception of being viable prior to the Democratic convention in Chicago, and persuade those Kennedy delegates, including Governor Harold Hughes, to switch their allegiance to the vice president. Both were going to be difficult.

State Senator Minette Dodderer of Iowa City urged me to contact Dr. James Van Allen, the renowned astrophysicist best known for the Explorer spacecraft, and Forest Evaskeski, the famed former head football coach at the University of Iowa. Both were celebrities in the state and highly respected. I convinced them to become co-chairmen of the Iowa United Democrats for Humphrey, which received state-wide press coverage. During that period I met two Robert Kennedy partisans—Larry Scalise and Jim Brick, who became my friends. Scalise had been attorney general of Iowa, while Brick was a much sought after political organizer. With my urging and that of Tom Hart, who was the campaign's Midwest coordinator, they joined the Humphrey team. We also recruited Art Hedburg, another lawyer and Kennedy delegate to be our main political organizer. Patty Sarcone, a member of a prominent Democratic family operated the campaign office. We had less success with Governor Hughes, however. About one week before the Chicago convention, he endorsed McCarthy. Hart and I also made a quick trip to Omaha to shore up the Humphrey support in Nebraska. Two or three Kennedy delegates, including a future U.S. Senator, Jim Exon, switched to our side. It was a very hot summer, but it would get even hotter—at least politically.

The Democratic convention got underway in Chicago on August 26th. Hart and I shared a room at the Hotel Knickerbocker, just off North Lake Shore Drive and across from the Drake Hotel where the Iowa and Nebraska delegations were staying. Every morning, very early, we had meetings at the Hilton Hotel with the Humphrey campaign team to conduct our state-by-state delegate count. We appeared to be in good shape and likely were assured a first- ballot victory. I noticed that I was probably the youngest staffer in the room, followed closely by Hart. All serious business, those sessions were basically headed by Lawrence O'Brien, with assistance from Robert McCandless, a Washington-based lawyer from Oklahoma. There didn't seem to be any blacks on staff.

Some of the state delegates were literally divided, not only between the Humphrey and anti-Humphrey forces, but also the twin issues of the Vietnam War and race, which were at the forefront of the nation's consciousness. Even among the Humphrey staffers and loyalists, there was a marked division. Hart and I were in the minority, we questioned the Vietnam War. So we were encouraged when the Humphrey leadership, including the vice president, had agreed to allow the moderate anti-war plank pushed by Governor Hughes to be voted on before the delegates on the floor. Both of us thought it was a good move to put some daylight between Humphrey and the President Johnson's policies. We had told our delegates basically they were free to vote their consciences. Late that night, however, we got a rude, surprise telephone call. We were notified by the Humphrey camp that we had to switch our delegates to vote against the minority plank. We were told that this was a test by the Ted Kennedy forces and if the minority plank vote was successful, it would give a boost to his candidacy on a floor vote. We both thought it was a ruse and not believable. Still, we began notifying our supporters to vote against the plank. Most of them did not believe our direction. Everyone was somewhat demoralized. Years later, we found out from various published reports that we were right. Johnson had sent his top emissary and staffer Marvin Watson on a plane to Chicago to notify Humphrey that the peace plank was unacceptable to him. Johnson had been observing the convention on television and grew incensed by the Democratic efforts on the floor. It was reported accurately that Watson had summoned Humphrey to his suite, giving him Johnson's message. Humphrey believed he needed Johnson's support; so he followed the directive. That definitely reduced the ardor we had for Humphrey, having been made to appear two-faced.

After working the floor one evening with the delegates, I walked off to get some refreshments and passed a small anteroom on the corridor where I noticed my friend and delegate Larry Scalise of Iowa with another Humphrey delegate, Phil Toliver from Kentucky; they were sitting next to each other. Behind them were two towering men both six feet tall and at least two hundred pounds. Being curious, I stopped to say hello but sensed something wrong. One of the gentlemen told me to get lost. They were cops, Scalise told me, adding that they had been detained for the alleged offense of trading delegate passes. Scalise told me quickly to get O'Brien upstairs. I ran out, got on my walkie-talkie and told Eiler Ravenholt, his assistant, what had occurred. I waited while our own security came and had Scalise and Toliver released. This was when I first learned of the apprehension consuming the auditorium. Mayor Richard Daley was certainly controlling the activities. I found out later about thug activity occurring within the convention from the television newscast of respected broadcaster Walter Cronkite. Dan Rather and Mike Wallace, then floor reporters for CBS, had been roughed up. Some delegates had received equally bad treatment from so-called security forces. It appeared the targets were to be those most left of center, including the media.

The majority of the delegates were older males, particularly from the South and Midwest. It seemed only New York, California, the District of Columbia and a few other states had delegates of color. The Rev. Channing E. Phillips, who headed Robert Kennedy's campaign in the District of Columbia and whom I had met briefly at the Poor Peoples' March in June, was a delegate at the convention. He allowed his name to be placed in nomination as a favorite-son candidate. He was the first black to be nominated for the presidency. He received sixty-seven and one-half votes. He said his candidacy was meant to show "The Negro vote must not be taken for granted."

Within the Iowa delegation, Hart and I had allowed Governor Hughes to have one more vote for McCarthy and then to shift to Humphrey. He was grateful, since he was the head of the whole delegation; but Hart and I knew we would need his support in the general election. Moreover, he was running for the U.S. Senate; he didn't want to antagonize the Humphrey forces. We did not realize it at the time, but the situation for the Democrats would get much worse.

On the night of August 27, I ran into my friend Dennis Brack, a well-known photographer who had taken a picture of Charles Robb and me at the White House. It had appeared in local papers in Iowa. I saw De Sibour about the same time and asked the photographer if he would take a quick picture of us on the convention floor. We never saw the photo, however. That next day, I went to the convention floor again for a while and then back to the Knickerbocker Hotel. Early that evening, I decided against returning to the convention. It was a fortunate decision. I called Larry Scalise, who was not feeling well and was not going down to the convention. So, I went to his hotel room, ordered some food and, hoping to relax, started watching the proceedings on television. The scene had turned ugly.

Over ten thousand demonstrators, mostly anti-Vietnam protestors, were met by twenty-three thousand police and National Guardsmen. That night's police riot would mark the 1968 Democratic Convention. Scalise and I watched horrified. It was a complete melee with demonstrators, innocent bystanders, and reporters being clubbed by police. I discovered later that my photographer friend had been chased by a policeman and, while attempting to defend himself, had placed the large camera on his head. With one blow, the camera was destroyed. It saved Brack's head, however. Fortuitously, de Sibour called, telling me she was headed back to her hotel room at the Conrad Hilton. I warned her not to go near that hotel but to stay with friends away from the area. She took my advice. After watching more than I wanted to see, I bid goodnight to Scalise, went to my room, knowing we had lost the election to Nixon that night.

The next morning, I went to the Conrad Hilton Hotel. The area looked like a war zone: a main ground floor window was completely shattered. The stench of tear gas was still in the air mixed with the smell of human vomit; I wanted to leave Chicago. De Sibour had driven her 1964 Volkswagen Beetle to the city. I had asked her to bring it with the idea of buying it to facilitate my work in Iowa. It served as our escape from the 'Windy City." I paid her one thousand dollars for the vehicle and gathered my luggage. We drove that day to my parents' farmhouse in Iowa, relieved to be away from the turmoil, the madness. After a couple of days, I gave her a ride to the Cedar Rapids airport and then drove to Des Moines.

Tom was already in Des Moines; we both knew we had a big hole to crawl out of in order to be competitive in the general election. We became creative. We started with two salesmen for a local Des Moines country radio station that came by our offices. I decided to cut a radio ad for their station using a segment of a Humphrey speech with my voice over at the end, seeking financial contributions to be sent to a local post office box. The buy time for the spot was very cheap. Also, since it was a small station, I did not expect large returns.

With a lead about a donor in Sioux City, Hart and I leased an airplane and flew up, speaking at a local Democratic meeting, begging for donations by passing the proverbial hat. Later, we met with the donor—an elderly gentleman who arrived at a local bar wearing very dark sunglasses and a well-worn dark suit. About this time, Hart and I had perfected what we thought was a clever play. We both had telephone pagers, allowing us to call into the number and leave a voice message. While Tom was speaking to a group or an individual, I would excuse myself, to a payphone and, disguising my voice, would say, "Tom, please call Larry O'Brien immediately." The audio beeper always impressed the audience with such messages from famous people. They were a new mode of communication. Cell phones were a long way off. As an aside, when I had my first cell phone in the mid-1980s they were huge in size. I needed one because I had to be in periodic touch with my cable television company technicians. I remember having lunch at Paul Young's restaurant in Washington, D.C. with Doug Kiker, then a well-known NBC news broadcaster. I was a little embarrassed having to place that large and heavy phone on our lunch table. It would not fit in any suit pocket.

The fundraiser for Humphrey in Sioux City went off well. After we collected fairly large checks, we got back on our chartered plane to Des Moines, arriving late at night. I also designed a peace pin with Humphrey's triple initials which sold well to a limited group of individuals. I met with a group of farmers who gave us hundreds of stamps for mailing purposes.

As we pushed ahead, Hart asserted that we needed better personal quarters. He persuaded a local motel owner, a Democrat and a friend of Scalise, to rent us a small suite without any deposit. It was only a few blocks from the headquarters. We now were more comfortable; we also had place to entertain dignitaries and volunteers. Since Wisconsin was one of our assigned states, Scalise and I made a trip to Madison and Milwaukee, which Muskie, the vice presidential candidate, would visit. In Madison, we met the state Democratic chairman Jim Wimmer, who was a dedicated professional. Together, we went over all the pros and cons of the state Democratic organization. He felt we had a reasonable shot, but that the Chicago convention had not been helpful. Wimmer had plenty of campaign experience, having managed Senator Gaylord Nelson's successful race for the U.S. Senate in 1958. Scalise and I subsequently drove to Milwaukee from Madison since Muskie would be coming there within twenty-four hours.

We met up with Muskie's advance team, headed by Ted Venetoulis, who we politely informed we had a small but influential group of dairy farmers who wished to meet Muskie at the airport in Milwaukee. Scalise handled most of the communication. The farmers were concerned with the Democrats' views on subsidies; the price on milk was way below what it should have been, so they were experiencing economic hardship. Wisconsin had a large block of rural voters. Those farmers were important. They were sympathetic to the Humphrey/Muskie ticket but wanted some assurance that the national ticket understood their plight. Scalise not only faxed information about their concerns, but also spoke to Muskie's chief of staff.

When Muskie arrived, he was escorted into a small conference room. Scalise introduced the group of approximately fifteen farmers representing various organizations, then sat next to Muskie; I was behind them at the long table. When questions started coming from the farmers, Muskie turned to Scalise and whispered, "Who are these folks?" Scalise was taken aback and appalled Muskie did not know the purpose of the meeting. We somehow all "slogged through" the meeting but it was very embarrassing. We asked ourselves later whether Muskie had been ill-served by his staff or was he simply clueless.

This would not have happened with a Kennedy, Humphrey, Hughes or Culver, we said to each other after the meeting. Four years later, when Muskie failed in his ill-advised campaign to seek the Democratic presidential nomination, I was not surprised by his lack of success. I always remembered that farmers meeting. The rest of his trip to Milwaukee was passable but not spectacular. Since he was of Polish ancestry, he visited the heavily Polish district.

Toward the end of his visit, I went back to the elegant Pfister Hotel where the advance team had a small set of adjoining rooms. As I entered the main room, hearing no one, I proceeded into an adjacent bedroom where I came upon the advance man from Washington locked in a romantic embrace with a young woman, who had appeared the day before to volunteer for the campaign. I slowly and quietly backed out of the room. Muskie was still in the city, and it was unbelievable to think that the lead advance person was more interested in a quick romantic tryst than the vice presidential candidate. Later, I called back to Washington and politely informed people that that guy should never be allowed to serve on the advance team for Muskie or Humphrey again. Without getting too specific in my description, they understood and were even more disgusted than I had been. I am certain that individual never figured out why he did not receive another assignment.

As soon as I arrived back in Des Moines, I received a telephone call from Robert McCandless who was O'Brien's principal deputy. His boss wanted me to check in on the Humphrey campaign in Minnesota. They were not getting adequate information from operatives in that state and wanted a more objective person to assess the situation. I was a little surprised since I thought that if we had problems even in Minnesota, Humphrey's home state, how could we expect to win? I took a late flight the next afternoon.

The Minnesota organization had been told I was arriving and I was met by Paul Thatcher, the thirty-three year-old assistant to Dwayne Andreas, then chairman and CEO of Archer-Daniels Midland Company, a large well-known processor of farm commodities in the United States. He was also a very close personal friend of the vice president. Thatcher met me at the airport in his shiny black Mercedes Benz. As he was giving me a ride to my hotel, I mentioned I needed to call a friend in Washington. He told me to pick up his phone on the console and call directly; he had an unrestricted WATS line. Very few people in 1968 had telephones in their autos, let alone with WATS (Wide Access Telephone System, which were 800 numbers). For some reason Thatcher and I hit it off, but I was a little self-conscious about the attention I was receiving. The next morning I went to the downtown office of the Humphrey headquarters where I met the state director Wendell Anderson, who eventually became governor of Minnesota, and his deputy, David Lebedoff, a young attorney several years older than I. We discussed the overall plan to win Minnesota; they were pretty emphatic that they had things well in hand, and, therefore, didn't need outside supervision. They also asked me if I would go to the 7th Congressional District, the largest city being Moorhead, in the far northwest section of Minnesota. I knew they were trying to get me out of campaign headquarters. But they also did need assistance in the most rural part of the state, which was like my part of Iowa—all white. I went along with their advice, after I was convinced that they had the operation well in hand.

I flew to Moorhead and took a ride to the Holiday Inn where the local organizer, Mike Pintar, had reserved a room. Having not eaten, I went over to the adjacent restaurant and bar to have a drink and dinner. Sitting at the bar having a Jack Daniels, I struck up a conversation with the bartender. He asked "Are you single?" Somewhat confused, I nevertheless said yes. He then stated there was a private party taking place in the room behind him. He stated that local girls from Concordia College were having a mixer and they were very short on male attendees. As I entered, I was immediately surrounded by coeds who were impressed when I told them I worked for the vice president. Besides having a great time that evening, I recruited a large number of young volunteers. When Mike Pintar appeared early the next morning at my door, I was a little groggy. We went over extensive plans for the 7th Congressional District. Bob Bergland was the candidate that year. He failed to win but recovered two years later in 1970, after which he later became President Carter's Secretary of Agriculture. Pintar and I helped plan for Muriel Humphrey and Jane Muskie's tour of Minnesota, including Moorhead. Volunteers implemented a quick poll to determine support in the District. Humphrey came out fairly well. I knew we probably were not going to win but would be competitive with Nixon. After seventy-two hours, I flew back to Minneapolis.

Anderson and Lebedoff thought I should accompany Mrs. Humphrey and Mrs. Muskie on their tour. I knew that they wanted to get rid of me but they also knew that the candidates' wives needed political guidance on this trip. I dutifully obliged. That morning I boarded the chartered plane and introduced myself to both women as well as perhaps fifteen or twenty reporters who were on the trip. Our first plane stop was to be Moorhead with a sit-down planned at eleven o'clock in the morning for an airport rally organized by Pintar. I took a seat at the rear of the plane along with the three Secret Service agents. Having been involved in the day's planning, I was aware we were on a tight schedule. Also, I could tell from the press's comments that they assumed this trip would not be on time. The general perception about Humphrey and his organization was that they were almost never on time. I did not want to validate that view.

As we approached the airport, the plane started its descent. I looked at my watch; we were early by at least fifteen or twenty minutes. I walked hurriedly to the pilot's cockpit. Everyone else on the plane seemed preoccupied or disinterested. As I somewhat hesitantly entered the cockpit, I asked the pilot to circle the airplane over the airport. I understood if we landed ahead of time, the advance team wasn't going to be ready on the ground. "No problem, sir," the pilot said, responding to my request. There I was, a twenty-seven year-old kid, giving an order to a fortyish pilot. That maneuver caused us to land nearly at the scheduled time. We were greeted by a high school band and an enthusiastic crowd of between three hundred and five hundred people—a considerable sized group for a small town. From the airport, we went to a local college where a lunch was to be held for the spouses. I finally got an opportunity to pull Pintar aside and told him of my asking the pilot to delay the landing. Pintar breathed a huge sigh of relief. The crowd had not gathered before the planned arrival time of 11 am, nor had the band, and overall, he said; it would have been a disaster if our entourage had landed early. This was an obvious example of how important the element of timing could be in a successful political campaign.

Later that afternoon, we gathered everyone on board and headed for Duluth, which was a prime Democratic stronghold. It was home to various ethnic groups including Slavs, Poles, Finns, Swedes, Danes, Russians, Serbs, Norwegians, Germans, Irish and Italians. Many came to work in the Mesabi iron ore range. Few African Americans were present in the city. We were met and escorted onto a large bus by Manley "Moonie" Goldfine. I thought it strange that with so many different ethnicities in the area, a very prominent Jewish businessman would be the main contact in Duluth. I was very impressed with his enthusiasm and smartness, however.

We arrived at the Duluth Arena Auditorium, where over three thousand people had gathered. Adding to all that, Senator Walter Mondale was also in attendance. The early evening's program was very well choreographed with the usual political speeches. Toward the end of the program, a young woman came rushing up to me, identifying herself as a local television reporter. The Secret Service agent had sent her to me, saying that I would have the final word. She explained she just wanted a short on-camera interview with Mrs. Humphrey but had been rebuffed by her assistant. Sometimes, certain aides were over protective. I told the reporter that I would ask but that she would only be allowed five minutes. Mrs. Humphrey granted the request. The reporter, meeting me as we were leaving the auditorium, thanked me profusely. Frankly, I thought she was doing the campaign a favor as we received some positive media, without any cost.

On our flight back to Minneapolis as Mrs. Humphrey sat alone, I considered approaching her to discuss the Vietnam War and the racial issues affecting the country, hoping she might persuade her husband of the need to reach out more to minorities and young Americans. But taking that action would be overstepping my boundary. Two reporters seated in front of me seemed pleased about the trip's end: "Can you believe?" they stated. "A Humphrey trip on schedule; we are going to be home on time." I smugly and silently took it as a compliment.

The next day, I took a flight to Des Moines. Being able to fly as needed on commercial or chartered flight was a great asset. The Humphrey campaign was very sensitive to the fact that political operatives had to move fast at times. I am sure the debt after the 1968 election was due, in part, to large unpaid airplane flight charges. But at least we were not cut off before the election. I drafted a quick report regarding our events and results to Claire Stewart, who was one of the "boiler room" girls, as they were called in that day; she was one of five women assigned to serve as coordinators in the country who had the job of relaying state-based information daily to Bob McCandless and Larry O'Brien. Stewart had been one of the Robert Kennedy assistants during his campaign, and had lots of experience.

When I arrived back in Des Moines, a volunteer, Jonnie McClain, told me that the local post office had been trying to locate me. A little perplexed, I couldn't for the life of me comprehend why. Then I realized that I completely forgot about the post office box where contributions were to be mailed in response to our radio advertisement. Patty Sarcone, the office manager, went to gather the envelopes. She came in about an hour later with a huge box. Hundreds of envelopes, filled with small contributions, had jammed the post office box to over-flowing. They were anywhere from five dollars to fifty dollars. The total haul was probably three or four thousand dollars—a nice take for so little an investment. It taught me the power of radio ads with the right message.

Hart had been speaking almost constantly to Stewart. They had struck up a sort of mutual attraction via telephone. He persuaded me we needed a break. Let's go to Washington tonight, he said. It was a Friday; we could make it back the next day. I had not seen De Sibour for a long time and he wanted the four of us to go to dinner. I was very hesitant. He said he already had the tickets and we needed a break. I finally said yes and we flew back to D.C., where the four of us had an excellent dinner. He and I flew back the next day. We told no one of our overnight trip. That Monday a call came from Washington that we had been expecting. It was not about our secretive trip. McCandless told us we had to abandon

Iowa; there was little hope we could win there. Hart was to go to Ohio, taking Jim Brick along with him. I was to head for California, namely Santa Barbara.

We still needed someone we could trust to run the Iowa operation. Art Hedberg was reluctant to accept the assignment. He had a family, plus a profitable and time-consuming legal practice. He had said no before, but Tom and I had a strategy. We asked Art to meet us for drinks at six that evening at Babe's, a downtown Italian restaurant in Des Moines popular with politicos. Hart had cooked up a "good guy, bad guy" scenario. First, we asked Art nicely if he would handle the operation. He firmly said no. Then, with me playing the "bad guy," I went off on him, saying that he was letting down us and Humphrey. I accused him of being a coward and not having any guts. I told him I had given up law school to help Humphrey. He should be willing to give up his law practice for a month to do the same. I finally stormed out of the restaurant acting mad. Tom told me that Art was taken aback by my anger. Then Tom soft-soaped him in my absence, lauding him in every possible way. Art, feeling very guilty, finally acceded to Tom's praises and pleadings. Later that night, we had a good laugh and a Jack Daniels to celebrate our successful ploy.

The next day both Hart and I packed for our flights from Des Moines to our respective destinations. I knew we had an outstanding bill with our rooms at the motel. The owner had treated us very well. I told Hart he had to settle up with the owner before we left. I don't know why I placed the burden on him, but I wanted to protect our reputation. I am sure the bill was well into the five figures. I pressured him until he agreed to go downstairs and settle out the account. Ten minutes later, he came back to the room, saying the account had been paid. We grabbed our bags and got into a waiting cab.

After we checked in and were waiting to board, I realized that a new pair of black dress shoes I had just purchased had been left under my bed in a shoebox. Telling Tom, I started for a payphone to call the motel and have them saved for me. As I was dialing the motel's number, Tom abruptly depressed the telephone button. "I would not call them if I were you." I realized then that he had not paid the bill. I was mad at him but also realized we actually had no money to pay for hardly anything. About a year later, I convinced the Democratic National Committee to pay the motel bill, so my conscience was somewhat mollified.

Arriving in Santa Barbara was like a breath of fresh air. Scalise had found a headquarters and had made contact with Humphrey supporters. He also had arranged for me to stay with his parents, Albert and Mary, who had moved there from Des Moines almost fifteen years earlier. They had a beautiful home overlooking the bay, and they were the perfect hosts.

I made contact with different labor unions in the area, soliciting money to operate a get-out-the vote campaign and to place political ads. I thought I had commitments for five thousand dollars total from the different labor unions, but I quickly learned otherwise. Each of the unions was claiming the same one thousand dollar contribution. So instead of five thousand dollars, I had only one thousand dollars. Money was hard to acquire because the common belief was that Humphrey could not win. Also there had been some fall-out from the Kennedy-McCarthy primary in June. There were different Democratic groups in Santa Barbara County— Humphrey supporters, of course, and then those of Kennedy and McCarthy. There was still very bad blood between McCarthy partisans and the Kennedy group. McCarthy folks were primarily located in the

Center for the Study of Democratic Institutions, a think tank headed by Harry Ashmore, Harvey Wheeler and Robert Maynard Hutchins, who were basically very liberal and very influential in California.

The Kennedy faction was headed by Assemblyman Win Shoemaker, who was a major ally of Speaker Jesse Unruh who had headed up operations for Robert Kennedy in California. I got along better with Shoemaker and his staffers who wanted Humphrey to win. On a call back to Washington, I recruited Joe Rauh, a well-known liberal and former head of Americans for Democratic Action. Rauh had been a big supporter of McCarthy and agreed to come out to California to assist Humphrey, who had been his long-time friend, although they disagreed on the Vietnam War. Rauh came for a meeting with the Santa Barbara liberals, who were critical of his switch.

I received a call from J.D. Williams in Los Angeles, asking me to come down to a meeting with top Humphrey organizers. That same day I was pondering two major issues: staffing the office, and finding another four thousand dollars for my budget. The first was resolved somewhat quickly. A young black man appeared in the office and wanted to volunteer. He said he was originally not going to vote or he was voting for the Black Panther Party. But the threat of Nixon being president had convinced him to be more practical and help Humphrey. He seemed genuine and eager; I placed him in charge of the office when I was absent. I also found out that I should stay the night in Los Angeles since Sammy Davis and other entertainers were having a large gala for Humphrey at an amphitheater there. I drove down and met with the other Humphrey organizers later that afternoon. That evening, I went to the gala and had a backstage pass courtesy of Charles Hoffman, my friend and one of the main coordinators of the Poor Peoples' March. Besides convincing Sammy Davis to perform for Humphrey, he also organized Watts for Humphrey. Hoffman was white but he could organize politically tough situations. It was an admirable talent. I met Davis before he went on stage and was amazed how short and frail he was. He also seemed to smoke cigarettes non-stop. But he put on a terrific performance for the audience, which had paid a steep price for admission.

The next morning we had another meeting; my friend Don Joel, the media advance man in Des Moines was in attendance. As the meeting broke up, he asked me if I wanted to join him and three of his colleagues for lunch. I accepted and we took a table in the hotel restaurant. During lunch, I remarked that I needed several thousand more dollars for my budget for Santa Barbara and the surrounding counties. I felt a slight kick under the table. I looked at him he motioned to me to put my hand under the table; I obeyed. He gave me a sealed envelope. Without the rest of my table mates noticing, I put it in my suit pocket. After coffee, I bid everyone goodbye, wishing us all good luck. I went to my car, locked the door and unsealed the envelope. I counted out five thousand dollars in cash. I was truly grateful. Years later, I found out from Joel that a rich California oilman had given Joel over fifty thousand dollars from a wall safe in his office to help Humphrey. On hearing my tale of woe, Joel had decided at the table to help me since he knew the cash would be put to good use. I was learning the power of cash in campaigns. I did put it to good use by purchasing those needed ads.

Humphrey began gaining traction in the area. Democrats were realizing that Nixon could become president. Johnson was making an all-out effort in Texas and Senator McCarthy had endorsed Humphrey. I went into the headquarters and the office was jammed with new volunteers. I could no longer make telephone calls in private nor was there room to work. Even though there was no space or privacy, I was thankful for the new out pouring of support. I knew we had a shot at California. I also had enough money to pay for the phone banks and some newspaper advertisements.

On election eve, I decided to take my friend Shirley to a restaurant in Montecito, next to Santa Barbara, owned by Arturo Perez, a successful businessman. Although a Republican, she was fun besides being Perez's friend and very pretty. That day I also had a call from a friend in Los Angeles telling me secretly that the Los Angeles Times had a poll showing Humphrey close to overtaking Nixon in California. About midway through our dinner Arturo came over to our table asking me if I was interested in going fifty-fifty on a bet with a bookie who was sitting in his bar at the time. The bookie was giving odds of more than 4 to 1 to one that Nixon would take California. He was betting one thousand six hundred dollars against four hundred dollars. I mulled it over for maybe fifteen seconds, and then told Arturo I was in for two hundred dollars; he placed the bet.

The L.A. Times poll surely had to be accurate, so I concluded we had a good chance of winning. Plus, I thought the eight hundred dollars would pay for my law school tuition the coming year. I am sure I also wanted to impress Shirley with my level of confidence in the election.

The next morning, Election Day, the telephone began ringing at six thirty. Mary Scalise woke me and said Arturo was on the phone. A somewhat sleepy Arturo told me to look at the L.A. Times; I immediately picked up the newspaper from the front porch. The headline splashed across the page in bold black letters said simply: "It's Even Steven" meaning Nixon and Humphrey were tied in California. Arturo stated that his bookie friend had called him in a near panic after seeing the headline. He wanted to withdraw the bet. Arturo asked me what I thought. I said, "No, stick with it." Arturo readily agreed; letting the bookie sweat gave me some joy. Larry Scalise had come out to California the day before. So after we determined that we had done all we could that election day, we drove down to the Los Angeles headquarters. We met Don O'Brien, another

Iowan and head of the campaign in California. An old Kennedy hand, he had joined Humphrey at the urging of Larry O'Brien.

Around eight that evening, Larry and I grabbed a late flight to Minneapolis. The Humphrey headquarters wanted all of us to be in Minnesota. As we flew out that night, I had the sinking feeling we were going to lose. The War, the Chicago Convention, the race riots, the assassinations had taken a huge toll on the campaign. Nobody really loved Nixon but the country was unsure of the Democratic policies, especially on the war.

When we arrived at the Leamington Hotel, it was fairly evident that Humphrey had lost. Nixon would now be the president. I also found out the next morning that my father had lost his re-election bid for his state senate seat by fewer than five hundred votes. Nixon won California, which meant I had lost the $200 bet. Governor Hughes had barely won his seat for the U.S. Senate over a fairly weak Republican. I felt badly that I had not been there for my father to help him more. But I would make it up to him in two years.

Quite honestly, 1968 had been an exhausting year, full of many lows. After the riots as well as the Chicago convention, I knew that for Humphrey to win would have been almost impossible. Where was Nixon going to lead the country? We still had a major war and huge social divisions. The only thing I was sure of was that I would be re-entering law school the coming winter. My focus definitely had narrowed.

I had drinks with Scalise and a few others, including de Sibour, then went to bed. The next morning Scalise and I headed back to Des Moines. I was depressed and dreaded the fact that I had to close the headquarters there. Unknowingly, my next stop would be the snow in Colorado. I was going from a highly placed political operative to a lowly ski bum.

CHAPTER TWELVE

Losing: A Difficult Companion

LOSING is never easy. As I adjusted to that fact, I simultaneously decided my next move. I knew I had to start law school in February and find work unrelated to the farm. Quite frankly, the campaign bug remained in my system. But I had to wait for the right opportunity. I wasn't quite twenty-eight years old, so I arrogantly expected things would come my way. It was hard to ignore the dissension in the country, however. Still, I needed cash for law school; whatever employment I accepted also couldn't require spending too much. Don't ask why, but Vail, Colorado seemed the logical choice. I tracked down my friend Terry Ferry, who was working as a waiter in a local restaurant there. He invited me to stay with him while I looked for a job. Shortly after Thanksgiving, I drove my 1964 Volkswagen Beetle to begin another short-term venture, finding work at a popular nightclub, Nu Gnu, owned and operated by Paul Johnston, who became a good friend but who has since died. That stint began my attraction to the Vail Valley. I worked as a combination waiter, bartender, bouncer and, probably most important, cleaned up daily in the afternoon, following my skiing routine. The whole experience that winter was a complete drop-out from politics. I almost missed going back to law school on time.

One morning, I woke up and realized it was time to move forward. I needed to register for law school in Iowa. Friends helped me dig out my Beetle, which had been parked in the same spot all winter in more than four feet of snow. I went first to my parents' farm to exchange my ski apparel for clothes more appropriate for school. Arriving at the University of Iowa Law School the next day, I went immediately to enroll for the second semester. The assistant to the dean of the law school, a wonderful and charming older woman, recognized me from three years earlier. She told me that the second semester had begun three days prior to my arrival. I immediately panicked. Being enamored with Colorado skiing was going to cost me dearly. The law school had told me that I had to enter in February, otherwise I would have to take the whole first year over again because there could not be more than a three-year gap in law school attendance. The dean's assistant must have read the worry on my face; she quietly and discretely shoved my application across the desk. "I will take care of it, just start class tomorrow." I breathed a sigh of relief.

Prior to the Vail trip, I had bought a house in Iowa City, using five thousand dollars I had saved as down payment. I thought it was better than having money in the stock market. It was only two houses from the original home of Grant Wood, the American painter, who had been born in Iowa and was best known for depicting the rural Midwest, especially the 1930 painting, American Gothic. I lived on a lovely street and in a fairly substantial house. It had four bedrooms upstairs as well as one on the first floor; a large front and back yard; and a detached garage. My talented father also installed a shower on the first floor. I rented out the upstairs bedrooms to female students at the university. So the transition back to law school was fairly easy, as I took up residence in my own home.

The student body had changed. I was perhaps the oldest in my class and I felt worldlier than the others, and believed I had more in common with the professors. Most were Democrats and were impressed that I had lived in Washington and worked for Humphrey. I noticed immediately that there were a few more women and African Americans—though not many. I became friends with one of them, Howard Porter. We both realized that we had Eastern connections, plus he was an avid skier. Porter had attended Middlebury College. He wore glasses, had a medium complexion and possessed a wry sense of humor. He was also well traveled and attuned to urban living. Who knows how he got to Iowa. Years later, he ended up in Washington as a government agency attorney. We made preliminary plans to go to Vail the next winter at Christmas break. But while things were better financially, I still had to work to help pay my way through law school. I obtained a law clerk job with one of my professors, James Meeks. He and I also double dated. I was twenty-eight years old and he was in his early thirties. So in some respects we were contemporaries. He had gotten married in 1965 to an Iowa coed. Within a few weeks, however, I was approached by Ed Mezvinsky, an Iowa State Representative. He was running for Congress from the 1st District in Iowa. I had met him briefly the previous summer. He had a fabulous resume and a photogenic family. He wanted to hire me as a consultant for him in the 1970 campaign; I accepted.

Politics were in my bones, failed season or not. I had an opportunity, I thought, to perhaps reclaim victory, even if it wasn't for my father or Humphrey. Mezvinsky was in a three-way primary, with a college professor from the university and a county sheriff named "Blackie" Stout from Davenport in Scott County. We established a district-wide organization, and I traveled almost the entire area, recruiting coordinators in each county. Mezvinsky had cultivated a reformer reputation in the Iowa State House; it was fairly easy gathering activists to his campaign. But, even if we won the primary, we were going to have to defeat a popular two-term incumbent, Fred Schwengel, who was a moderate Republican.

Additionally, the previous summer in 1969, a friend, Patrick White, an attorney in Iowa City, asked me to help him win a seat on the Iowa City council. He had been encouraged to enter a crowded competitive primary. The top two vote-getters would acquire the two open council seats, and the person with the greatest number of voters also would be declared mayor. I convinced White he had to campaign door-to-door in precincts I had targeted. Despite my earlier losses, I had become very adept at retail politics, similar to those I used after my father's experience in 1964. As I mastered the design, I combined it with precinct data to identify specific voters who could be captured by White. He finished second barely missing out on the top position. It was clearly an upset. But White was well liked and his family had been residents for decades. Sometimes candidates win just because people like them.

I persuaded Mezvinsky to follow the same campaign approach I designed for White, but in larger cities like Davenport, where he was not well known. I also began learning how to use free media effectively. The press always needs stories. I found out that in Mezvinsky's case, newspapers in smaller towns were curious about him. Thus, we leveraged that, along with our door-to-door campaign, to build name recognition. Law school was easier for me during this period than it had been in my first year in 1964. I took full advantage of the extra time to hone my campaign skills.

That Christmas break I decided to drive to Vail to ski. I asked my law school friend, Howard, if he still was interested in going with me. He offered to drive, which I accepted since he had a newer vehicle. I wanted to leave one evening about six o'clock, but Howard said he could not leave until after nine. We didn't actually depart Iowa City until after ten that night. As we were driving across Iowa on Interstate Highway 80, he told me that he was down to about a quarter tank of gas. Of course, by then, as was customary during those days, almost all the gas stations were closed. I knew we had to get to Council Bluffs, Iowa where there were 24-hour stations. We were far from there. Shortly after we had passed Des Moines, with no open stations, Howard hit a patch of ice on the road. The car went into the median ditch headed in the opposite direction. I then subtly offered to drive since I had more experience driving in winter conditions. By then, we both knew we were going to run out of gas before Council Bluffs. Eventually the car sputtered to a stop; I managed to get it onto the shoulder of the highway. It was almost midnight and freezing cold, with probably five to six inches of snow on the ground. Over in the distance, I spotted a farmhouse with lights on.

Porter and I looked at each other, knowing we had to get help there. It was also clear that I would be the one, leaving unsaid that it would be problematic for both of us to approach a farmhouse at midnight. It could have been outright dangerous for Howard, since he was black and we were in rural Iowa. I climbed over the woven-wire fence and trudged through a snow-covered field, knocking on the front door with great apprehension. Someone was watching me. As I glanced to my side, there was a huge German Shepherd dog about thirty feet away. A teenage girl opened the door, allowing me to quickly step inside while preventing the dog's entrance. She was the babysitter. Within moments a vehicle turned into the yard. A farmer about forty-five years old came through the door along with a woman I assumed was his wife. I explained my predicament. He retrieved a gasoline can and placed probably three gallons of gas in it. I offered to pay him, but he declined to accept any cash. He had one curious question: Had the dog made any movement toward me. No, I said. He shrugged, noting the dog had a mean disposition and, in fact, that hardly anyone could get out of a car when it was present. I shuddered, thankful that I had met a charitable farmer but also a dog who, for whatever reason, had remained passive. The farmer told me to get on his tractor; we drove back to the car where Howard was waiting. The farmer, seeing my black friend, offered no reaction which was surprising given what Howard and I had anticipated. After we emptied the gas can, we thanked him profusely and drove off to Council Bluffs.

We arrived in Vail early that next morning. . We skied for the next ten days with great snow cover. Howard, with his great people skills, was clearly accepted by the citizens of Vail. In that era, he was a bit of an oddity, since one did not see many blacks skiing. And Porter was a very good skier—better than I.

Within a day or two of returning to the drudgery of law school, I received a call from my old friend Tom Hart. He was in Bridgeport, Connecticut. Unlike me, he hadn't taken a break from politics. He was up to his neck in the 1970 Democratic U.S. Senate race. He had been recruited by his friend Mike Monroney, the son of Oklahoma Senator Almer Stillwell Monroney. They were trying to get Al Donahue elected in a Democratic Primary. A wealthy industrialist from Stamford, Connecticut, he was running for political office for the first time. Tom insisted that I join him; money was no object. I agreed to come around Easter break for four or five days. I got an okay from Mezvinsky to leave his campaign for a short time.

When I got to Bridgeport, Tom was working feverishly to move the campaign headquarters from Bridgeport to Hartford. The former was a backwater town, and Donahue desperately needed to get some momentum. He had two opponents in the primary: Ed Marcus, a state senator from the New Haven area, and Joe Duffey, an anti-war, university professor who had run Eugene McCarthy's race in Connecticut in 1968.

Duffey was the most liberal of the three. Connecticut was very divided along ethnic and even religious lines. Back then, in 1970, it was common for people to refer to a "mixed marriage" as basically between an Irish individual and an Italian. Race was secondary. During that year, Congressman Emilio "Mim" Daddario ran for governor. He, of course, was the darling of the Italian community. A major complication was the fact that the U.S. Senate seat was held by Thomas Dodd, who had strong backing from the more conservative wing of the Democratic Party. Senator Dodd (whose son Chris later became a U.S. Senator and a friend of mine) was urged to drop out of the race because of hints of political scandal. Most Democratic leaders thought he would siphon votes from Duffey. Initially, he refused. Eventually, he dropped his name from the Democratic Primary, finally realizing he didn't have a chance of winning that contest. But he ran as an independent.

I went back to Connecticut twice more before I completed law school in July. I had taken the state bar exam in June and I passed. I would tell Mezvinsky he had gotten through a tough three-way primary, easily out-distancing his two opponents. I wanted to move on and eventually get back to Washington, where my future awaited me. Unfortunately, Mezvinsky lost the general election that fall to the Republican candidate. In the next election cycle he was successful. But eventually he would serve several years in prison for mail, bank and wire fraud, ending what would have been a stellar career.

After law school, I rejoined the Donahue campaign and remained through the primary. Every town in Connecticut became a fight for delegates all the way to the state convention. While there, we recruited Nicholas Carbone, who was an emerging leader in the rugged politics of Hartford. My area of focus became urban and ethnic politics, including serving as the de facto contact with black politicians. The political structure in that community was machine-like: block coordinators were assigned ten to fifteen voters and would ensure that they came out to vote. Precinct coordinators had twenty block coordinators for which they were responsible. Both groups worked with a ward chairman, who at that time was Clyde Billington. Everyone got paid. The Donahue forces won the Democratic Party's endorsement at the state convention, but it proved to be a hollow, short-term victory.

Both Duffey and Marcus won enough delegates to qualify to enter a Democratic primary in August. Although we had the party's endorsement, Duffey won the primary as the reformist candidate. Donahue may have been likeable, but he wasn't the best campaigner. That loss resulted in bitter feelings among the Irish voters. The day after the primary, we began getting reports from our supporters and coordinators that they were never going to vote for Duffey in the general election. Many of them felt that Daddario had stabbed Donahue in the back by not actively supporting him, and that Duffey was "too left" for their politics. They decided they were going to vote for Dodd in the general election, and maybe Daddario for governor.

Tom Hart had already flown back to Washington. I was planning to leave the next day when I received a call from a local supporter, Tom Reynolds, asking me to meet him for a farewell drink at Frank's Restaurant in downtown Hartford. I gained another lesson in ethnic politics. Allegedly, Frank's was the local hangout for politicos, unsavory types like bookies, and other Damon Runyon-type characters. It was also a reputed Mafia hangout. Anyway, when I got to the restaurant and its adjacent bar, Gerald Cummins, a very close friend of Donahue's, was also there in a somewhat mellow state fueled by liquor. He was shaking a paper bag asking quizzically "Is that you in the bag, Daddario?" It was an outtake on a Jack Anderson column in the Washington Post, suggesting that Daddario was indebted to the mob. With Cummins carrying on like this very loudly, I knew that Frank's was the last place to bring up the idea that maybe Daddario was mob connected. Reynolds implored me to get Cummins out of there quickly, as the other bar patrons, many Italians, likely did not like the dialogue. I, along with Jim Brick, who had joined us from Des Moines, said loudly that we going to a nightclub in a suburb outside of Hartford. We piled into two different cars. Brick, Reynolds and I were in one; Cummins, and two other consultants, Tom Baker, and Mike McClister, were in the second one. Everyone was headed for the club. When we arrived, the place was extremely large and crowded. The car in which Cummins was riding hadn't arrived. We took a booth in the back and waited patiently. After about ten minutes over the loudspeaker came a message that a Gerald Cummins was wanted for an external telephone call. We looked at each other puzzled as to why he would be receiving a call. Tom and Jim said I should go answer it. I did immediately, thinking perhaps it was from a friend or his spouse. Picking up the house phone and saying "Hello," I heard a very deep gravelly voice say "Is this Gerald Cummins?" Thinking quickly I said, "No, he's headed back to New York."

"Oh, I see," said the male voice. "He is not there?"

"No," I said. "Who should I tell him called?"

I then heard a sinister reply "Just tell him that Jack Anderson called." I realized then that it could be trouble for Cummins. Turning around I happened to look outside and saw two large black Cadillacs pulling up in the parking lot. I scrambled back to our booth to join Brick and Reynolds. Settling into my seat, I saw huge men walk across the dance floor, who, at six feet five inches tall and over two hundred pounds, caused dancers to part, creating an aisle especially for them. They surveyed the crowd. Reynolds recognized one as being a local mob enforcer. I was thankful they didn't see us or at least didn't recognize us; after a few minutes, they left. I later learned that Baker and McClister had persuaded Cummins to leave town. I also was glad to get out of Connecticut, having learned a lot about northeast ethnic politics.

Back in Washington, and staying with my friend David Lambert in his townhouse apartment, I received a telephone call from Carbone, asking me if I would speak to Joe Duffey's managers about joining their campaign. While flattered, I had had enough of Connecticut. A good friend of Carbone's, Richard Suisman, called asking if I would speak with Anne Wexler, the campaign manager for Joe Duffey. She was well-respected and wanted me to help Duffey. "No," I said politely, telling them they had to get Dodd, who was an independent, to drop his bid or they would certainly lose. She said very strongly that they wanted Dodd in the race against Lowell Weicker. I was somewhat surprised by her strong reply to the contrary. I knew the Irish and many of the Italian voters were not going to support Duffey. And, they didn't. In the November election, both Republicans won handily: Lowell Weicker for Senate and Thomas Meskill for governor.

Finished with Connecticut, I had a bigger challenge: What was I going to do in Washington? A Republican held the White House and my job prospects looked bleak.

CHAPTER THIRTEEN

Black in Business

WHEN Sterling Tucker called that fall day in 1970, asking me to meet him at a place in the Southwest section of Washington, D.C, I never imagined it would be another campaign job. I was tired of traveling and wanted to have a permanent location in the city. Further, with the Republican Richard Nixon now president, there wouldn't be many opportunities for a Democratic operative like myself. Settling in the nation's capital, the center of politics, allowed me to stay connected, however. The experience in the Humphrey campaign also helped me to understand that I wanted to affect things on a national level, even if at that moment I was averse to jumping into the rigors of yet another political effort. I did not know responding to Tucker's call meant not only employment but a return to the course on which I had unofficially set for myself nearly seven years earlier.

While I had been away from the city for only two years, it seemed a longer time. There was a different air about the District of Columbia. Demonstrations against the Viet Nam War seemed to have been at a lull. Richard Nixon was firmly ensconced as president. In a place where titles and positions are considered important that meant Republican notables had ready access to the best restaurants, galas and other significant social gatherings. I, like many Democrats, felt left out.

Still, I was determined to plant myself in the city and found a large studio apartment on 33rd Street in Georgetown, an area that had been a separate settlement in 1751; it predated the city of Washington and was once an old tobacco port. After the Civil War, many African Americans moved to Georgetown, seeking a stable community. Many had been living in a network of shacks hidden in the city's alleys. In fact, in the late 1800s over 17,000 people, or 11% of Washington's population, lived in deplorable alley dwellings that were breeding grounds for all manner of health problems. Fortunately by the early 1930s, a public housing authority had been established, whose aim was to move blacks out of such conditions. Today, there still are remnants of alley housing, including Snow's Court in Foggy Bottom and Gessford Court near the Union Station.

By the time I moved into Georgetown, it was different. There were only a few African Americans residents. They had been pushed out by whites with money, as they had been in the Southwest quadrant of the city by urban renewal. Georgetown had become a Mecca for pricey boutiques as well as exclusive clubs and upscale restaurants. Clyde's, Mr. Smith's, and the Third Edition were all trendy bars. My apartment was on a lower level of a townhouse, with a separate entrance from an alley, a fire place and enough room for the furniture I had retrieved from the house I owned in Iowa. I also brought my 1967 Buick to the city. It had been left in the garage, but when I placed the key in the ignition, it magically started, reinforcing my belief in American made products. In my absence, the family to whom I had leased the house trashed it in the few months they lived there. They also cheated me out of rent money. Fortunately, they left the premises.

On my way back to Washington, I stopped in Joliet, Illinois, to attend the wedding of my close friend Terrance Ferry who was marrying a local girl. The wedding was an elaborate affair with an outdoor tent for a sit down dinner. My former employer and still good friend from Vail, Paul Johnston, attended and proceeded to lift a tad too many glasses of Scotch. Not wanting to drink and drive that evening, and feeling the pressure to get back on the road to D.C., I decided to hold off on the alcohol. Johnston decided he was going to accompany me, asserting that I needed company. I accepted his offer and I drove all night to get back to Washington. By morning, I was glad I had him in the car. He was definitely sober and able to assist me in unloading the U-Haul of furniture into my apartment.

Finally settled, I renewed my search for employment. Bill Oldaker, the friend who had driven his Jaguar through the King riots with me, and Jim Mooney put me in touch with Warren Cikins, who was executive director of the Former Members of Congress (FMC). He had been selected by the Princeton Seminar, which was a liberal group that put on working election forums for college students. It was headed by David Hertzberg, a well-known political science professor from Princeton who had encouraged students to become involved in the electoral process. But Cikins really didn't have the contacts to recruit political consultants and speakers. We reached an agreement for my involvement. I plunged into organizing the seminar, which was to be held at the Marriot Hotel in Arlington in early October. I recruited then-Senators Robert Packwood of Oregon and Fred Harris of Oklahoma to be the main speakers, along with Richard Scammon, Sam Brown, Lance Torrance and other political notables from both parties. I also called on Matt Reese and other consultants like Mel Cotton to lead group discussions. We had approximately one hundred active student leaders attend and most thought it was a great success. I also met individuals such as James Johnson, who in later years became the head of Fannie Mae and a confidant of Senators Walter Mondale and John Kerry.

While the seminar proved successful, I still lacked a permanent job. My friend Charles Hoffman from the Poor People's Campaign Solidarity March and the Humphrey campaign called; he was executive director of the Institute of Scrap Iron and Steel and was heavily involved in recruiting members of his organization to train the hard-core unemployed, mainly African Americans, for jobs in the scrap iron industry. He persuaded me to travel to Columbia, South Carolina, to call on one of his members to convince that person to sign up for the program. I visited for three days, making the only black-owned motel in the town my temporary home. It must have been somewhat of a shock to see a young white man from Washington staying and eating there. It was very clear to me that Columbia was still a segregated city. I had a good experience, however, and got local members to enroll in Hoffman's program. The potential employers, the junk men, made personal commitments to hire blue-collar blacks to work for them; they would receive decent wages and educational training. It became a good partnership.

Years later, Hoffman was arrested by the FBI on embezzlement charges. He had written fraudulent checks payable to several of his friends including myself. None of us had received any of the funds. They were for his personal use. I found out much later that he actually had been acquitted. He told the judge in the case that the money had been used for anti-Viet Nam War causes. He was certainly very much against the war, as were many of us. However, using his friends in such a scam was not honorable.

Back in the District of Columbia, I thought I had snared a permanent job through my friend Tom Hyde. He was the chief financial officer at the League of Cities, which had been established in 1926 as an advocacy association representing cities and towns across the United States. Besides providing training to municipal officials, it frequently lobbied Congress. He told me the decision wouldn't be made for another month. But he assured me I was the front runner. I lacked the cash to pay rent and buy groceries. Fortunately, Hoffman had given me work editing one of his training books as well as the trip to South Carolina, keeping destitution at bay. Then, my fortunes changed. I found out the position with the League had gone to someone else.

The Fauntroy campaign was a blessing. I enthusiastically jumped at the opportunity. It seemed all the campaigns on which I had worked prepared me for what I would encounter in trying to get him elected as the District of Columbia's first representative to Congress, albeit a nonvoting one. I had shaped campaigns where the candidates were mostly novices challenging history or community preferences; there were a dearth of experienced or competent workers; and a lack of money. In many respects, his election operation would be a compilation of all of those, demanding that I use my entire tool box of contacts, skills and strategies. Pulling off a victory wouldn't be easy.

We found ourselves dealing with characters inside the campaign and external forces which seemed designed to harm the budding black political power. Early one morning, for example, as I came into the office, Mary, the office assistant, notified me that C&P Telephone company technicians were in the building. We had not reported any problems, so I found their presence strange to say the least. I went into my office and looked out the window. From that vantage, I noticed an unmarked white paneled truck parked across the street. After a few minutes, I picked up my telephone to place a call. Before dialing, I heard two distinct male voices on the line. I listened quietly: "Well, you know what we have upstairs: more of them n———-s," one remarked. That prompted me to shout back "What are you sons-of-a-bitches doing here?" After slamming down the phone, I went to the outer offices but most of the campaign employees hadn't yet arrived. I thought I might need some support, since I wasn't quite certain what I was up against. I walked out to the hallway and pushed the button for the elevator, having decided to find out who the hell was in the truck. They had seen me first, however. Two males fled from our building, jumped into the truck and raced away.

I thought back to my experiences at U.S. A.I.D. Telephone tapping was, indeed, rampant in the nation's capital. I hadn't had any similar experience in any of the democratic campaigns on which I had worked. Privacy had become a foreign concept. I didn't know how or when it started, but each citizen seemed subject to becoming a victim of the federal government's obsession with surveillance. I wasn't sure how to handle the problem, except to continue our campaign and perhaps adjust how much and what we talked about over the telephone.

I couldn't permit whacky occurrences to take the campaign off track. It had taken us a few weeks to pull together an energetic staff, trained by Jerry Fitzgerald, who I had brought out from Iowa. John Wilson, my co-campaign manager, had brought in a young dedicated African American to assist in the precinct organization. Tutt Tate had been active in the southern civil rights movement. We were always tight for money, with either workers hammering us for pay or the practical needs, like media coverage, demanding our attention. We certainly needed to figure out how to get free press.

A Georgetown professor once explained that neither Fauntroy nor his campaign had used race or racial discrimination to raise a host of issues that had the potential of attracting the media. I asked him to put the issues he believed were critical in draft press releases for me. I thought we needed to paint a visual picture, using a unique location to place Fauntroy on reporters' radar. We chose the Federal Bureau of Investigation (FBI) as a great Goliath to Fauntroy's David. Under its director J. Edgar Hoover, the agency had developed an antagonistic relationship with African Americans and women. After Rev. Martin Luther King, Jr.'s murder, we came to understand how unrelenting Hoover had been, recording the civil rights leader's private conversations and actions and threatening to use information gathered from his illegal wire taps to destroy King and his family.

In 1971, the FBI was constructing a new building at 9th St. NW and Pennsylvania Ave. NW, a monstrosity that would occupy an entire city block. There had been recent articles about rampant discrimination against workers. We decided it would be a great issue for Fauntroy; so we told him to show up early one morning at the building and walk down into the excavation site. We told the press we were going to have an announcement at 7th St. NW and E St. NW. Without disclosing the substance, we were told them privately that something was going to happen and they should arrive at the building at 7:00 a.m. sharp. Fauntroy gave a statement about racial discrimination in the F.B.I.. It was an instant hit with the reporters. Four or five years later, in his syndicated column in the Washington Post, Jack Anderson pointed out that F.B.I. agents were monitoring that press conference and Fauntroy's movements. How did they know we would be there? I had kept it all very confidential for that reason. Their presence confirmed that the telephones at our campaign headquarters had been tapped.

Getting press coverage improved significantly as we brought in experts, like Johnny Allem, who had been introduced to me by David Apter, Fauntroy's public relations person. Allem understood messaging and how to use all segments of the media. He had come from a successful U.S. Senate campaign in Indiana where he had assisted Senator Vance Hartke in getting re-elected. He was a master in his field. I knew we needed an inexpensive method of telling Fauntroy's story. Allem came up with the idea of using a newspaper format. A newsprint broadside was given to precinct captains and ward coordinators who actually distributed it to people in their communities. With a meager budget, we achieved real success. I also thought we needed a simple, coherent message. Many of the whites thought the theme was demeaning, but "He is going to get it all together" caught on. We bought extensive time on soul or African-American radio stations in the city. The mainstream media were beginning to provide fairer critiques. David Boldt of the Washington Post, Joe Volz of the then Daily News, and Steve Green, of the now defunct Washington Star, wrote objective articles about the campaign.

A week before the January 12, 1971, Democratic Primary, I spoke by telephone with an official at the D.C. Board of Elections and Ethics. It was clear he didn't understand what was supposed to take place on Election Day. Local law permitted each campaign to place two poll workers at each precinct. He kept saying that the District government would provide those workers. No, I corrected him; those are poll watchers, which is a major difference. After that exchange, I pulled in Fitzgerald, telling him elections employees needed a tutorial. I had neither the time nor the patience to tolerate uncertainty. He followed though in his usual smooth manner, persuading elections staffers to allow him to provide some education. It was fast becoming apparent that we had to educate nearly everyone associated with the election, whether they were inside our campaign or not. The District had been starved for democracy. It had been stripped of its local elected mayor in the 1800s. Another one wouldn't come along until after the Fauntroy election. That made it unlike any other jurisdiction I had been exposed to in my short political career. Everything was new for the elections staff and nothing could be taken for granted.

On election eve, we went over our plans. We had set up a bank of over twenty phones that was operated and managed by Jerry Clark, the AFSCME political director. We identified where our precinct priorities lay. We had created teams that would provide food for workers. Every two hours I wanted an absolute count of actual voters who had voted; that tallying would continue until closing. Not overly confident, I predicted a 40 percent turnout for Fauntroy, which is what he needed to avoid a runoff. Election Day, dawned with the usual problems. Some people just didn't show up; not only our own workers but District of Columbia officials who were supposed to open and man the polling places. Then we had the usual reports of harassment of voters from certain parts of the city. We anticipated such challenges and had a detailed plan. I was concerned because I knew that in the more affluent parts of the city Fauntroy's opponents, Channing Phillips and Joseph Yeldell, were strong. Therefore, we needed respectable numbers from precincts where there was a preponderance of African-American blue-collar voters, if we were going to win.

When reports of trouble came in, we would rush hefty-looking black union members to the scene. We also had workers from Marion Barry's organization, Pride Inc., which had strong relations in select poor and working-class neighborhoods. His followers were not people to mess with. Two incidents still stand out for me. In Ward 5, a man, identified as a Yeldell supporter, was distributing dollar bills in front of a polling station, while telling potential voters "a dollar in, a dollar out." A group of our supporters took his roll of bills and escorted him from the area. In the other case, we received word that a large African American male was blocking voters from entering a far northeast precinct. Our poll watchers had alerted a nearby policeman who did nothing. After more frantic calls, we detailed four Pride workers to the scene. They simply escorted the gentleman to their waiting station wagon and drove off. I didn't inquire about what happened to him. Plausible deniability was effective even then. We all had been on edge all day. We were relieved when the polls closed. Fauntroy won with over 40 percent of the vote.

Never a fan of post-election victory parties, I wasn't looking forward to the Fauntroy's celebration. But there was much to feel good about. Reluctantly I made my way to Pitts Motor Lodge, where we had scheduled the event. I remember walking into Fauntroy's private room and having him hug me effusively. Back then men didn't engage in such displays; we were way too self-conscious about how it might be perceived. Bill Lucy, the executive assistant for the president of AFSCME, came into the room while we were locked in each other's arms. Quickly, we disconnected, and I said that it was a joyous night. But we still had a general election on March 23.

During the post-primary period, I decided to terminate the contract with the two white individuals who had handled the press relations. Wilson and I agreed we needed a more professional operation. Yvonne Williams took on those duties. We hired another black woman named Joni Franna to handle scheduling. Yet another African-American female became our receptionist. With a win behind us, money became a little easier to raise. We also reached out to Fauntroy's opponents, Phillips and Yeldell. We recruited David Marlin from the Phillips group. We wanted Bruce Terris who had been Phillips' campaign manager, but he was still sulking. Yeldell's followers were much easier to lure. We were readying for a battle. Julius Hobson of the Statehood Party was on the ballot as was Douglas Moore, a very active militant who later became an elected city councilman. Further, there was the Republican candidate, John Nevius, a white, well respected civic leader and businessman. During the course of the campaign, through Wilson, I met Warren Graves, who was actively working for Hobson. Despite our differences we became good friends.

Although my tendency was to take nothing for granted, it appeared that we would cruise to a general election victory; registered Democrats accounted for an overwhelming segment of the electorate. But we suffered a mild hiccup. I had placed a staffer to set up the arrangements for the post election party at the Hamilton Hotel located at 14th and K Streets downtown. I believed things were progressing well until I got a telephone call from a volunteer handling the arrangements, informing me that the hotel manager had said we didn't have the authority to proceed with the party. When I got that manager on the phone, he told me that John Hechinger said we had not been given responsibility to arrange the post-election event. I hung up and immediately dialed Hechinger, verbally exploding at him. A well-respected and rather wealthy businessman, Hechinger had been, throughout the campaign, more of a hindrance than a help. He had constantly interfered with operations. The party episode was the last straw for me. I told him if he did not call back the Hamilton manager, Hechinger would suffer the consequences. What they would be, I was uncertain at that time. But that threat and my profanity were enough to catapult him into action. The affair went off as planned.

Fauntroy handily won the general election with 57 percent of the vote. But I had not heard the last of Hechinger. Right after the election, Max Berry, a stalwart fundraiser and adviser, called asking if I would have a private meeting with Hechinger. Two nights later, he and I sat down at the Carroll Arms Hotel bar, which was an after-work hangout for congressmen, lobbyists, and Capitol Hill staffers. While somewhat dark and smoky, I enjoyed the spot. As we ordered drinks, I asked Hechinger what was on his mind; he seemed somewhat uncomfortable with the face-to-face but slowly began the discussion, noting our differences and asserting that he had heard I had made anti-Semitic slurs about him. "John," I said, "I like you but you have to understand the following. I'm here to win elections and that is my job. An individual can bring two things to a campaign. One is campaign skills and the other is money. You, frankly, do not have the campaign skills. You do have the money. But you did not give nor did you raise enough money. And you always seem to want to tell us how to spend it. Further, I am one of the last people who would be anti-Semitic. But I apologize to you if I did utter something that may have been construed as anti-Semitic." He also apologized. We ordered another round of drinks and parted as friends; we maintained our relationship until his death in 2004.

With Fauntroy elected, the focus turned to hiring staff for his Capitol Hill office. I had worked hard and thought I might have a role, but equally important, I could help identify individuals to be employed. I became concerned when Harley Daniels, who had been Tucker's legislative assistant at the D.C. Council, had been tapped to serve a similar role for Fauntroy. Harley, who was a friend and highly competent, had discretely told me that two other city employees also had been offered jobs. All of this was happening without my fore-knowledge, and that concerned me because Fauntroy lacked an organizational mind. Meanwhile, Tucker told me I would be Fauntroy's administrative assistant.

It appeared to me that loyal campaign workers were being left out in the cold. Hoping to redirect and perhaps halt the unfocused hiring, I leaked to a reporter for the Daily News information about six employees that would be hired. When the story appeared the next day, Fauntroy was furious and suspected I had been the person to talk to the press. Actually, none of those people had been offered jobs, but they should have been, and my action forced Fauntroy's hand. Consequently, he hired Yvonne Green, Yvonne Williams, Geraldine Boykin, Bill Brockenborough and the campaign's former receptionist. Oh yes, and me, as chief assistant.

We were assigned an office on the top floor of the Longworth Building, which was commonly called Siberia. For me, it was more like a plantation atmosphere. Everyone was cordial and Fauntroy was certainly someone they would have to get used to. We had barely settled in the first day when William "Fish Bait" Miller, the House of Representative's doorkeeper appeared in our offices. He asked us if there was anything we needed; he was a bit too patronizing. Fauntroy had a formal swearing in ceremony on the Capitol steps, with many dignitaries in attendance, including other House members and Coretta Scott King. I immediately noticed a striking African American woman who was outgoing and friendly. Somewhat captivated, I started a conversation, only knowing her first name, Nancy. Fauntroy came by commenting to both of us and chuckling "Well Doug, it did not take you long to start a conversation with Nancy." I realized this was Nancy Wilson, the famous singer and song stylist. I was at a loss for words and immediately became tongue-tied, as I often did in the presence of a famous person I had long admired. I found out later she was divorced, so maybe I should have gotten over my stage-struck condition and asked her out on a date.

My time as chief assistant wouldn't last long, however. After nearly three months, I moved on. Fauntroy settled on a new top assistant, Delano Lewis, who was coming over from the office of Senator Ed Brooke, the only black Republican in the Senate. On my last day, I remembered that Yvonne Williams wanted to have a private word with me. She told me that she had really enjoyed working for me, but she also wanted to move on to another career. "Why?" I asked. "This Hill atmosphere is strange and it is like a plantation," she answered candidly. So, I was not alone in my observations. It was time for me to go.

The Patton Family—John, Alma, sister Lois and me—1942

At my grandmother's farm, 1943 with my sister Lois and cousins JoAnn and Sheryl.

Relatives and friends at my Aunt Joyce's and Uncle Dutch's tavern for New Year's Eve, 1954

Terrance Ferry and myself just after arriving in London 1963.

My father and me unloading bales of hay on our farm in June 1979.

The family farm, 1952 with the old farm house; my former one-room schoolhouse that my father purchased is in the foreground.

Me and my prize-winning pigs on our farm in 1956.

My Uncle Gerald Becker and me pheasant hunting on our Iowa farm in 1990. Pheasant hunting is an annual tradition.

In Vail, Colorado during the winter of 1968 through 1969.

I am attending a going away party in Washington, D.C. for me in June 1968, before I went to the Vice President Hubert Humphrey presidential campaign. With me are Mike and Jean Fitzgerald and Stephanie De Sibour.

Close friends at a party in 1967 in the Madison Hotel for Charles Robb and President Lyndon Johnson's daughter, Lynda Bird Johnson.

"The Wild Bunch" with Chuck Hoffman and his son along with my friend Bill Oldaker and me.

DC Mayor Anthony A. Williams, David Marlin, Max Berry and me in 1998. Together Berry and I helped usher in nearly every African-American mayor in the District of Columbia.

At an Atlanta night club in 1972 with Stephanie and Agnes, who worked with me in David Gambrell's U.S. Senate campaign.

Charity event in Washington D.C. with friends, including Delores Pruden, Avery Brooks and Carolyn Lewis.

At a private party at the Capitol in 1989 with House Speaker Jim Wright and Clerk of the House Donnald Anderson.

The Rev. Walter Fauntroy and myself on the day we shot a television commercial on Capitol Hill for his 1971 Congressional campaign

On the Costa Brava beach near Barcelona, during my 1963 European sojourn.

A 1967 photo with friends left to right, Mike Fitzgerald, Bob Price, yours truly, David Lambert, Ted Brown in Washington.

Bill Hamilton, Johnny Allem and myself, who comprised the political consulting firm of Allem-Hamilton-Patton.

The Poor Peoples March in Washington D.C., which I helped organize in 1968.

A fundraiser for Fauntroy in the National Democratic Woman's Club in 1971, with Speaker Carl Albert, me, John Wilson, John Hechinger and Senator Ted Kennedy.

The Ed Mezvinsky Congressional campaign staff in 1970 in Iowa City.

At a 1989 Hotel Association Dinner with my wife Nancy and friends, including John Wilson on the left.

As D.C. Deputy Mayor for Planning and Economic Development, I cut the ribbon in 1999 for a new Dress Barn store on Connecticut Ave, part of an effort to spur development in the city.

Charles Robb and myself at the White House in 1967.

Yours truly working the phone for the "Black Delegate Concern".

In Hartford, Conn.at the local AFSCME office
in 1975. My cigar habit began quite early.

CHAPTER FOURTEEN

An African-American Offensive, Sort Of

IN the winter of 1972, Congressman Fauntroy approached me about establishing a non-profit organization. He wanted to secure grants to train African Americans in how to become delegates to national conventions, regardless of whether Republican or Democratic. He intended to advance black empowerment beyond his office. Ensuring that more people of color were delegates would provide them an opportunity to affect the platforms of those parties and to have influence over who actually was elected to office. I embraced the concept of a political offensive that would strengthen the role of blacks in the country's democracy. The Rev. Martin Luther King Jr., and other civil rights leaders, including Fauntroy, had successfully pushed federal elected officials to pass the Civil Rights Act of 1964 and the Voting Rights Act of 1965. But it would take much more to translate those laws into real power that could restructure the relationship between blacks and the American political class. Oddly, the request from Fauntroy would become a destiny of sorts for me. I would be pulled deeper into providing training for African Americans and continuing to advance their political involvement.

Months before Fauntroy called me into his office I had returned from a brief vacation in Martinique and had begun working for Senator Harold Hughes's 1972 presidential campaign. I was still on the mission to elevate what I considered sensitive, humane leadership in the model of John F. Kennedy. Hughes was that kind of leader. For once, I was involved in a campaign that wasn't strapped for cash. It wasn't flush either, but there was enough to pay me well. I made several trips on behalf of the candidate, including to West Virginia where I met the future Senator Jay Rockefeller. I also went to Wisconsin, Iowa and North Carolina. The latter was particularly interesting. With the assistance of James Hunt, who would later become the state's governor, serving four terms, a large group of forty to fifty supporters were assembled; they were diverse, representing multiple socio-economic groups, genders and age. When I returned to the District the next day and went to the Hughes campaign office, Alan Baron, a top assistant, asked me about my trip. I thought it went well and told him so. After his inquiry, I told him who hosted the meeting.

"Doug, probably every one in that room was a member of A.A.," he said. Interestingly, Hughes was never a public member of Alcoholics Anonymous.

"Well, if Hughes has that kind of support across the country with that many A.A.'s working for him, he can become president," I replied.

Actually, that campaign and, thus my employment, were short-lived. I had heard rumors that Hughes was rethinking his decision to run. Then, I was summoned to a closed-door meeting in Hughes' Senate office that was chaired by Ed McDermott, a senior partner at the Hogan & Hartson Law Firm. Others in attendance included Jack Reilly, a former commissioner with Federal Trade Commission, Park Rinard, probably Hughes' closest advisor, Edward Campbell, another trusted advisor and friend, Alan Baron, Eli Segal, Patti Knox from Michigan, Sandy Berger, and Joe Rosenfeld, the finance chair. (Segal and Berger would eventually serve in President Bill Clinton's administration. Years later, after leaving the White House, Berger would be caught removing documents from the National Archives.) Hughes said he had decided not to run. Money wasn't an obstacle, he said, noting that fellow Senator Allan Cranston from California had begged him to have breakfast with two of his wealthy constituents from California. They later called Campbell saying they would raise $100,000 immediately and $50,000 each month as long as Hughes remained in the race. So what was behind his strange decision to bow out? Who really knew or knows to this day? Reportedly, he had attended séances where he had communicated with his longtime dead brother. If that kind of information had been made public, it certainly would not have been well received and would have led to a more controversial ending of his campaign.

After his announcement to campaign staffers, a few of us adjourned to the Carroll-Arms bar, hoping to drown our disappointment. That's when we discovered that not only was Joe Rosenfeld, the wealthy department store magnate, raising tons of money but so were his friends and colleagues, like Martin Buxbaum and Warren Buffett from Omaha, whose fame was just beginning to blossom. I received six weeks of severance pay, which served as testimony to the campaign's financial health.

Ted VanDyke, a top McGovern staffer, called the next day. He had been a close confidant and staffer to Hubert Humphrey, so I was a little surprised at his involvement with McGovern. Ted invited me to their offices on Capitol Hill and, after a brief conversation, offered me a job as one of the four regional coordinators. He said all the McGovern staffers wanted me onboard. While we were talking, campaign manager Gary Hart, who later became a U.S. Senator, walked into Van Dyke's office and reiterated the offer. It was common knowledge that many of the Hughes staffers were going to jump to the Muskie campaign, including myself. I still harbored severe doubts, although he was the front-runner. I had never forgotten that Milwaukee trip where Muskie and he couldn't remember why the farmers were seated before him. I told McGovern's folks that I thought he would get the Democratic nomination. But I really had no interest in presidential campaigns. I think I was becoming more and more enamored with state and local elections.

Within forty-eight hours of turning down the McGovern offer, I received a telephone call from my old friend in Hartford, Connecticut, Nick Carbone, who had ably assisted me in the 1970 Senate primary with Donahue. He wanted my help with a city council primary scheduled for September 1971. He had assembled a slate of candidates. George Athanson was vying to become mayor. Carbone, Richard Suisman, George Levine, Bill Di Bella, Mary Heslin, and Allyn Martin were city council candidates. Martin, a dentist, was the only African American on the ticket. Carbone and Di Bella were Italian, Levine and Suisman were Jewish, and Heslin was Irish. Athanson was of Greek heritage. Upon arriving in Hartford, I had to move quickly. I had no experience in running a slate of candidates. Any candidate had imperfections that could be overcome. But, I was challenged with seven and trying to sell them as one coherent body. Further, the opponents were no slouches.

Wilbur Smith, for example, was a well-regarded African American from the North End of the city. John Murphy was a popular and liberal Irishman. Both would be thorns in Carbone's side if either was elected. Murphy was a kneejerk liberal while Smith was smart and plain mean. After gaining experience in Hartford politics the year before, I knew we needed to get a significant black vote to offset Wilbur Smith's standing in the African-American community. For delivering a clear message, I reached out to

Jerry Lowengard, a friend of Suisman's who ran an advertising agency. He assigned Bill Gorton to the campaign. I immediately had Bill obtain a photographer and we spent a good part of a day taking pictures of the candidates. It wasn't easy, since they were not used to being instructed on how to pose without looking as if they were posing. Athanson was the easiest because he understood we needed action shots and lots of them. My biggest headache was George Levine, who did not even like to campaign let alone sit still for photographs. But I also ended up staying in George's huge home for long periods and we both loved martinis and cigars. That part was good.

Lowengard's firm, following my instructions, designed a very nice brochure as well as effective radio ads that were perfect for the Hartford media market. After I had done the precinct targeting, I asked Carbone to recruit African Americans for a telephone bank. I was not taking any chances on purely relying on the Democratic machine to turn out our vote. All seven candidates were victorious. Winning the Democratic primary was almost tantamount to ultimate victory since there was a lack of Republican opposition. Still, I stayed through the general election.

Back in Washington, D.C., Johnny Allem approached me about forming a political consulting firm. Along with William Hamilton, a well known pollster and friend of Allem's, we formed Allem/Hamilton/Patton, commonly known as "AHP." But just as we were starting that effort, I was side tracked by Fauntroy's request to help train blacks.

Through Ken Bode, a well-known liberal Democrat, I met Stewart Mott, a wealthy political activist. With the legal assistance of David Bonderman, then a partner with the prestigious Arnold and Porter law firm, I established the federal tax-exempt Black Delegate Concern (BDC). Bonderman eventually would become one the richest and most successful businessmen in the United States. Essentially, I had made the right connections for the organization's financial success. Mott's organization gave us a $15,000 grant. That and a smaller donation, allowed me to set up an office on Capitol Hill and hire an all-black staff, including Carolyn Lewis, who was my assistant, Ed Darden, a part-time operative, and Phoebe Haddon, a Smith College graduate, who served as an able intern. Among our first efforts was presenting a seminar in Little Rock, Arkansas, where I met Tony Harrison, another African-American political activist. When meeting blacks like Harrison, I knew they had uneasiness about a youngish white guy trying to persuade African Americans to be delegates. There was also some internal tension. My staff met with me complaining that I was a tad too insensitive and had not included them sufficiently in discussions or decisions that were being made. I adjusted accordingly, quieting the criticism and creating a more inclusive environment. BDC was successful in getting more African Americans to attend the conventions that year. (Phoebe Haddon eventually went to law school, and later became the Dean at the University of Maryland Law School. Darden became a successful realtor.)

Meanwhile, Ed McDermott, from Hughes' campaign, reappeared. This time he wanted me to go to Japan. He was legal counsel to the Japanese embassy; they needed a political consultant to come to Tokyo and teach American campaign methods to members and staff of the Liberal Democratic Party (LDP). Candidly, I liked the fact that I was getting the opportunity to do exactly what I hoped to do: strengthen democracy—not just in America but potentially around the world. When Kennedy was assassinated that November afternoon, I was so devastated and worried that the country was decidedly on the wrong track. But by the early 1970s, I was becoming confident again in who we were as a culture and as a republic. Could I help the Japanese adopt the best of us? I wanted to try.

The Liberal Democratic Party was the ruling political party in Japan and was intent on adopting certain American campaign methods in order to win more elections. With Allem's assistance, we put together materials including slides on campaign techniques—comprehensive polling, targeting, voter identification, organizing at the precinct level, and effective use of the media. I gave both large lectures and smaller seminars, with groups of LDP members, who essentially were representatives of the country's Congress; their immediate staff also often attended those sessions. The last lecture I gave was where I learned what I considered my toughest lesson. Before probably three hundred or more attendees in a large auditorium, I was proceeding through the types of media spots— thirty second, sixty second, five minute documentaries, etc. I had not previewed a longer five-minute political piece on Hubert Humphrey. As I was standing to the side watching the short film and listening to the commentator, I saw and heard the commentator make reference to the end of WWII; a scene of the atomic bomb exploding over Hiroshima appeared on the screen. I wanted to crawl under a rug. Still, that evening they treated me to a large banquet at an upscale restaurant complete with much Saki. They were very gracious. But I was never invited back to Tokyo by the Liberal Democratic Party. How could I say I was sorry? It was a very stupid mistake. I learned a cardinal rule: preview everything.

Soon after arriving home, I received another call from Harley Daniels, in Fauntroy's office, who wanted me to meet Bill Craig, a lawyer from South Carolina. He wanted to challenge U.S. Representative John McMillan, the chairman of the District of Columbia House Committee, an infamous racist, who had opposed all things related to civil rights. In 1967, when then appointed D.C. Mayor Walter Washington, submitted the city's budget, McMillan sent a truckload of watermelons in response. "I will definitely meet with him, anything to rid us of that despot," I told Daniels. But I had several other races I was involved in at that time including one for my friend Ed Mezvinsky in Iowa as well as State Treasurer Emily Womack in Delaware, who was running for governor. Our firm was also the main consultant to Jay Rockefeller, the gubernatorial candidate for West Virginia. Further, we were engaged in David Gambrell's race to retain his seat as the U.S. Senator from Georgia.

I met with Craig and signed an engagement letter with him. He never really honored it nor did he ever pay us. I went to South Carolina once for about three days and advised him on how to set up his campaign organization. I realized at the end of those three days that he was a real hustler. He had some good people helping him, but he was a compulsive liar. I went back to Allem and Hamilton, urging them to forget him. We all wanted to get rid of McMillan, but I was not sure what we were getting from Craig in return. McMillan won narrowly. He was forced into a runoff with John Jenrette from Myrtle Beach on the west side of the 6th Congressional District. Craig had finished third and subsequently endorsed McMillan in the runoff. But Jenrette won by about one thousand votes. Unfortunately, Jenrette lost the general election to a Republican. In 1974, he ran again and won. He served until he was defeated in 1980. He was convicted of accepting a bribe that year during a federal sting known as ABSCAM. He went on to serve thirteen months in prison.

Mezvinsky in Iowa and Emily Womack in Delaware were far better candidates. Mezvinsky won that year; she was a different story. A sitting treasurer, she wanted to be governor. The nominee was selected through a convention process, dominated by older males. She never had a chance. Womack was probably one of the best and most qualified candidates I ever advised. After that unsuccessful try she became a respected banker in Washington D.C. As I write this, no woman has ever been elected governor, U.S. Senator or U.S.

Representative in Delaware—one of only a few states not to elect a woman, which had included my home state. But, in 2014, that trend ended in Iowa, when Joni Ernst, a Republican, was elected to the Senate.

Gambrell, who I had been working with since mid-July at the request of Allem and Hamilton, was locked in a tight senate race in Georgia with then former Governor Ernest Vandiver and State Representative Sam Nunn. Gambrell had been appointed by Georgia Governor Jimmy Carter to fill the seat left vacant following the death of Richard Russell. Not only a distinguished attorney, Gambrell had been treasurer of Carter's campaign for governor. He operated out of the "Heart of Atlanta" motel complex, which, I later discovered, was somewhat infamous. Touted as one of the finest hotels between New York and Miami when it opened in 1956, its owner Moreton Rolleston, a lawyer and strict segregationist, refused to rent rooms to black patrons. When Congress passed the Civil Rights Act of 1964, the owner sued claiming the act violated his rights as a private businessman. The Supreme Court ruled against him in a unanimous opinion, leading to the dismantling of segregation across the South, including the Heart of Atlanta motel. By 1972, the motel had lost much of its glamour. Later, I concluded that Gambrell had intentionally chosen the motel as its headquarters, sending a not-so-subtle message of his conservative credentials to the rest of Georgia. I immediately met with the campaign chairman Conley Ingram, a true gentleman who later became a Georgia Supreme Court Justice, and John Girardeau of Gainesville, Georgia, who would become a senior justice of the Superior Court in the Northeastern Judicial Circuit of Gainesville. They advised me to work at the advertising agency that had been hired by the campaign.

The agency's director was Gerald Rafshoon, who became famous as Carter's media man in the 1976 presidential election. Jerry was affable and funny; we hit it off right away. I also was probably correct in my assumption that the campaign wanted me "not to be seen but also not heard," particularly since I was basically a Yankee from Washington. Unlike today in which many political consultants and so-called strategists always seem to be in the spotlight, in the 1960s and 1970s, an invisible consultant was the desired standard. One of my key tasks for Gambrell was bolstering his support among black voters. The campaign had a young African-American political operative, Benny, who generally knew and understood campaign mechanics.

Former Governor Ernest Vandiver was the most liberal candidate in the race while Nunn appeared the most conservative. Gambrell had a good shot at black voters, particularly since he was connected to Carter who was fairly popular with African-American leaders in Atlanta. I asked Benny if he could recruit a few black women to staff a paid telephone bank. After we put them in place, I treated him, and a couple of the workers, Stephanie, and another woman, Agnes, to lunch. As we became friendlier, the two women announced they wanted to treat me to an evening out, escorting me to an area called "Underground Atlanta," which was six historic blocks of bars, restaurants and lounges. We took a taxicab there, and immediately entered a very large lounge and bar where we were guided to a prime booth located almost in the middle of the place. I was the only white person in the club. The band was headed by a black songstress, who sounded exactly like the famous Aretha Franklin. Other club patrons nodded to us as they passed the booth. Only one person actually stopped and introduced himself as the photographer, asking if we wanted our pictures taken. Of course, I said, and paid him five dollars; I still have the photograph. We had a great evening; there were no incidents of any kind, although I was the only white male with two very attractive African- American women. An observation I made then about race in Georgia was that whites and blacks interacted well, both politically and socially. At one local fundraiser for a white city council person I attended there were many blacks in attendance. That was where I met Andrew Young, the future African American congressman and delegate to the United Nations. I also became friends with Stony Cooks, his top assistant, who on a number of occasions gave me good advice on Georgia politics.

Surprisingly, Carter's popularity with blacks did not help Gambrell's campaign in the first election on August 8, 1972. He brought in 31.4 percent of the vote while Sam Nunn had 23 percent. We were a little surprised that Vandiver was third with 20.53 percent. Most of us anticipated that he would have finished a strong second. Since Gambrell hadn't received over 40 percent, I knew we were in trouble for the run-off slated for August 29—three weeks later. Political history had never been good to candidates who had to face run-offs after finishing first in the initial election. Frank Moore, one of the Gambrell staffers was assigned by Girardeau the campaign manager to travel to South Georgia to gauge and drum up support for the senator. After three days, he reported back to us. His briefing was succinct, very little support. "I am not going back, not only do they dislike Gambrell, but they hate the governor." I thought to myself if Moore is scared and well over six feet tall and probably weighing 200 lbs., we are not going to win. I was right.

Before election night, I had picked out three key precincts from around the state. They were swing precincts historically; whoever won those precincts would win the election. I found three volunteers that I planned to post outside polls when they closed at 8 o'clock. Once they had the results from voting machines, they were to call a pre-assigned telephone number in the office I would be occupying. All three numbers were on separate phones. At almost 8:02 all three telephones rang. They reported the results: Nunn was winning narrowly. The gap didn't matter. It still was a loss for Gambrell. I immediately called Conley Ingram, the campaign chairman. I knew he was with the senator. I told him Gambrell had lost.

"What do you mean Doug, the polls just closed?" asked Ingram. He had confidence in my abilities, but still repeated, "Are you sure?"

"Positive," I replied.

He handed the telephone to Gambrell. I repeated the bad news. He was quiet. Finally, he said "Thank you, Doug," and hung up. Nunn won with about 54 percent of the vote and served in the Senate until 1996.

CHAPTER FIFTEEN

On the Road, Once More

I wasn't a vagabond but I was living like one: constantly on the road, training one group, trying to get yet another person elected, often under rather difficult conditions. As 1972 wore on, I realized things wouldn't change much, especially after the telephone call from Bill Welsh. The legislative political director of AFSCME, he wanted me to go to Memphis, Tennessee, to help J.O. Patterson, Jr., an African American pastor and son of a bishop from a distinguished Memphis family, get elected to the U.S. House of Representatives. I felt no warmth for that city. After all, it had been where the Rev. Martin Luther, Jr., took his last breath. The assassination left a bitter taste in everyone's mouth, particularly African Americans who believed it was a conspiracy. James Earle Ray may have been caught, but few people believed he acted alone any more than they were convinced that Lee Harvey Oswald had been the lone shooter that day in Dallas. I have wondered a million times what would have happened if King, John and Robert Kennedy had not been cut down in their prime, at a time when the country was turning away from the segregation and the hatred it wrought. How might we have evolved? What would have been our humanity quotient?

The only thing that made a trip to Memphis less difficult to take was the fact that African American men weren't marching in the streets as they had been that day King was murdered with placards that read "I Am A Man" hanging from their necks. Blacks were gaining more and more power, as evidenced by Patterson's campaign. Truthfully, he was not the best candidate. He wasn't an aggressive campaigner. In fact, at times he didn't even seem interested in campaigning. I met individuals from the advertising firm he was using and was impressed with the African American who was the younger partner in that small company. After a few days, he invited me to dinner at a restaurant on the top floor of a Holiday Inn, asking me to escort one of his employees, an African American woman. His date, however, was another employee, an outgoing white woman. As we were seated, I could feel the stares of the patrons, who were all white. We thought it all amusing. Customers probably did not realize my date was the African-American woman.

I found myself constantly amused by the south and its quirky ways. Once when I needed a haircut, I asked Dotty, a woman who worked for AFSCME, to recommend a barber. When I entered the shop, I realized all eight of the barbers were African American. I had never had my hair cut by a black barber. But I noticed several customers in chairs as well as those waiting were like myself—white. White southerners allowed blacks to cut their hair, care for their children, cook and serve their meals, drive them to various destinations and perform other personal chores. Yet they did not want their children to attend the same schools as African American children. It made me angry. What's more, I didn't like the white section of Memphis. Frank Jackson, a friend I had known several years earlier in Washington, was an attorney in Memphis. He came from one of the city's old-line families. He and I had dinner one evening; three nights later, he invited me to a party at a large fashionable home in the very white section of Memphis. There were perhaps seventy-five people, mostly young white couples. Some members of the group were constantly using that the infamous "N" word. While I had heard it before and even some African Americans used it liberally, the way it was being thrown around at the party made be uncomfortable. I made an excuse, telling Frank I didn't feel well. He called me a taxicab.

After a few more days on the ground, I was positive that Patterson didn't have much of a chance in the election. I caught a plane back to Washington. He subsequently lost to Republican incumbent Don Kuykendall, who was white. In 1974, the Democrats nominated Harold Ford, Sr., a young black state representative who won the seat. The Ford Family kept that seat until his son Harold Ford, Jr., decided in 2006 not to seek re-election.

I managed only one victory in 1972; that was in Hartford. Carbone had asked me to come to the city yet again. An important referendum on funding for the Hartford Civic Center would be on the ballot. We won but by fewer than 100 votes. In politics, a win is a win. Returning to Washington with a slight smile on my face, and a desire to put down some roots, I purchased a small townhouse on Reno Road in Cleveland Park. My funds were tight, but the political consulting firm—Allem, Hamilton and Patton—was in decent shape, with AFSCME as a consistent client. But there was political pandemonium related to a burglary of the National Democratic Committee headquarters in the Watergate office complex on June 17, 1972. The crime had been committed by Republican Party operatives, working at the behest of President Richard Nixon and his key staff. The congressional investigation that ensued was explosive. Eventually, 48 people were found guilty and sentenced to prison. During that period, I was in frequent contact then with Barry Sussman, the city editor of the

Washington Post. He and I had become friendly during the Fauntroy race. He was also the immediate boss of Bob Woodward and Carl Bernstein, the two reporters who broke the Watergate story and covered its aftermath. Sussman would call occasionally, asking me whether a rumor or leak had reality in political campaigns. He relied on my experience in campaigns to determine whether a story had any possible truth-in-fact. Everything was off the record of course.

Finally, after intense reporting and scrutiny, Nixon resigned in 1974. After two years of nonstop scrutiny, it was almost anti-climatic. Nevertheless, it made me sad for the country. I wondered what would have happened had voters elected Hubert Humphrey president in 1968. Would the nation have been better off? Certainly the trajectory of my life would have been very different. I likely would not have been able to be so intimately involved in the political empowerment of African Americans. Despite the high political drama, things for me didn't stand still. AFSCME's president Jerry Wurf, along with his chief assistant Bill Welsh, had determined that their national union had to be more aggressive politically. That meant training their members on how to become active in campaigns. Once again, our firm designed workshops, slide shows and manuals. It took weeks, months even, to formulate them and implement our plan. Since I had some acting experience, I performed the voice-over on many of the slide shows. We had the services of a man named Bart, who reminded me of Burl Ives; he was very bright and entertaining but extremely overweight—maybe three hundred pounds. He also was non-political and pretty naïve. He owned a production company in Merrifield, Virginia; he was a true magician with audio tape. He called one day from his recording studio, telling me he had been visited by two conservatively dressed men who said they were from the White House. During a thirty-minute interview, they asked about various techniques involving audio tape usage, including splicing and editing. It all sounded a little strange, prompting me to call Sussman, relaying the details of the visit. He attempted to locate them. Unsurprisingly, they had provided Bart false telephone numbers and addresses. Only later, after it was revealed that President Nixon had recorded, as a matter of course, all conversations in the Oval Office, did the nation learn eighteen and one-half minutes of critical dialogue was missing. Reportedly they were accidentally erased by his personal secretary Rosemary Woods. Almost everyone who knew about the Merrifield visit believed there was a connection to it and the missing minutes.

Bill Lucy, an assistant to the president of AFSCME, had become chairman of the D.C. Democratic State Committee. He asked me to spearhead a fundraiser for the group. We had it at the Shoreham Omni Hotel, attracting almost one thousand attendees. We imported performing acts from Stax Records in Memphis, which had become famous with the emergence and subsequent death of Otis Redding. The company also had other great artists, including Issac Hayes and comedian Richard Pryor. Through Lucy's friendship with the management, Stax sent its house band, Booker T and the MG's, a racially integrated group of musicians. We also enlisted the services of the noted African-American flutist Bobbie Humphrey and the well-known white comedian Mark Russell. It was a fabulously fun evening. We didn't net a big profit, however, teaching me another lesson: While entertainers are providing their services free, nothing is ever free. There are costs for technical support and hangers-on who help rack up large hotel bills including room service. Putting that aside, the event bolstered Lucy's stature, which was one of the primary goals.

No sooner had I recovered, when I received yet another call from Carbone wanting help with the 1973 mayoral and city council races in Hartford.

I also was contracted to assist Victor Mambruno, the sitting mayor of Waterbury, Connecticut. While in Waterbury one evening and having dinner with Frank Santaguida, Mambruno's main campaign advisor, I was told my Washington office had been trying to reach me. I immediately called Bill Hamilton at his home. His girlfriend Claire explained that Jill, a woman I was dating who was from England, had been attacked and stabbed in her Georgetown apartment on 35th St. NW. in Washington, D.C. I took the earliest flight out the next morning, rushing to the Georgetown Hospital and proceeding to the fourth floor where I had been told her room was located. I noticed an armed, uniformed policeman sitting on a chair between entrances. He nodded but watched me closely as I went past the second doorway. I glanced in and saw a young woman in the bed. "Doug, is that you?" The woman called out, causing me to turn back and enter. Jill's face and head were extremely swollen. I didn't recognize her.

She told me what happened. As she was moving into her new apartment, a young black male, slipped behind her and struck her with a large mirror that was in the entryway. He repeatedly asked for money. Using a paring knife from the kitchen, he stabbed her multiple times in her upper torso. Fortunately, none of her vital organs were pierced. Hearing her screams, a neighbor raced downstairs. The assailant fled. An ambulance was called.

After two days at the hospital, Jill went to recuperate at a friend's country farm in Virginia. I flew back to Connecticut, but returned a week later. By then Jill had recovered enough to make a trip to the D.C. police headquarters, where she was escorted into a private room; officers insisted that I remain outside. They wanted details of the attack and had her look through mug shots, hoping she might identify her assailant. I was peeved that she was forced to re-live what was one of the worst moments in her life without having me at her side. As I sat in the waiting room, a plainclothes police officer approached me, asking if my girlfriend was the woman who had been attacked in Georgetown ten days ago. Yes, I said. He was a homicide detective but he had been called to the scene and accompanied Jill in the ambulance. He was amazed, he said, adding that, no one believed she would survive.

Jill returned with me to Hartford for a few days, but was plagued with recurring nightmares, sometimes waking me by her cries in the middle of the night. It greatly affected me, inspiring a negative reaction to each young black male I encountered in public and prompting in me thoughts that he might have some criminal intent. I am not proud of that but I could not ignore the attack on Jill. Those harsh feelings took a while to dissipate.

After winning both the Waterbury and Hartford contests, I retreated to my Washington home that fall, unsure of how many clients we could procure in 1974. I soon found out. Johnny Allem asked if I would be willing to leave the firm and live in New York working for AFSCME. Bill Welsh the political/legislative director wanted me to be an assistant director for AFSCME in New York State. Agreeing to meet, he told me Jerry Wurf, AFSCME's president, wanted desperately to defeat Nelson Rockefeller, then governor of New York. He needed someone who could work with the large District Council 37 in New York City, which had over 100,000 members—the largest public employee union in the city—that was headed by Victor Gotbaum, a well-known figure in New York political and social circles. His assistant director and second in charge was Lillian Roberts, an African American. She was also a close friend of Bill Lucy who was by then the National Secretary/Treasurer of AFSCME. Welsh said I was the ideal person to help their political efforts in New York State. The union had some smaller District Councils in Rochester and Buffalo. I accepted the position knowing, of course, it made sense for Allem and Hamilton to reduce their overhead while gaining an even firmer position in the national union. I kept my home in Washington but rented an apartment in the upper east side of the city on 81st Street. The national union paid me well and covered housing and meals.

As was typical, I plunged into the job, finding a small office in the union's headquarters while establishing a satellite office in Albany. Then, I started recognizing the tensions between Wurf and Gotbaum, which affected my role. Both rose through the New York City local and were friends, but they seemed to distrust each other; that feeling carried over to their respective staffs. Meanwhile, President Gerald Ford, who had assumed office after Nixon resigned in disgrace, appointed Rockefeller as his vice-president; he had to step down as governor. Malcolm Wilson, the lieutenant took the reins. The joke was that I had only been in New York a short time and already I had accomplished the mission of getting rid of Rockefeller.

On the Democratic side of the ledger, Howard "the Horse" Samuels, a wealthy industrialist who co-founded the Kordite Corporation, best known for plastic bags like the Hefty, and Hugh Carey, a seven-term congressman from the borough of Brooklyn, announced for the democratic nomination for governor. It appeared to me that Gotbaum wanted to endorse and support Samuels, who was a good friend. However, I believed Carey had a better chance of winning. Also, my friend Gerald Cummins had been appointed Carey's campaign manager, placing me in a bind. I shared my opinion with Wurf and Welsh, albeit off the record. I really wanted to help Carey and Cummins, but felt my hands were tied. By this time I had become more acquainted with AFSCME's rank and file members. They, too, had discretely expressed their own support for Carey.

At the Democratic Party state convention on June 13, 1974, in Niagara Falls, New York delegates had chosen Howard Samuels as the designee for governor. However, Carey secured enough delegates that, based on the rules, meant a primary election had to be held. I got to know Samuels staffers, primarily Ken Aulettta, his campaign manager. Mario Cuomo, the Lieutenant Governor designee, was on the ticket with Samuels. As we were holding one campaign training session for our Rochester AFCSME local that summer, I invited Cuomo to give a little pep talk to about forty members at a Rochester hotel. Always a very good speaker, he gave an excellent talk to the members, many of them Italian American like himself. After he had departed, a staffer told me of an interesting conversation she had overheard in the back of the room. One person, whispering to the President Local 66 Anthony Gingello, said "Hey, Tony, this guy Cuomo can't be Italian, he speaks too good." In 1982, Cuomo became governor of New York.

I had the feeling union leaders did not take Carey seriously enough in the race against Samuels. I told them I was concerned particularly about upper New York State voters. All through the summer, we were constantly training the rank and file members of AFSCME in the campaign techniques of voter identification, polling, and get-out-the vote programs. Some of the locals were very resistant to change; moreover, there were also some small-time mobsters or, at least, criminal elements in their leadership.

During my travels and work, I got to know two African-American leaders who became friends and political allies. One was Charles 'Charlie" Hughes, head of Local 372 in New York City which represented lunchroom aides, crossing guards, and other school employees. He would become a political supporter and advisor to three mayors, including Rudy Giuliani. Unfortunately, years later, Charlie Hughes's career ended when he was convicted of corruption and went to prison. He subsequently died of a heart attack in 2009 at the age of 68. The other black person was Arthur O. Eve, a state legislator from Buffalo, who I helped in the primary races. Never a fan of the established Democratic machine, he still rose to be deputy speaker of the New York State Assembly. He was a strong advocate for liberal causes and was invited to be an observer and negotiator by inmates during the 1971 Attica Prison Riot. Arthur retired in 2002 after an illustrious public career. As I had predicted, Carey won the September primary against Samuels and went on to defeat the Republican Wilson in November. He and I continued to be friends. Cummins became chairman of the New York Thruway Authority. Ella Grasso, a congresswoman who was running for governor of Connecticut and whose campaign I had been helping through my friend Carbone, also won; she became the first woman elected governor and the first woman to be elected governor of any U.S. state "in her own right." Others had been appointed to succeed their deceased husbands. Grasso defeated Congressman Robert Steele, Jr., by more than two hundred thousand votes.

During my involvement in the New York race, I also assisted about fifteen individuals running for state senate and assembly contests. Most of those for whom I raised money went on to win, resulting in Democratic control of the State Legislature. So, 1974 proved a good year for my political organizing. But once again I faced that ever present question: "What do I do next?"

I had been out of Washington most of that year. The city had held its first election for mayor following passage of the Home Rule Charter Act by Congress. Walter Washington edged out Clifford Alexander, a prominent African American attorney. Alexander had been a major backer of Fauntroy's, but he did not have the blue collar appeal or the common touch Fauntroy possessed. I was re-entering a new political environment in D.C. of which I had not been a major part for over three years. But many of the people who Fitzgerald and I had trained during Fauntroy's campaign were beginning to take the next rung up the political ladder. It wouldn't be long before I would return to an influential position, working in the background to help black empowerment.

But first AFCSME had another assignment for me. In addition to continuing the nationwide political campaign training of union members that my firm and I had developed, I was to lead major lobbying efforts in Connecticut, helping to pass a collective bargaining bill for public employees. I knew the importance of the legislation for Jerry Wurf, although lobbying was quite a new task for me. With the aid of my ally Nick Carbone, we were able to forge an effective coalition with the Connecticut Teachers Association and the State of Connecticut public employee association. Tom Mondani, the head of the National Education Association, became the principal spokesperson for the coalition. Mike Ferrucci, the head of the major AFSCME local was also part of the coalition. We drafted the legislation ensuring it was acceptable to all players. There was only one obstacle, however: Governor Ella Grasso.

While she had relied on Carbone to help her win the general election, she was always antagonistic towards me. When she would encounter me in the hallways of the Capitol she would always ask me, within earshot of the staff and reporters, "Doug, are you now finally registered to vote in Connecticut?" By highlighting my outsider status, I think she hoped to discredit me and my work. I laughed to deflect the question. It wasn't just me, however. She had a bad temperament. Once, when ten of the coalition members attended a meeting in her private office, she, visibly angry at our position, uttered loudly, "I don't care what the f—- you think." We were all aghast, since it was the first time many of us, certainly I, had ever heard a woman politician, indeed the governor, use profanity. She apologized, somewhat, for the outburst, particularly to the women who were in attendance.

But as the heat over the collective bargaining bill increased, I called Bill Welsh from a staff phone in the Capitol. He told me President Wurf wanted to speak with me. "Where are you calling from," he asked me.

When I told him where I was, he told me to hang up and go to a pay phone outside the building. Later, Wurf told me that whenever you get in a similar situation, you have to remember conversations are always being tapped. We eventually got the bill passed, but without her support.

After Connecticut, I went to Maine to assist with in the re-election campaign of Senator Edmund Muskie. He was supposed to speak at an AFSCME training session, but abruptly cancelled on the day of the event. I called Welsh in Washington, asking him if he had any ideas about a substitute. Call George J. Mitchell, he told me, noting that he was one of his friends. Mitchell came and presented excellent welcoming remarks. Little did the participants—or I for that matter—know that Mitchell would be elected senator from Maine in 1980, and eventually become a very effective majority leader. After leaving the Senate, he had a distinguished career as a diplomat.

I was worn out, and having earned almost a month of vacation time, decided to take a trip to Europe, including Eastern Europe. It was an opportunity to revisit Germany. I had been away for a decade. I wanted to see how much had changed. I hoped to reacquaint myself with some of the people I met during my first trip. I ended my tour by attending my close friend Jerry Pritchett's wedding to Claude Michelin in Provence, France. She was French and a member of the famous Michelin family. They married in a small ceremony. My wife and I still visit them in France and Washington, D.C.

Arriving back in the nation's capital in late summer 1975, I knew I had had enough of being on the road, even for pleasure and certainly for political campaigns. Additionally, my year long relationship with Margie McNamara had come to an end. I decided to look for a new career. No sooner had I made that wish, it was granted. Two friends, Susan

King and Bob Moss told me about a position at the Federal Election Commission (FEC).

Established by Congress, the FEC set rules and had oversight of federal elections. It included two ex-officio positions, one from the Senate and one from the House of Representatives. Moss, who was the counsel to the Clerk of the House, was serving temporarily as the House designee. He urged me to seek the post. But I needed political support from House members. I contacted my friend Jim Mooney, who was the top assistant to Congressman John Brademas; he was a deputy whip under then-Speaker of the House Carl Albert. I met with Brademas who agreed to support my application. I also called Marshall Lyman who was the top assistant to Congressman Jim Wright, an influential House member from Texas. I remember Wright calling me to ensure I would be loyal to the House as an institution. Many members, if not all, were very leery of a so-called independent body like the F.E.C. overseeing their campaigns. The agency had an uneven reputation over the course of its history. Many friends, including King and Moss wanted someone at the commission who knew something about political campaigns and how they actually operate. I thought it was a natural fit for me, and that I could instill more confidence in the commission with congressional representatives.

After failed attempts by select individuals to sabotage my appointment, I finally left AFSCME and became the designee of the House of Representatives on the Commission. I was there only a short time when the famous decision by Supreme Court came down that stated major provisions of the FEC statute were unconstitutional. There was a rush in Congress to implement legislation that would retain current FEC members while providing remedies to cure an imperfect statute. During the 1976 national election, I had almost weekly conversations with Robert Lipshutz who was the legal counsel to then candidate Jimmy Carter. Lipshutz's daughter had worked for me during my campaign in Georgia in 1972, consequently, he trusted me with regard to election law questions. I had also begun to work with different House members and perceived myself in a lawyer-client relationship with them on specific issues. There were, indeed, characters: Charles Diggs, an African American Congressman from Detroit, Michigan, always called me directly with the usual greeting, "Diggs, Michigan." That was it and after my acknowledging him, he would ask his questions. Congressman William Natcher from Kentucky, who later became chairman of the House Committee on Appropriations, would always called my private line with the opening "Am I bothering you, Doug?" in a very courtly manner. He would not allow his own staff to ask even the most elementary questions about his political campaign activity. There were many other contacts with both Republican and Democratic members, many of them highly sensitive, at least politically,

The election commission rapidly became a bureaucratic agency with almost all of its initial employees being white and many from offices on the Hill. There may have been two minority workers; neither was in top administrative positions. I mentioned this to a friend and colleague who at that time was an assistant legal counsel; he agreed it was a problem. He said he was having difficulty hiring minorities. Moreover, high quality African Americans were going to major law firms where the pay was much better and career paths more defined.

I broke away from the minutiae of election regulations to attend the 1976 Democratic Convention in New York. I got in touch with my old friend Gerald Cummins, who said he was very busy, but would meet at the Bull n' Bear Restaurant Bar in the Waldorf-Astoria Hotel on Park Avenue at five o'clock. I thought this was a somewhat unusual venue since I usually met him at Rose's, another landmark in Manhattan or the legendary 21 Club. When I arrived, Gerry was standing at the bar with three other men: New

York Governor Hugh Carey, his aide and friend Tom Regan and Jimmy Breslin, the author and well-known columnist. After the usual hellos, they proceeded with their loud and sometimes profane conversation. I looked around the well-attended bar but no one else seemed aware or even took notice that the governor was enjoying his friends and partaking of a few Scotches. The men did not slack up, at least not while I was there. Today it likely would be impossible for a New York governor or any other high profile elected official to toss back a few drinks in a public setting like the Waldorf.

Tip O'Neil became the new speaker of the House in early 1977, and Brademas became the Chief Majority Whip under him. Later, my other mentor, Jim Wright, became Majority leader by one vote, replacing O'Neil.

During my years at the F.E.C. and the House of Representatives, I paid little attention to Mayor Walter Washington's administration except when it affected me personally, like getting permits, for example, for my house renovations on Reno Road or trying to restrict traffic on my street. Then in late 1977, the environment changed again, or at least expanded.

CHAPTER SIXTEEN

Ushering In Real Black Power

MARION Barry called one evening in late 1977, asking me to meet him privately. By then, he had been elected to the D.C. Council, after serving on the D.C. Board of Education. Nearly all the people who worked with me during Fauntroy's campaign had effectively used the skills they learned during that time as well as details about the city's electorate to win office. In addition to Barry, Willie Hardy, John Wilson, Nadine Winter and several others were serving as elected officials or had developed as political players behind the scenes. The blue-collar or working-class blacks, who had helped Fauntroy win office, had been behind Barry's victory. He had been adept, first with Pride Inc, a nonprofit organization, working mostly with low-income residents. Using that same constituency he had led an effective bus boycott. While I hadn't been involved with his career on the council, we hadn't lost touch. Our network of operators intersected, providing a source of information about each other's activities. I told him evenings were better for me and offered my house as the place to talk. I knew he had his sights on the mayor's office. He had gained some notoriety, after being shot earlier that year during a takeover of city hall by members of a radical sect known as the Hanafi Muslims. The group, led by Hamaas Abdul Khaalis, had also seized control of the B'nai B'rith, the Islamic Center and the District Building. They had 149 hostages and, in exchange for their freedom, were demanding the release of prisoners who had been convicted of killing several of Khaalis' relatives, including children. The group also wanted the destruction of the movie Mohammad, Messenger of God, which they called sacrilege. Ambassadors from three predominantly Muslim countries helped in the negotiations, persuading the gunmen to surrender. By then, however, Maurice Williams, a reporter from the Howard University owned WHUR radio station, who had stepped off the elevator on the 5th floor during the height of the siege at the District Building, was dead. A security guard later died in the hospital. Barry had been rushed to the hospital. Hearing noise in the hallway, he had gone to investigate and also was shot; the bullet lodged near his heart. He was lucky to have survived. That feat alone cast him as a modern folk hero. Obviously, he understood the moment and didn't waste it.

At my home, I offered him a drink and some snacks. He accepted a beer but never finished it, which would be at odds with his reputation in later years as a heavy drinker. Maybe he was just too busy laying out his election scheme and how I might fit in. He wanted me to co-manage his campaign with Ivanhoe Donaldson, a savvy operator who had been involved with the civil rights movement and who was a friend of John Wilson. Barry was convinced that he needed a black/white co-manager arrangement in order to win. I didn't agree. One manager was enough, I told him, although I was appreciated that he thought so much of my skills and expertise. Donaldson could do the job. What's more, I wasn't eager to give up my lucrative F.E.C. job for yet another low-paying campaign position. After an hour-long conversation, I pledged to support him, while asking a series of questions about how he intended to win against both Walter Washington and my old friend Sterling Tucker, who, interestingly, had not asked for my assistance. Finally, I asked Barry a rather personal question: "I had the feeling during the Fauntroy campaign that your former wife and business partner, Mary Treadwell, didn't like white people. Is that true? How do you reconcile that with having been married to her? Will that be a problem for you in the white community?" He was silent for fifteen or twenty seconds. "Doug, you should understand that Mary doesn't like a lot of people, period." I laughed, relieved and greatly amused by his candid response.

Eventually I became part of Barry's advisory team. I already knew my friends Max Berry, David Abramson and Delano Lewis were on board. I respected their judgment and abilities. The former two were part of a cadre of whites, myself included, who had helped build the black government of Washington, D.C., from the ground up. As we had done with Fauntroy, we met regularly to advise Barry's team. I hosted one or two gatherings on Saturdays at my home. Often the group included Berry, Lorraine Whitlock, Jan Ichord, Phil Ogilvie, Betty King, Sybil Hammond, Rob Robinson, Jim Gibson and a few others. Ivanhoe Donaldson and Barry chaired the meetings.

We had also assembled a formidable finance group, which included Gilbert and Anne Kinney, a socially prominent Georgetown couple, Jerry Lustine, a local realtor, Jeff Cohen, a young developer, Joe Sharlitt, a prominent attorney, Stuart Long, a local restaurateur, and Conrad and Peggy Cooper Cafritz, of the notable real estate family . We also had the support of two prominent African-American artists—Sam Gilliam and Lou Stovall. They produced art works, the prints of which were used as fundraising items. I still have both of those paintings today. An event at my home raised about $7,000—a nice sum in 1978.

Barry was presumed to be running third behind Tucker and Washington. Then the Washington Post leveled the playing field substantially by endorsing Barry. It became a horse race.

I had done much of the precinct targeting for the campaign based on past elections so I could gauge turnout and support using such statistics. On Election Day, I took up residence at the Barry headquarters, which was on the lower level in a midtown building. Courtland Cox, a friend of Barry's, also helped monitor returns. At that time, each campaign was allowed monitors at the city's election headquarters to observe the vote counting. At midday, officials gathered all the ballots from all the precinct locations and brought them under security to their headquarters where counting took place. John Gibson, a brother of Jim Gibson, was one of three monitors. During the process, he called describing, three piles of ballots that were about the same dimension. We were encouraged, believing that meant there was a close three-way mayoral race. By the time the polls closed, I had completed my analysis and was fairly confident Barry had won. Many of the campaign workers had left for the hotel near Howard University, the location of the victory celebration. Cox and I lingered for about an hour, rechecking key precincts and the voting totals. Certain of my assumptions, I got in my car and headed for the hotel.

I entered Barry's suite, immediately seeing David Abramson and Max Berry sitting in an outer living room area. They didn't seem to want to tell me where I could find Barry. I knocked loudly on an adjacent closed door. I opened it slightly; a large African-American man blocked full entry. Barry sat on the bed with Effie, who he had married just a year earlier, after divorcing Mary Treadwell. Several other individuals, whom I did not know, were also in the room. I realized then I was the only white face. With my data in hand, I quickly told Barry he had indeed won the election. He nodded appreciatively; I got the feeling my words did not register with him. It was almost as if he were in shock. I did not observe any other members of the main advisory group in the room. For the first time, I realized Barry had different circles of people who never interacted with each other; that was a practice he maintained throughout his career.

I am certain that if some of his white supporters had realized he had relations with shady people, he may not have received their help to realize his political ambitions.

The race had been close enough so that there was a recount. Barry had clearly won the election, with a fifteen hundred vote-lead over Tucker who came in second, barely beating out Washington. As had been the history of the city, since even before it achieved quasi-independence through what came to be called Home Rule, whites had voted for Barry in droves. They returned him to office a second time, before many finally abandoning him during his third term, following rumors of drug abuse. In 1978, however, they were still in his corner for the November General Election. Barry beat Republican candidate Arthur Fletcher, who had been in the Nixon administration and was credited with developing the affirmative action public policy that eventually helped expand the black middle- class.

I returned to my white enclave—the Federal Election Commission. There wasn't any question a pattern had developed in my life: I would slip out of my comfort zone to advance some political careers usually involving an African American pushing to get to the next level. I trained a crew of second-tier operatives, who stayed behind to continue the work, and then moved to the next challenge. It was no different with Barry's election.

After his victory, I headed for Vail, Colorado, staying, as I often did, at the Christiania Lodge, of which I was part owner. I may not have made a ton of money when I worked on campaigns but as I stabilized my employment my finances improved and I invested wisely. My friend Bill Oldaker and I skied on New Year's Day 1979. When we got part way up the mountain and off the lift we learned it was twenty-eight degrees below zero with a minus eighty degree wind-chill factor. We quickly skied back to the Village. At lunch time we went to Sweet Basil, a very good local restaurant, which is still in operation. I noticed a very beautiful Asian woman sitting alone at a nearby table. I told Bill that I thought it was the same woman I had seen earlier that morning in Gorsuch's clothing store, another Vail landmark. As we were getting ready to leave, Bill encouraged me to go speak to her. "What do you have to lose?" Nancy had been skiing in Vail for a few days but was leaving the next morning. I tried to persuade her to stay longer; she had to return to Austin, Tex. where she worked at IBM. I got her telephone number and persuaded her to allow me to visit. Ten days later I was in Austin.

After many months of traveling between Austin and Washington, D.C., I proposed to her in late October of that year. Together we flew to New York to purchase a ring in the diamond section of the city on West 47th Street. As we settled into the flight, I slipped on her ring finger one of my cigar wrappers, telling her this would serve as an engagement ring until I had purchased the real thing. She laughed. The bond was sealed. My bachelorhood ended.

On January 1, 1980, a year after our first meeting, Nancy and I married in Vail. She moved from Austin to Washington, D.C., and we settled into our new house on Cathedral Ave. NW. She had a new position at IBM, and I accepted an unpaid political appointment by Mayor Barry to the Board of Zoning Adjustment (BZA), which oversaw and ruled on zoning matters within the District. Interestingly, I replaced an African American, Leonard McCantz, with whom I had worked on the 1968 Poor People's March, becoming the only white person on the board appointed by the mayor. Most of the BZA staff was white except for the clerical assistants. The prime authority was Walter Lewis, an older African American. The five members rotated weekly, serving on the BZA at its separate meetings as required by statute. Lewis and I became very good friends. He probably forgot more about zoning than I would ever learn. He also provided me with many stories about growing up in the South and the extreme prejudices he had encountered. But he was almost always in great spirits. Once, the zoning panel held a hearing on a parking lot appeal from a small local owner who was white. It was a contested case in a near northeast neighborhood. I asked the owner who supervised activities on the parking lot. He said "I have my boy look after it almost daily." I kicked Lewis under our hearing table, surprised by the demeaning answer. Lewis asked, subtly highlighting the owner's prejudice, "Is this boy your son or a member of your family?" The owner appearing befuddled said, "No, he works for me, he is my boy." We issued a bench decision denying the parking extension. At lunch, I was visibly angry by the exchange with that owner. "Doug," said Walter, "I see it all the time, I am used to it." Well, I wasn't.

Barry had an excellent first term as mayor, hiring good deputies and inspiring a new spirit to government service. He also developed the city's first budget prepared independent of the federal government. And, when he moved his home east of the Anacostia River to Ward 7, an area often forgotten by many in the city, he helped instill a sense of pride among its residents. Still, he faced serious opposition in his 1982 re-election. He was challenged by Patricia Roberts Harris, a former Secretary of the Department of Health and Human Welfare under President Jimmy Carter and later an Ambassador to Luxembourg. Many middle-class African Americans weren't quite enamored of Barry. They didn't like his dress or his southern dialect, which sometimes seemed garbled. He wasn't their kind of politician. Harris was more representative of what native, black middle-class Washingtonians saw as their type. With Ivanhoe Donaldson as his chief strategist, Barry nevertheless reached out to them, promising to bring them deeper into the government, providing more jobs. Nancy and I held a fundraiser for him that year at our home on Ellicott Street. He won handily and for many years held onto that section of the electorate.

His second term got off to a great start. But in short order, it all went south. Stories began to emerge about his night-time activity. I paid little attention to those rumors. One evening that year, I remember getting a call from the mayor asking me to join him at 7 o'clock the next morning at the Jefferson Hotel on 16th St. NW. He wanted me to come to the Rev. Jesse Jackson's suite. When I arrived, I found the two of them and a few staffers who wanted a tutorial on federal election laws, particularly around presidential campaigns. Ten minutes into the presentation, Jackson disappeared. His aides and Barry remained; at the end, he thanked me profusely. Little did I know then, Jackson was preparing to run for the democratic presidential nomination in 1984.

I wasn't enthralled with Jackson. I responded to the request mostly to help the mayor. There were times when I had to reach out for his help. One time a laggard D.C. agency seemed determined to force me into personal bankruptcy. I had begun a cable television business in 1983. I could not persuade government executives to make a decision on a possible satellite dish location in the Southwest, which was under the jurisdiction of the Redevelopment Land Agency ("RLA"), a throwback from the 1960s urban renewal programs. Believing I had exhausted all avenues, I finally called Barry for help. After I described the situation, he got his city administrator Carol Thompson on the telephone. She was also the designated city agent who had the power to sign an order allowing for the installation of the satellite dish. The mayor simply said to Carol, "Tell Doug yes or no, and tell him quickly." In two days, I heard from the RLA that Thompson had given me a yes vote. Not only I was relieved, but I was able to continue with my business. Barry had helped make it happen, and I always would be grateful.

Meanwhile rumors persisted about Barry, who was becoming the peripatetic mayor. The ad-hoc advisory committee that had been established during his first term continued to include myself. Max Berry, David Abramson, Delano Lewis, then head of C&P Telephone Company, Robert Johnson, founder of Black Entertainment Television, two or three others and rounded out what was a sort of kitchen cabinet, which also held periodic off-the-record meetings with the mayor. Once such a gathering, called by Abramson, took place in the mayor's personal office. Barry was expected to arrive at 8:30 that morning. He strode in an hour late, not looking in his most alert state. We were all irritated. As the he sat down at the conference table, Abramson threw down a copy of the Washington Post, which contained a very negative story about how Barry had met a woman on the west coast and, on his own and without much thought, offered her a position in his administration. She appeared to have few qualifications other than his attraction to her. We told him to meet her at the plane and tell her she had no job. It was a fairly embarrassing confrontation. The group then informed him quite succinctly that he had to clean up his act or this group would abandon him politically and personally. As we exited the meeting, Berry was optimistic that we had made a definite impression. Barry assured us that he would change. The next day, we learned the woman had returned to the West Coast. So we were at least successful in that in that effort. For a while, he stayed out of the spotlight. But there were constant rumors about women, drugs and alcohol. Other than an occasional meeting I had my own life to live.

By 1985 my business was faltering and needed my undivided attention. I resigned from the BZA. The next year, my father suddenly suffered a severe stroke, requiring me to travel frequently to Iowa to see him in a nursing home while helping to care for my mother, who had become distraught over his condition. Then in March 1989, while my wife and I were skiing in Vail, I received news my father had passed. I flew to Iowa the next day to help my mother make the necessary funeral arrangements. At my parent's home for two days, the telephone rang around 7:30 a.m. I heard the caller ask "Is this Doug Patton?"

"Yes. Who's calling," I asked. Failing to understand the answer, I asked again. The caller became slightly irritated. "This is the mayor, Marion."

Surprised, I apologized for the confusion. Barry was always a mumbler, and it could be difficult understanding him on the telephone. He told me that he had not seen me around the District Building or in the city and had asked about me. Someone told him that my father had died. He was simply calling to offer condolences. I was touched. Though I never asked, I wondered how he had found my parents' telephone number. His empathy and thoughtfulness always has been remembered.

Later that year, in 1989, I was asked to serve on the Redevelopment Land Authority, a District agency that controlled government owned real estate. It required confirmation by the D.C. Council, particularly the Committee on Economic Development. Its chairperson, Ward 4 Council member Charlene Drew Jarvis, blocked my confirmation. Perhaps as consolation prize, I was named to the Lottery Board. In the interim, Barry had decided to run for a fourth term. Kay McGrath, an old friend who was working for the mayor, called asking whether Nancy and I could come to her house for a small reception that evening. We were leaving the next morning for a vacation in Colorado. Kay persisted, saying she wanted some loyal Barry supporters at the event because she was concerned many of the attendees would pose negative questions. The group of about forty people was more concerned with specific neighborhood issues like traffic, health accessibility, and street crime, however. Barry demonstrated an impressive command of those issues, presenting himself as ready to govern for another four years. On our way home Nancy wondered how someone with such political skills and knowledge could have a drug problem. His mental faculties were extremely sharp. .

After two weeks of skiing, we headed back home to Washington, D.C. During the drive from Dulles International Airport, we heard media reports that Barry had been caught and arrested in an FBI sting at the Vista Hotel in Washington for smoking crack cocaine. The evening took on a somber tone. The rumors had been true.

CHAPTER SEVENTEEN

Back Together Again

THE majority of D.C. residents had assumed Barry would run for re-election in 1990, and win. That was no longer the case. His arrest sent many politically ambitious people racing to file papers to enter the contest. Some folks were urging Fauntroy to mount a bid; he asked Harley Daniels to call me to determine whether I would manage his campaign. I already had my prestigious and highly visible position on the Federal Election Commission. I needed to talk about it with my wife Nancy and consult several close friends. Eventually, however, I decided, at least conditionally, to accept the offer. I sought to obtain a leave of absence without pay from the House of Representatives. I consulted with my immediate boss, Donnald Anderson, who was Clerk of the House. He was very supportive since he personally liked Fauntroy. But ever the political realist, he advised I should get an okay from Speaker Tom Foley; that meant asking for approval from his wife and unofficial chief of staff, Heather Foley. She was supportive but questioned why I wanted to take on the task. Somehow I felt that she didn't believe Fauntroy could win, and felt it was odd that he would leave his comfortable perch in the House of Representatives where he had achieved measurable success, including helping found the Congressional Black Caucus.

After securing approval from those key gatekeepers, I joined Fauntroy's campaign and began duplicating the same tasks I had performed in previous operations: finding a headquarters on I Street between 16th St. NW and 17th St. NW, and shoring up the staff. Fauntroy had resigned from Congress and had begun campaigning, but lacked the fervor he had demonstrated in 1971. I hired my old friend and former partner Bill Hamilton to conduct a poll. I assembled a fundraising framework to raise early money. In two weeks, Hamilton came back with his polling results. The news was not encouraging. Fauntroy had way too many negatives that were impossible to overcome. That reality and the fact that I was having problems with the campaign organization, particularly with a close female friend of Fauntroy's who was countermanding my instructions, caused me to question whether I should remain.

I reached my decision one evening as I was giving Fauntroy a ride home. He confided that he had a malady somewhat akin to tuberculosis and was under heavy medication. Two weeks earlier I had noticed him dozing off during meetings or paying little attention to the substance of discussions. Other than his spouse, no one else was aware of his condition. That made it clear he probably should not have been in the race. I started making my move to leave the operation. He went on to lose his bid. But he became actively involved in the political affairs and citizens campaigns in Africa, including South Africa and the Sudan. In 2011, Fauntroy made many visits to those countries as well as Libya on what was billed as a peace mission; at that time Libya was experiencing a violent civil war. His presence in the country became controversial. (Most baffling, perhaps, were reports in 2014 and 2015 that he either couldn't or wouldn't return to the United States, leaving his wife without proper financial resources. There were fundraisers to help her cover living expenses. As I wrote this book, Fauntroy was living in Dubai.)

I called Heather Foley and Donnald Anderson the next morning. They were very pleased I was returning. I informed Fauntroy as well as my friend Harley Daniels of my decision. I felt sorry for Fauntroy, but I was left with no alternative. The press basically ignored my stepping down, for which I was thankful. Fauntroy's campaign slid downward. I learned later that many of his close supporters also had stepped away after I resigned. They told me that without a professional manager his candidacy was hopeless. I believed it was hopeless in any case.

Sharon Pratt Kelly, a former executive from **PEPCO**, the utility company, had taken the lead in the mayoral race, with her reform rhetoric and agenda. Residents, particularly those in the white community, had been disturbed by events during Barry's final term. They were on the hunt for someone unconnected to that regime and seemed to reject the other candidates, including current and former council members. She had used a broom as a visual symbol of her determination to sweep out old players as well as ineffective policies. The Washington Post liked what it heard and offered her a series of endorsements, which contributed, in no small way, to her victory in the September Primary. She went on to win the general election.

But while she was long on pronouncements during her campaign, she proved unable to govern effectively. She made misstep after misstep. Her cabinet was as inexperienced as she. The District government suffered serious financial woes under her.

Meanwhile, Barry had been convicted and sentenced to six months in federal prison. He served most of his time in a facility in Pennsylvania, but not without controversy. Once he was accused of having oral sex with someone in the visitors' quarters. That resulted in him being moved to another facility. Still, working-class blacks and some of the middle-income residents remained supporters, asserting that the FBI had set him up. That kind of thinking set the stage for a political comeback. African-American Baptist cleric, the Rev. Willie Wilson, members of his congregation and others organized a major caravan that met Barry on the day he was discharged from the prison. He returned to the city in 1992 like the prodigal son. In short order, he plotted his resurrection. He decided to run for a seat in Ward 8, one of the poorest sections of the city. That meant challenging a former ally: four- term incumbent Wilhelmina Rolark. He easily won 70 percent of the vote. At the time, he swore he wasn't interested in returning to the mayoral suite. That was just talk.

Early in 1994, it was apparent Barry was seriously considering a fourth run for mayor. During a dinner with Bill Lucy, I casually mentioned to him that I might support Barry. Since I had not spoken to the mayor for maybe two years, Bill said he would set up a meeting. Our lunch took place at the Washington Hotel on 15th St. NW, across from the U.S. Treasury building. Barry actually appeared on time, which was unusual. Without equivocation, I told him that I would support him and also raise money for his campaign. That pronouncement seemed to put him at ease. Perhaps he thought he would have to persuade me. As we left the luncheon, the Clerk of the House's driver, Roger, an African American, was waiting outside the hotel to take me to a meeting on Capitol Hill. When he saw Barry, he came over to the car introducing himself. I realized, once again, Barry's broad appeal and history. Roger told me he was thankful because Barry, as mayor in the early 1980s, started a summer jobs program for many youth. He received one of those jobs, which kept him out of trouble and provided income that helped him and his family.

Despite Barry's mistakes, there was no denying the contributions he had made to the city as it struggled to assert itself as an independent municipality. Further, he remained a key figure in the story of black political advancement; a story of which I, too, had played a role, albeit at that point unacknowledged, even by Barry. From time to time, when things hadn't gone his way, he had pointed the accusatory finger at white people. I would chuckle, knowing that when the full and objective story of the city's political development was told, white folks would have a major role. They helped train the future leaders, funded campaigns and provided sound advice, in many cases asking for nothing in return, except the opportunity to make the nation's capital a diverse democracy where every person was judged, as Rev. King had pleaded, by the content of his character, not the color of his skin.

After my lunch, I began the task of fulfilling my commitment to bring money to Barry's fourth campaign. It wasn't easy. Many people had lost confidence in him. What's more, the city council had passed a law that limited contributions to one hundred dollars. A lot of telephone calls had to be made to raise any significant amount. I found out after the election there was an independent expenditure committee that was raising lots of money; that effort was not subjected to the $100 financial contribution limit. It also expended a large amount on Barry's behalf. As I continued my fundraising, I brought in an additional $500 in contributions, which I decided late one evening to take to Barry's campaign office on Vermont Avenue NW. I stayed around for a while and, by coincidence, one of the campaign workers marched in with an early edition of the Washington Post.

On the editorial page, the Post had announced its endorsement of John Ray in the Democratic Primary. While the editorial board had featured Ray as the principal being endorsed, it actually also endorsed the incumbent Mayor Sharon Pratt (Kelly). It was somewhat confusing at best. Ray had been a Barry protégé, gaining a seat on the council years earlier. Now, for the second time, he was running against the man who could be characterized as his mentor.

Barry said nothing when he saw the endorsement. His workers seemed very downcast and surprised. I was not surprised at all. The Post was never going to endorse Barry again. His drug arrest had embarrassed the city and disappointed many of his supporters, including the paper's editorial board. I quickly read the editorial. I suggested to the campaign staff that they run-off between 50,000 to 100,000 copies of the endorsement and circulate them door-to-door in Wards 5, 7, and 8, and parts of 4 and 6. I was certain the Post's endorsement which ignored Barry and sought to buffer criticism against Pratt would be roundly trashed by residents in those communities. That would inspire them to come to the polls in droves. Eventually, the campaign hierarchy realized the positive value of my advice, and printed and distributed many copies of the editorial.

On Election Day, Barry won with over 40 percent of the vote, with large pluralities in the black precincts. Pratt received only 13 percent of the vote. His resurrection and restoration appeared complete. I decided to attend the victory celebration at the old convention center. I stood at the back since there were probably about two thousand citizens in attendance. However, I didn't go unnoticed. Mark Plotkin, a local commentator and friend, hollered at me. The crowd was at least 90 to 95 percent African American. I was probably one of the few middle-aged white guys in the room. Many of my black friends came around to congratulate me for supporting Barry. That next week in the *Washington City Paper* under the Loose Lips columnist Ken Cummins mentioned my name as having raised money for Barry. Obviously Plotkin had provided Cummins that background. Later, Cummins became a good friend, although I wasn't thrilled about seeing my name in print. I went home that night happy, knowing Barry had prevailed.

That elation died very quickly, however. Thornell Page, a friend and also a close Barry confidant, thought we should convene a small group of supporters for a private meeting. The word had gone out that the city was in deep financial trouble and that the U.S. House of Representatives, controlled by Republicans, was prepared to install some type of financial entity that would control the District finances. The conservatives also were alarmed that Barry was coming back to power. Page believed Barry wasn't taking the threat seriously enough. I agreed. I called Benny Kass, a well-known lawyer, a neighbor and Barry supporter, hoping he would help solicit influential citizens for the meeting, which was to be held at a hotel on 11th St. NW. Through our collective efforts, we had about twelve to fifteen people in attendance. Emily Durso Vetter, then director of the Hotel Association, arranged for a conference room. Everyone was sworn to secrecy. The main spokesman was James Gibson, who I had known since Barry's initial race in 1978 and who had been the city's first director for planning and development. He also went on to help found the D.C. Agenda and served as its president. The group, working under the auspices of the Federal City Council, addressed fiscal and governance problems facing the District. Gibson had a long record of civic involvement including serving as a director of Equal Opportunity Programs at the Rockefeller Foundation. In short, he was well- respected, thus the perfect individual to lead the discussion. Barry also came. He had inherited a deficit of over $700 million, created during Pratt's watch. Gibson warned that Congress was probably going to pass legislation to create a control board, perhaps similar to what already had been done in Philadelphia. The mayor listened. But I don't think he entirely believed the dire prediction and presentation. We met for a good ninety minutes. Barry said he was going to embark on a strategy to fix the looming deficit. Most of us left the meeting fairly certain that there would be a congressional takeover.

Barry asked Congress for a financial rescue; that seemed a shrewd move. But it backfired. Instead of cash, the feds enacted the District of Columbia Financial Responsibility and Management Assistance Act of 1995, which among other things established a control board. Its five members would be appointed by the president but approved by Congress. President Bill Clinton selected Andrew Brimmer, an African American and a noted economist as the panel's chair; he had been the first black to serve on the Federal Reserve Board. Other members were Steve Harlan, Constance Newman, Joyce Ladner, and Edward Singletary. All, except Harlan, were African Americans. The group assumed control not just of the city's budget but also large swaths of the local government. Decisions made by the mayor and city council could be overruled by the control board. Thus began constant battles between that federally created body and locally elected officials. The fighting went on for the next three years.

It was difficult for an outsider, like myself, to determine who had the real authority. Many times, the lines blurred. What's more, a new personality was beginning to emerge. Chief Financial Officer (CFO) Anthony A. Williams had been appointed by Barry. It was assumed by many, even the mayor perhaps, that Williams would be under the executive's control. That did not happen, however. Congress invested the CFO with unprecedented authority and independence. Consequently, four power entities evolved—Barry, the control board, Williams and the D.C. Council, which occasionally sparred with the other three.

Needless to say, the public was roundly confused. Divisions across the city grew. Barry retained only a few white supporters; they opposed him on nearly every subject. Even the world outside the District of Columbia had grown less tolerant. I remember during this period when I was in Vail, I would refrain from telling tourists on the ski-lifts where I lived. Invariably making any such reference invoked nasty remarks about Barry.

Meanwhile, the Republicans were victorious in the November elections and had assumed total control of Congress. My FEC job would likely end by early January. The incoming Speaker of the House Newt Gingrich always had me in his sights. Fortunately, I found part-time employment with four Democratic House members until I secured a position at the U.S. Agency for International Development (USAID)—the place, ironically, where I had interned in 1965.

Tom Hart, my close friend and a former aide to Senator Robert Byrd, convinced me to set up a small lobbying firm to be named Patton Hart. Tom was a real salesman and already had three clients in tow. Eventually, we found space to rent at O'Connor Hanan, a respected downtown law firm. The political and jurisdictional battles between Barry and the control board began in earnest in 1995. The media was constantly playing up the differences. I stayed away from the fray until a firm from New Jersey approached me about tax lien securitization. It appeared that major commercial buildings and private residential owners were not paying their real estate taxes due to loopholes in the D.C. tax law. Along with the O'Connor Hanan law firm, they retained us. Unfortunately, Barry was losing or had lost much of his power to correct the problem. I approached the staff for the control board with a proposal to raise money by securitizing unpaid taxes. They initially awarded the project to another firm. I became aware that the control board and its staff did not want to work with individuals who had been or were friends of Barry. We eventually acquired most of the work, however.

In late 1995, someone mentioned to me that a commission called the Business Regulatory Reform Commission (BRRC) had been created that year by the city council and the mayor had signed it into law. The commission was established not only to identify legislation to eliminate but also to modify outdated or inconsistent business statutes and regulations. Additionally, it would recommend administrative changes to improve the processing of license and permit applications. In short, it would not only improve the D.C. business environment, but would also help individual citizens navigate the bureaucracy. Its twelve members represented business, industry and government. Several of my friends encouraged me to ask Barry if he would appoint me chairman. I had a private meeting with the mayor in early 1996. He appointed me to the post, but told me there was no District money to help support the commission in its mission. We had a one year sunset provision; that meant we had to move quickly.

Our first meeting was held in August 1996. We had a very cohesive group of leaders, evenly split between blacks and whites. Harold Nelson, an African American, was my very able vice-chairman. Charles Lowery, an aide to then city administrator Michael Rogers, was also available to me. I acquired the services of Mary Wilmot from the Department of Consumer and Regulatory Affairs (DCRA), and hired an outside consultant, Rose Mathews. All were African Americans. We spent countless hours examining statutes, regulations and interviewing agency personnel. We held four public hearings and conducted site visits to Baltimore, Philadelphia, Fairfax County, Virginia, and Prince George's County, Maryland. We were all determined to find the best practices and use them in the District. Our commission had learned through sources that the control board was also in the process of calling for an independent study of the regulatory process in Washington.

Many of the commissioners were incensed; the board's study would be duplicative and unnecessary. We officially asked for a meeting with Chairman Brimmer and the board's staff, who were ensconced in lush and large offices while we were struggling to pay our small incidental expenses. I was accompanied to the meeting by five other commission members, including Madeline Petty, who once had managed the DCRA. She was African American, tough, and at the time headed The Enterprise Foundation. I asked her to take the lead. She immediately quizzed Brimmer about why the board was having a separate, expensive project similar to ours. He was smoothly evasive, but Petty did not let up. She told him we would have the better study and knew more about the changes that needed to be accomplished. After fifteen minutes, we left. Money remained an issue for us. Consequently, I went to Michael Rogers, the city administrator, and asked him for $15,000. I told him I would raise another $20,000 from private entities to secure our small budget of $35,000. A week later, he told me he had squeezed the money from his budget to accommodate me; as promised, I raised the remainder needed for me to pay Mathews, the consultant, as well as cover the cost for producing our report.

In our commission meetings, we had discussed several controversial topics, including rent control. Most of our members thought the whole issue was one of complete mismanagement within the rental offices, which hurt property owners and tenants equally. Someone mentioned that we should go see Eleanor Holmes Norton, D.C's delegate to the U.S. House of Representatives, about the issue. She had succeeded Fauntroy and had taken office in 1991. One of the members, Pedro Alfonso, knew her well and said he would set up a meeting. Commission members Sanford Britt, Nelson, Alfonso and I met with her in her congressional offices one morning. Alfonso posed the rent control issue and our recommendations. He hardly got out his third or fourth sentence when she exploded. She leapt from the sofa, walking briskly to her desk, shouting at our group. She pulled out a drawer while yelling for us to forget about rent control. We quickly excused ourselves. Once we were outside, Alfonso exclaimed, "So much for that. I thought she was going to her desk to get a gun." We all laughed a little nervously. In reality we were glad to be safely out of her environment. Over time, Norton gained the unofficial nickname of "wild woman." I never knew whether she was acting or was for real. But, she had a real reputation for being volatile.

As we were coming to the end of our year's study, and prior to printing the report, I requested another meeting with Mayor Barry, during which I provided a short summary of our work. "Do not hurt my D.C. street vendors," he said to my surprise.

"Marion," I said, "over 75 percent of the street vendors live in Virginia and Maryland. They are not D.C. voters." I also pointed out to him that at least 66 percent of D.C. government workers do not live in the District. This was an amazing turn around in twenty years; he seemed unaware. He simply nodded, obviously surprised by the retort, and I left.

We issued our full report in September 1997, making our deadline. It received favorable reviews. We also found out the study commissioned by the congressionally created financial control board cost over $800,000, most of it going to local D.C. legal firms. Even the Washington Post proclaimed that our study was superior—and it cost only $35,000. Ironically, in three years, I would become a member of one of the legal firms hired by the control board, Holland and Knight. Eventually many of our recommendations were passed by the council and signed by Barry. The Business Regulatory Reform Commission, our little commission, had done its job and quieted initial skeptics.

I continued my lobbying with Tom Hart on Capitol Hill while working on D.C. issues on behalf of two local clients. Barry had announced he was not going to run for reelection. The field for mayor in the 1998 Democratic Primary exploded with candidates. CFO Williams, an African American lawyer and accountant, was being courted by a large and diverse group of residents in what would be the only official draft movement in the city's history.

CHAPTER EIGHTEEN

Bringing in a New Era

BARRY'S win in the 1978 mayor's race was not only a culmination of his rise to power. It was part of the political ascent of many who had been involved in the first city-wide competitive race in 1971. There had emerged an entire tier of political operatives and leaders in the District of Columbia that would change the politics of the city, and, I dare say, the country, over the next twenty years. The list of African Americans who emerged as political leaders was not short and began with my friend and mentor Sterling Tucker, who was elected chairman of the D.C. Council in 1974—just three years after I had helped him get the Rev. Walter Fauntroy elected. Others from that campaign, people who had been trained by my team, who found their way into elective office included Nadine Winters who in 1974 won the seat for the Ward 6 representative; Willie Hardy who became the Ward 7 council member; John Wilson who was elected by Ward 2 residents, while Polly Shackleton became the member from Ward 3. David Clarke, who was white, won in Ward 1 and later would become council chairman. Even Julius Hobson, who ran against Fauntroy as a member of the Statehood Party, won a position in 1974. He soon died and was replaced by Hilda Mason. Harry Thomas Sr. and H.R. Crawford were later elected as ward representatives.

Warren Graves, who in 1971 managed Hobson's campaign, would be appointed to various senior positions in the government. Anita Bonds became head of the local Democratic State Party and eventually an at-large D.C. Council member. The foundation indisputably had been set in 1971 for black political empowerment in the District. Those were impressive people. Ironically, it was white people behind the scenes who taught them the ropes and gave them the tools. It wasn't until 1998 that that initial burst of African American leaders would peter out, making way for a new crop.

The art of city campaigns had taken on a new sophistication. The campaign methods and techniques taught by my crew and adopted by Fauntroy became the template used by subsequent candidates. For example, the targeting of heavy turn-out precincts bolstered by door-to-door voter canvassing, which we had introduced into the local political lexicon, became the norm deployed by many candidates, including Barry. Radio advertising, particularly on stations with predominantly African-American listenership, also was used to reach new voters. Clear concise messaging, in not only literature and radio spots but also in press releases, campaign stationary and mass telephone calls, that had been mastered by us during Fauntroy's campaign was duplicated in Barry's 1978 mayoral bid, and was later replicated by other political aspirants.

None of that was surprising. What was awful for me, however, was John Wilson's suicide on May 13, 1993. He had risen to the post of chairman of the D.C. Council when he hanged himself. I was in Iowa, caring for my ill mother, when my wife, Nancy, called to tell me of his death. My friend Max Berry had called me a few weeks earlier, asking if I would serve as campaign counsel for Wilson's possible 1994 mayoral run. Berry said he asked Wilson about a matter in which I was interested. Wilson said he would help on the condition that I would be his counsel. I said I would.

Frankly, in spite of his sometimes unpredictable temper and chaotic personal life, I thought he would be a good mayor.

I asked Nancy, who was fond of John, to please attend his funeral services, which she did gladly. I learned later that our friend Warren Graves, who was one of the ushers, had spotted her in the huge crowd. He made sure she got a seat in the church.

Even before then, a new group of political candidates arrived not just in Washington but also in other cities across the country. For example, by 1993, there were over 8,000 black elected officials nationally. Of those, over 300 were mayors. Washington, D.C. had definitely been an early trendsetter. But things would soon make another shift—this one away from the Barry style of leadership to a new one exemplified by Williams.

Max Berry called, asking me to come to his office in Georgetown to meet Williams. Throughout my efforts to assist in black empowerment in the District, Berry seemed as much a constant as I had been. We were unofficial partners, believers in the dream, dedicated to its realization. When he called, I never hesitated to respond. A friend of his, and later mine, Marie Drissel, had arranged the meeting. A scheduling conflict prevented my attendance.

Nevertheless, Berry had agreed to the meeting as a personal favor to Drissel. Instead of an hour-long meeting, he and Williams had talked for three to four hours, leaving Berry very enthusiastic. He told me that he had invited Williams back to his office for another meeting that Friday afternoon and wanted me to be there. Berry told Williams about me and also paid me a sincere compliment, noting he wanted my help not only because of our friendship but also because of my extensive campaign background.

From Williams's arrival in 1995, filling the congressionally created independent chief financial officer seat, he and Barry were constantly in the news fighting over the District's finances. Undeniably, Williams had successfully steered the city's finances in a better direction, moving from a nearly seven hundred million deficit to a surplus in fiscal year 1997. The rumblings of a draft movement weren't exactly surprising. Frankly, I initially thought he did not have a chance. Council members Jack Evans, Kevin Chavous and Harold Brazil were all seeking the nomination. I had even given them campaign contributions without really backing any of them. But Williams had something none of them had. He inspired voters from all sections of the city, who were so excited about him, they were launching the District's first and only legitimate draft movement.

At the meeting, the first question I asked Williams was "Why do you want to be mayor?" It is a routine question political consultants pose to every type of candidate. Many candidates don't provide good answers. I remembered commentator Roger Mudd asking the late Senator Edward Kennedy that same question when he was challenging Carter for the presidency in 1979. Kennedy had bungled his answer, failing to provide a clear and concise reason.

Williams gave a sufficient, though not overpowering, answer. After about a half hour, he and Berry left for another session in an adjacent conference room. Berry asked me to join but made clear it was off-the-record. About a dozen individuals were in attendance including Max Brown, Marie Drissel, Paul Savage and others from across the city, who were leaders of the draft committee. Some were a tad uneasy about my presence, especially since they had been told by Berry that I had not officially come on board in support of Williams. But after an hour, I was brought into the fold, self-tasked with helping to find a campaign headquarters and assist in fundraising. It was already June, the primary was in September. We had to raise money quickly. We assembled an extensive group of fundraisers holding weekly meetings in my law office. Most of the finance group was essentially new to the D.C. political scene as far as political contributions were concerned. The usual suspects were already locked in with other candidates. With Max Berry as chair of the finance group, however, we had assembled a formidable cross-section of the city. We had a few long time citizens like H.R. Crawford, Valerie Pinson, Gwendolyn Hemphill and Peggy Cooper Cafritz. But we also had newer individuals like Sandy McCall, Joe Moravec, Michael Allen, Rod Heller and John Richardson. All were dedicated to raising money to get William selected.

Through my real estate friend Duke Brannock, I found a headquarters at 17th St. NW and I St. NW in a basement. A campaign staff was quickly assembled. We raised considerable funds but almost 25 percent of it came over the transom without solicitation. The citizens were anxious for a change. Williams won handily with over 50 percent of the vote in the six-candidate Democratic primary. In the November general election, he won by a 2 to 1 margin. Other than raising money and providing general campaign advice, I kept apart from the operation of the campaign. I paid particular attention to the financial management. Additionally, we were fortunate in that the candidate's wife, Diane, was a very able accountant as well as a shrewd judge of people. She was great to have on the team.

Williams' impressive victory was a distinct break from the past—somewhat identical to Barry's in 1978, when he won against Walter Washington and Sterling Tucker. Clearly voters wanted change, since Williams also beat out several council members in the primary.

We had a very smooth inauguration which was ably handled by Robert Jones. A D.C. political operative, we called him Bilko after that 1950s television protagonist Sergeant Bilko, played by Phil Silvers. Like that character, Jones could procure anything you wanted. No one dared asked how he did what he did. He recruited several of his friends who all had done many advances for the Clinton White House, so the logistics were made easier by experienced people like Joe Ruffin and James Day, both African Americans, and a Latino, Gus West. The city had come a long way since my first experience in 1971 during the Fauntroy race. The many political campaigns in almost thirty years had experienced waves of black and other minority operatives, a very healthy diversification.

After Williams was sworn into office, many of my campaign friends like Berry and Richardson urged me to take a position in the administration. I had mixed emotions, but I wanted Williams to succeed and the District government to improve. Since I had performed in several roles—the Board of Zoning Adjustment, the D.C. Lottery Board, and the BRCC—all under Barry—I knew a fair amount about the internal workings of government. I knew, for example, that one should combine the offices of planning under a strong deputy mayor for economic development. So, I approached Williams privately telling him of my interest in that position. Almost simultaneously, the hiring partner at Holland and Knight approached me informally about possibly joining their firm.

In early January, Williams announced many of his new appointees at a press conference. Unfortunately, the angle of a photograph of the new staff that appeared on the front page of the Washington Post made it appear that that most of the appointees were white. That, of course, was not the case. I knew many, if not all, of the new staff, except for his new Chief of Staff, Reba Pittman, an African American. My friend Warren Graves was head of the inter-governmental affairs group. Still, there was an outcry from many in the black community. I waited almost two weeks to hear back from Williams regarding my own appointment. I knew his supporters desired an experienced individual in his administration who knew something about governance. When I sat down with him in his private office I explained that I needed to know one way or another whether he wanted me in his administration. He paused slightly and, aware of the recent photograph in the Post, I put forth the following question and statement. "Mayor, if it's because I am white and you obviously are concerned about too many whites in your administration, I will offer that I probably have more black friends in this city than you do." Without missing a beat, he replied, "Well, that is very low bar." We both laughed. Then, he said, "Let's do it. Start when you are ready." With that, I went to work the next week. I was relieved, and appreciated Williams's humor. I had to move fast. I made it clear I only wanted to be a transition deputy mayor, stating that I would serve for only six months. I actually stayed for about eight months.

When I arrived at my offices at 441 Fourth Street NW, then the seat of the government, things were in an absolute mess: Old furniture and outdated files contributed to the almost unbearable working conditions. I hired a staff immediately with African Americans such as Rose Lindsay and Kim Calvin as my two executive assistants. I also brought in Rose Mathews to serve as communications director; I liked her work at the Business Regulatory Reform Commission (BRRC). All the rest of the staff members were African Americans—except for Lindsey Williams, who was in charge of land use, and Mary Rudolph, my internal counsel whom I had known at the city council. I immediately contracted to have the offices renovated and to have different furniture brought in; photographs of Washington were placed on the walls. If you want new businesses to come to the District, you at least have to look professional I told my colleagues and staff. I also thought it was important for African Americans, who were District residents, to have priority for the positions.

I decided to have an informal group of advisors, something of a sub-cabinet to meet every two weeks. It was a racially mixed group that provided unfiltered advice about the city, both on development and political issues. Almost the entire group consisted of people I knew from past political campaigns and positions I had held in the city. Two members of the advisory group, Lloyd Smith and Carolyn Lewis, both African Americans, were invaluable. (Years later, I would attend both their funerals; the crowds reflected the respect that many in the city held for them. They were pillars of their communities and great assets to the District.)

Often I was in the office by 7:30 in the morning and stayed as late as 8:00 in the evening. A driver picked me up in the morning, but I usually took a cab home at night. The Williams administration sent the message that "We are open for business and the operation of D.C. government is changing." I reached out to John Tydings, then- director of the Greater Washington Board of Trade, as well as the D.C. Chamber of Commerce and the District of Columbia Building Industry Association. With the assistance of Dennis Archer then-Mayor of Detroit, we convinced Mayor Williams to attend the International Council of Shopping Centers (ICSC) in Las Vegas. The event was always well attended by the retail real estate industry. Also, all the major real estate developers from throughout the United States often attended. It would be the first time the mayor of Washington, D.C., or any of its leaders actually attended the event.

Our mission was simple: convince developers and the industry to locate in Washington. While at the ICSC meeting, we attempted to meet with the major developers as well as the different retail entities like Home Depot, Staples, and Kmart. We had mixed success partly because Washington was not perceived as a good market. I am sure there were racial reasons for that. We did succeed in getting a developer who was aligned with Kmart to come to the city and explore options. I felt like a beggar with a tin cup trying to persuade interested parties to meet with Mayor Williams.

We had many projects on the drawing board for which I was responsible. One of my main tasks was to recruit experienced individuals to serve on the National Capital Revitalization Commission (NCRC). The Commission had been created by Congress to promote economic development in the city. It was composed of seven members, three of whom were to be chosen by the president. I worked almost daily with Robert Nash, the head of White House personnel, who was African American. We vetted many persons until we came up with an acceptable list. Unfortunately, after I left, two crucial members had to be replaced: Peggy Richardson, a former IRS Commissioner and a tax expert, as well as Joe Moravec, a commercial real estate broker well versed in D.C. land matters.

Richardson's firm believed she would have a legal conflict and Moravec was rejected by Council member Charlene Jarvis, who continued to serve as chair of the Committee on Economic Development. I really never knew why she was against him. Both were major losses and probably had much to do with the future problems and deficiencies of NCRC.

There were many important projects that came to fruition during my short stay, and two are worth mentioning. I had barely settled in my office when I received word that a Fresh Fields (later renamed Whole Foods), was interested in locating store at 15th St. NW and P St. NW., a short block from the Studio Theater where my wife was on the board of directors. I knew the area well. I was told they were about to cancel their plan, which was their first entrée into the District. The typical government bureaucracy had posed too many barriers. I immediately sought the C.E.O. Chris Hitt, calling him directly and requesting a meeting. He was located in suburban Maryland; I committed to going to his headquarters. Lindsey Williams, my expert on land use, accompanied me. I remember he wore a long ponytail, although he was probably in his late forties or early fifties. We jelled immediately and I told him that the Williams administration would do everything in our power to make sure Fresh Fields had a home at that location. He seemed impressed by our sincerity. Within a short time, the company reconsidered, becoming an anchor for the area while attracting many new businesses and new residents.

The second achievement was not as quick to materialize, but was ultimately successful. I had become good friends with Americo "Migo" Miconi, the chief clerk of the D.C. House Subcommittee on Appropriations. He was sometimes called the "Mayor" because of the tremendous power he possessed over District financial matters on Capitol Hill. Bob Jones, who also was doing some special assignments for my office was also a friend of Miconi's. We would meet most weeks for drinks in the evenings either at Morton's or Smith and Wolinsky's, two popular restaurants. On one occasion, we scratched out on a paper napkin how we could finance a metro stop on New York Ave. NE. We came up with a 1/3-1/3-1/3 proposition. One third would come from a House/Senate Appropriation; one third from the federal government; and one-third from major real estate owners along the corridor where the stop would be located. The last third would be the most difficult, but it was eventually achieved. Out of that threesome meeting, the New York Avenue stop eventually became a reality. A major part of it was that the three of us trusted each other, and knew we could get it accomplished.

By early October, feeling burned out, I was ready to move on. Certain other officials in the Williams administration were causing me problems. Also, though maybe not as important, the fall hunting season would soon be starting in the Midwest. Since I had been a young teenager, I had been a devoted bird hunter, especially the Chinese ring-tailed pheasant, which was abundant in Iowa. I had had conversations with the mayor about me acting as a consultant to the NCRC once I left the District government. I wanted to be certain it would be operational; I agreed with him on a six-month consultancy at $10,000 per month. I then announced my departure and was waiting in my office for my successor to hammer out the details of the consultancy. The mayor's chief of staff subsequently asked to see me. In a terse tone, he told me that the consultancy would not happen. I looked at him somewhat in disbelief. While I had helped Abdusalom Omer secure his position; I had grown to distrust him. I cannot remember all the exact details, but by the time he left my office, I remember my Irish anger had reached full throttle. I threw my cell phone against the wall, shattering it. Like most things in the city, the episode made its rounds in the D.C. gossip world. A basic agreement had been broken, in my opinion, placing me in an unfavorable position. Most importantly, I did not believe NCRC ultimately would be successful. My prediction eventually came true. The day after that encounter with Omer, I took off for the Midwest with my dog, Mookie, in my newly leased Ford Explorer. I couldn't wait to go hunting.

When that trip ended, I decided in early 2000 to join the Holland and Knight Law firm. I was not sure how I would do economically in a large firm. Still, I took the plunge. I was impressed with Dick Dunnels, the hiring partner, as well as some of the other partners. I almost immediately met Rod Woodson, an African American who was also serving as the chairman of the Alcoholic Beverage Control Board (ABC). I had helped affirm him as the nominee for Marie Drissel, who was head of the D.C. Boards and Commissions. There were a few other African Americans in the firm, including one who became the executive partner in the Washington office. I thought this was notable since twenty years earlier there were almost no blacks in such major firms.

My clients, including the Charter School Development Corporation headed by my friend Richard Thompson, were referrals. Their main concern was with the development corporation trying to utilize unused government properties to locate their schools. It would appear to be an easy issue; but it wasn't. Many entities, including the teachers' unions and the entrenched school bureaucracy, were opposed for obvious reasons. It was going to shake up the status quo, which was not in the least concerned with the plight of black children in the District.

I worked at setting up a meeting with Williams, since he was the only person I could legally lobby in the administration. He was the only person higher than me when I was deputy mayor. I had obtained a legal opinion from the corporation counsel's ethics office as well as one from my private attorney Robert Krasne, who was at the Williams and Connolly law firm. They said, specifically, I had to wait one year before I could effectively lobby other agencies and individuals in the executive branch.

We had the meeting with the mayor in his private office in June 2000. His educational advisor was present as well as another aide. A week later, I received a telephone call from my former assistant Rose Lindsay, asking me if I was aware that the *Washington City Paper* was going to run an article critical of me related to a meeting I had had with an individual from my former deputy mayor's office. It was untrue, I told her. Then, I remembered that meeting with the mayor on surplus properties. There was a person whom I did not know. I had assumed he was simply an aide, but in fact must have been from that office. I had been set up. I called the *City Paper*'s editor, Eric Wemple, with whom I had had a cordial relationship, explaining the specifics to him. I also subtly implied that I would pursue legal action against the paper if the story appeared. "There is no need to do that," he replied. He had determined, I guess, the paper was being used as a tool by someone high in the Williams administration. The story never ran.

Later, I discovered the person who tried to set me up by sending that innocent unsuspecting individual from my former office. I kept my distance after that incident, lobbying mostly the federal government and

Congress. I was pleasantly surprised at the friendly reception I received from Republican legislators, because that situation had been resolved and I didn't have any ethical conflicts.

In 2002, Williams was mounting a reelection campaign, and officials from that operation were busy raising money. I kept away from the campaign, although Nancy and I occasionally had dinner with the mayor and his wife. My friends, Max Berry, in particular, were urging me to get involved. Some people assumed I was on the outs with the Williams administration. I wasn't sure that was the case. Then over lunch Gwen Hemphill, who was co-chair of the mayor's campaign, implored me to be the counsel. I said the only way I would accept the position was if the mayor asked me personally. We arranged to meet for lunch at the Four Seasons restaurant in Georgetown. The day before the meeting, Gwen called telling me that the Williams was anxious that I would reject his offer. I laughed. "Do not worry, I will accept the offer if he makes it," I assured her. As we sat down for lunch, he and I exchanged small talk and the usual pleasantries. Then the Williams broached the subject somewhat formally, "Doug, I would be honored if you would be my campaign counsel." I was a little surprised at his formality but I readily said, "Of course, Mayor." He then relaxed and we had a great lunch.

Unfortunately, it was not going to be an easy ride. I attended some of the organizational meetings of the campaign, usually chaired by Hemphill. The campaign manager was Charles Duncan, who previously worked in the Clinton White House. I knew him but not well. He had plenty of campaign experience and had worked as executive assistant to U.S. Department of Agriculture Secretary Mike Epsy. But on July 15, all hell broke loose.

Dorothy Brizill, executive director of DC Watch, a local and respected government watchdog group, filed a formal complaint with the D.C. Board of Elections and Ethics, alleging that petitions signed and filed by the Williams campaign were invalid and fraudulent. A lawyer I knew to be really the only person with experience in this area was Vincent Mark Policy, who initially rejected my request to help us deal with the problem. He could be an excellent advocate for his clients' causes but he also could cause heartburn in others. Somewhat pugnacious, with an aggressive manner and focused intensity, he often didn't let go of an issue. I thought him perfect for our challenge. He later agreed to provide assistance. Meanwhile, I assembled a group of ten to twelve volunteers to examine all the signatures on the petitions. While there were close to 10,000 signatures on the petitions (only 2,000 were legally required), it was readily evident that many were forgeries; there were names of television stars, celebrities like Martha Stewart, and cartoon characters like Mickey Mouse. We still had over the requisite 2,000 signatures, which were presented to the Board of Elections and Ethics during a two-day hearing. Nonetheless, the board ruled against us. Its chairman was an attorney named Benjamin Wilson, who I found a bit too pompous for his role. Not only was the Williams campaign fined $277,000, the mayor was thrown off the Democratic primary ballot. We appealed to the D.C. Superior Court but lost.

The mayor appointed a new manager, Ted Carter, who I approved of, as did Berry and Williams' wife Diane. There were external rumblings about Gwen Hemphill and her role as the executive director of the Washington Teachers Union (WTU). She resigned from the campaign quietly in early October, almost at the same time the union demanded her resignation. Eventually, it was disclosed that she, along with President Barbara Bullock and the organization's treasurer, had embezzled over $5 million from the union. They had purchased expensive items like automobiles, furs, silverware and televisions to maintain their lifestyle. Gwen Hemphill was sentenced to eleven years for her infractions. Here was a black woman I had known since 1971, who was now a convicted felon.

Williams, with Carter's help, mounted an aggressive write-in campaign. It succeeded, with the mayor receiving over 60 percent of the vote; his only opposition was the Rev. Willie Wilson, who had been successful in helping to resurrect Barry's political career and had fought the control board, including Williams. In the general election, Williams easily beat Republican Carol Schwartz.

It had been a long tough election year. After, I went pheasant hunting in the Midwest.

CHAPTER NINETEEN

A Personal Crisis

IN early 2003, Nancy and I were deeply involved in construction of our new home in Colorado. To be honest, she was the person paying most of the attention to building details. I took time for my yearly physical examination with internist Dr. Linda Yau. A few days later, she reported I was in excellent health, except my P.S.A. (Prostate-Specific Antigen) screening test for prostate cancer had spiked from a normal of 2.0 to a 3.1. She advised that I see my urologist and longtime friend, Dr. Ian Spence. I had known him since 1966, when I used to call on him as a salesman or "detail man" for Easton Laboratories. He was one of many white physicians located in the I St. NW corridor. I made an appointment.

Dr. Spence recommended I have P.S.A. test through a different laboratory. That score was even higher at 3.4. He urged a biopsy. From my days at Eaton, I was very familiar with the functions of the prostate and aware of various medications. Without saying anything to anyone, I suspected what would be the outcome. There was a sort of perfunctory quality about how I went about following the doctor's recommendation for analysis.

A week later, I scheduled the procedure with Edward Dunne, a junior partner in his practice. I had heard it likely would be unpleasant, a tad painful, but I was given a sedative to reduce that affect. Dr. Dunne took "ten bites" or samples from all quadrants of the prostate. The last two were extremely painful. I remember wishing at the time that I had a bullet to bite down on, like the cowboys did in those old western movies. Perhaps I also should have had a shot of Jack Daniels whiskey. After the procedure, I intuitively knew my days of being cancer free had come to an end.

I received confirmation two days later. Dr. Dunne telephoned my downtown office. The biopsy test was positive. I had cancer. I burst into tears. Jackie, my African-American assistant, rushed in from the outer office, fearful that I had heard something tragic about my wife. She gave me a giant bear hug. I eventually regained my composure. I called Nancy, and then my sister in Waterloo, Iowa. It's curious how one reaches out to siblings in times of stress.

I had somewhat regained my composure when Nancy and I went to Dr. Dunne's office where he gave us the bad news together. He went right into the subject: Of the ten bites, he had taken, I had a Gleason score of seven on two of the samples and a six on two others. Gleason is a rating system of five to ten, reflecting the severity of the cancer. Sevens obviously is very serious; if you have eights, it probably means you should start writing your will.

I had cancer on four of the ten bites. Four more, Dr. Dunne told me, were in the precancerous stage. What does that I mean, I asked. Are you saying that four people are already on the train and four more are on the railroad platform waiting to board? Chuckling, he said "That is a perfect analogy. You have put it in perfect context."

He advised surgery as quickly as possible because he believed the cancer was very aggressive. He also said that if I used other forms of treatment, like the seed method, for example, and those methods proved unsuccessful, there was a risk of not being able to remove the prostate because over time, it becomes very hard, almost like stone. After listening to the explanation and having our many questions answered, Nancy and I agreed that surgery was the way to proceed. I did ask Dunne if I could get a second opinion. Without hesitation, he encouraged me to conduct additional research.

I went to see Dr. John Lynch in Georgetown. After examination and consultation, he offered the same opinion as Dr. Dunne. He also volunteered that if he needed similar surgery, he would go to my urologist. That was reassuring.

I remember calling Dr. Spence asking him if I could put off the operation until August when my law practice was less intense. There was a pause after I asked the question. "Doug," he said, "you cannot wait that long." That blunt response helped me understand the seriousness of my case.

Dunne had given me a large book about prostate cancer. It had stories about famous people who had had the surgery and survived. One of those people was a boyhood hero, Stan Musial, who played with the St Louis Cardinals. Not every case was a success story. There were tragedies: Telly Savalas, the actor who was famous for his lead role in the Kojak television crime drama, had put off his surgery and lost his life. I also consulted two of my friends who had battled prostate cancer. I spoke with Marion Barry, who had surgery in 1995, soon after beginning his fourth term as mayor. He and I had several private talks during which he shared information about his procedure. Finally, I scheduled my surgery for April, six weeks after the biopsy.

After two nights in Sibley Hospital in Northwest Washington, I went home to recover. Other than the inconvenience of a catheter, the pain and discomfort were tolerable. My client and friend Tim Chapman, Max Brown from the Williams campaign and Rod Woodson from my law firm, visited me at my home on the patio. I had confided in Woodson and Lloyd Jordan, two African Americans at the firm, who seized the opportunity to alert members of his fraternity about the need to be tested for prostate cancer. There is, actually, a greater incidence of the disease in black males.

The operation certainly proved to be the proverbial wakeup call to better direct my life and not to waste unnecessary time, especially in my professional career. I went back to the legal firm after about five weeks away. But on my first day back, by two o'clock in the afternoon, I was already very tired. I realized then that I was overly aggressive in trying to return to work. I went home and stayed there for another week.

By Christmas, our new home in Colorado was complete. I certainly considered myself a very lucky man. Dr. Lynch had mentioned that I should be very thankful that Dr. Yau sent up a red flag. Many internists would have dismissed the spike in the PSA because I was growing older. "Send her flowers," he told me. "You owe her."

CHAPTER TWENTY

Rock Solid?

JIM Hudson, an African-American attorney and friend, approached me in the summer of 2005 about supporting Adrian M. Fenty, the black Ward 4 councilman in Washington, D.C. The year earlier, however, I had mostly sworn off local elections, deciding instead to give national politics my attention. After all, it had been my concern about the state of the nation following the assassination of President John F. Kennedy that had lead me into the murky field, filled with wild and whacky characters, plenty of heart burn and barrages of profanity, including some of my own.

Consequently, I had raised money for John Kerry in his 2004 presidential bid. I brought more than $100,000 to the table. I thought it was a tidy sum. But I found out differently when I went to the convention in Boston that July. The Democratic National Committee, through the Kerry campaign, had given me only two lower level passes. National elections now demanded millions of dollars for a donor to appear on the radar. Times certainly had changed since my days working for Harold Hughes and Hubert Humphrey. Money was drowning out the voice of average voters.

In the local District of Columbia elections, I was informally helping Marie Johns, an African-American executive, who had been at Verizon; she had decided to run for mayor. I thought she had the experience and understanding of the city to do well. But I liked Hudson and told him I would meet with Fenty, who I personally liked. I met with them two or three times, giving them advice on fundraising in the District. We usually met at the Equinox restaurant on Connecticut Ave., about a block from the White House. At the same time, Linda Cropp, the sitting African-American chairperson of the city council was trying to recruit me into her mayoral campaign. She was the choice of the Washington political establishment, both white and black. I felt, however, that she had an uphill battle. I admired Fenty's determination and stamina and thought he could win. Johns' numbers in the polls were stagnant. About a month before the September primary, I politely told her I was going to help Fenty. I held a fundraising luncheon for him at my law office, collecting about $18,000. He performed well during that event, answering tough questions from the attendees. The Democratic Primary was a clear victory; he won all 142 precincts in the city and nearly repeated that unprecedented feat in the November general election, winning 89% of the vote.

Fenty's win was confirmation that District residents were satisfied with the change of politics and direction that had been ushered in by Williams. While he had endorsed Council Chair Linda Cropp, voters didn't share his view. Fenty not only was prepared to continue the course of government changes and socio-economic improvements instigated by Williams, he also displayed enormous energy and determination to shake up the bureaucracy. He was one of a class of young African-American leaders coming to the national stage, including Newark, New Jersey's Cory Booker.

During his term we met occasionally. Fenty was always cordial and responsive. I had access to other department directors, not unlike during the Williams administration. But, mid-way through his first term, some District citizens, particularly African Americans, began complaining that he was arrogant and insensitive to their concerns. The criticism persisted and was coupled with several missteps by Fenty's administration, including allegedly helping fraternity brothers on real estate deals in the city—not that other politicos hadn't done the same. Those disclosures and complaints weakened Fenty politically. He seemed impervious to the anger and animosity. It didn't help that his attorney general, Peter Nickles, who performed more like his personal counsel and political confidant, was equally brash and extremely unpopular. I could feel Fenty losing favor and the momentum building against him. Things may have taken a turn for the worst when he hired Michelle Rhee, a Korean American, as the first chancellor of the D.C. Public Schools, after the council had approved his request to take over the public education system. Her aggressive style and strong opinions constantly irritated many parents. I tended to agree with her objectives, but while her reform measures were sorely needed, they were seen by many as far too drastic and sharp-edged.

By then, however, I had returned to the national political stage. In 2008, Hudson extended the invitation to me to meet U.S. Senator Barack Obama, who, as an Illinois politician, had made a splash nationally four years earlier when he presented a speech at the National Democratic Convention. A group of fifteen people was expected to gather. The Massachusetts Ave. NW meeting room near Capitol Hill had the feel one of those low-budget campaign offices I had occupied hundreds of times over the years as a political operative and consultant. Drab with beige-colored walls, it flaunted attic-style furniture. The room would have been suitable, except the group mushroomed well beyond the anticipated fifteen. The majority in attendance were young blacks I had known for years, some of whom I had helped get elected. Then-at-large D.C. Council member Kwame Brown, who had his eyes on the chairmanship of the legislature, walked up to me and challenged my local allegiance: "I heard you're trying to get someone to run against me," he said menacingly. A man not more than five feet five inches tall has difficulty intimidating any one other than a midget. Further, I had faced more dangerous situations and individuals than he throughout my career in politics. Somewhat surprised by his approach, I jokingly replied "No Kwame, I am thinking of running against you myself. " He seemed startled by my response He turned and walked away, unsure whether I was joking. I was, of course. Interestingly, within a few years he would plead guilty to federal felony bank fraud and would be forced to resign.

Mayor Fenty's finance team—Darryl Wiggins, who was the campaign's treasurer and John Falcicchio, his chief fundraiser, also were at the Hudson meeting. Falcicchio was commonly called "Johnny Business" for his seriousness and attention to the financial operations. Frank White, a wealthy black business man, along with prominent white developers Chris Donatelli and Tim Chapman rounded out the group. It was crowded, hot and humid; I thought to myself "I am too old for this."

Obama finally arrived. Wearing a dark suit, he personified smooth and cool—not a hint of perspiration. His charisma was thick; his mere presence commanded attention. A room that had been filled with chatter moments earlier suddenly fell silent. After he made a few remarks, Hudson asked if there were any questions. There was an awkward pause. I raised my hand, hoping to break the ice and relax the crowd. I am a native Iowan, I told him, dropping names of a few of my friends working in his Des Moines office. He nodded, acting as if he knew the individuals I mentioned. He was a politician; they possess the skills not unlike those of an actor.

"How do you intend to win the Iowa Caucus?" I asked. "And, how will you handle the gun issue? Even when you win you'll have to deal with it in the general election. Iowans are hunting advocates."

Obama paused. Then, he explained he had performed well in Southern Illinois in his Senate bid. He thought Iowa demographically had the same sort of folks. He rambled a bit more, probably uncertain his answer was satisfactory. Then, he stated emphatically, "Don't worry, I am not going to take away your guns." He smiled. He thought I was a gun advocate and missed the thrust of my query. Further, he was wrong about the similarities between Southern Illinois and Iowa. I knew the state—and its politics.

While that encounter initially left me wondering, I grew more confident as his campaign proceeded. A few people thought me mad, but his superior organization persuaded me. Further, he had hard working people, like Paul Tewes, Mitch Stewart, and Emily Parcell, who knew Iowa and knew how to organize for a caucus. A former community organizer, Obama also knew how to build from the ground up. Hillary Clinton, the other Democratic contender, may have had a very able head in Iowa in Teresa Vilmain, but her organization was too top-heavy, filled with leftovers from President Bill Clinton's campaigns. Her operation was over-programmed and far too self-assured for Iowans. Hillary Clinton thought, or gave the impression, she was the presumptive nominee of the Democratic Party.

Oddly, while 1970s brought decentralized politics to Iowa, by the time Obama arrived, the state seemed to have come full circle. Activity was dominated by external forces, most often from Washington D.C. In his case, however, strings were being pulled from Chicago. Further, campaign workers weren't seasonal employees; they had become year-round operatives. And the variety of paid positions exploded: fundraisers, public relations and public affairs individuals, ward and precinct organizers, advance people, pollsters, and wordsmiths were all dependent on money raised incessantly throughout the country. Campaigns had become big business. The state caucus system may have changed, but most people didn't think Iowa had. They believe it as some white pristine state incapable of embracing an African American. It's true the state faced a unique situation in 2008 with a black and a woman running to become president of the United States.

Historically a woman had never won any party nomination for the top slot. Sarah Palin and Geraldine Ferraro were both vice presidential candidates. Shirley Chisholm, an African American from New York, ran for president. If past was prologue, there wasn't a chance in hell that Clinton would get the party nomination. With the choice in the 2008 election between a white woman and a black man, most bets were on the former.

After the meeting on Capitol Hill with Obama, I raised some funds for his campaign, mostly from personal friends. I recall I gave the maximum legally allowable over the course of his campaign.

I was at my home in Vail the night of the Iowa Caucus, snow was falling and coyote's were yelping. Colorado had been a sort of escape for me from the normal bustle of urban life and political activities. But on that cold January night in 2008, politics permeated everything. I paced the hall between the large screen television in the living room and the flat screen in the kitchen, watching CNN's and Fox News' coverage of the Iowa caucus. I had briefly contemplated going to Iowa to work for Obama's campaign. Despite my constant pacing, which suggested anxiety, I always believed Obama would win Iowa. He received almost 38 percent of the vote with John Edwards barely beating out Hillary Clinton for second. It was invigorating for me to have played a small role in his victory, and seeing him win was extremely satisfying. The state and the country had traveled a great distance since 1963. And, so had I.

EPILOGUE

IT now has been close to seventy-five years since I started my life as a rawboned farm boy from rural Winthrop, Iowa, when outdoor privies were the norm. During my more than five decades in politics, I have made significant sacrifices. All of them were absolutely worth it. Frankly, in the beginning, my intention was to make a minor contribution, giving my respect to President John F. Kennedy, a leader I admired and who inspired a nation in his inaugural speech in 1961 to ask not what the country could do for us but what we could do for the country. With his assassination those words gained greater significance for me, fueling my commitment to a new America. That personal mission began as an incremental involvement, one step at a time, evolved into pursuit of political equality and justice—hallmarks of Kennedy's life and the lives of others like the Rev. Martin Luther King Jr. It wasn't enough, I came to realize, to simply work in my own backyard to help advance the vocations and avocations of my friends—my white friends. Securing a better America meant I had to branch out into the larger world, touching and learning about people, who were fellow Americans but whose history and culture were foreign to me. Thus it was that I connected with African Americans, determined to expand their involvement in America's Democracy.

I was successful in helping to affect a second wave of black empowerment in the country. The First Wave, which often is overlooked, was the great advancement made by blacks just after the Civil War. During the Reconstruction Era, some former slaves or children of slaves gained a foothold in politics and in the government. Those gains were snatched away, particularly in the south by passage of discriminating Jim Crow laws.

But as my story demonstrates, I was not alone in my determination that the Second Wave would not replicate the first one. There were many whites who helped create the framework and foundation for a sustained political advancement of blacks. We were all behind the scenes, which did not diminish in any way our impact and influence. Through training sessions conducted by people like myself, and those I mentioned in this book, through fundraising events and media campaigns created to cast African Americans in a positive and impressive light, the number of elected black leaders expanded. That achievement and its attending narrative may have not been realized without a coalition of whites and blacks working together.

Lost in the contemporary telling of America's history is the fact that even during its most horrific history, during the days of intense Southern segregation and Northern discrimination against blacks, there was a strong, seemingly invincible group of whites and blacks working on behalf of the country's common good. Too often whites have been placed in the backrooms or carted out to the front porch to be excoriated as individuals who blocked black progress. Certainly there were many who did. But I, along with others with whom I worked, and even more I will never have known, were not among them. We rolled up our sleeves, sometimes endangered our lives and delayed accumulation of wealth to arrive at today's America where African Americans are playing a major role in the political and economic life of the United States. Those successful leaders are far too many to name. I certainly was involved with the first tier of individuals including Walter Fauntroy, Marion Barry, and John Wilson, among others.

Just as the work in which I and others engaged helped blacks secure the right to participate in the democratic process, it also afforded them the right to fail. I would be remiss if I did not admit my disappointment in the road taken by some. The sons of former Secretary of Commerce Ronald

Brown and the Rev. Jesse Jackson were convicted of crimes—crimes that reflected poorly on them but also injured the dreams and aspirations of other African Americans they were elected to serve. Former New Orleans Mayor Ray Nagin, U.S. Rep. William Jefferson and former Prince George's County Executive Jack Johnson also engaged in illegal actions that caused them to draw prison terms.

While I was troubled by these misdeeds, the political landscape always has been sprinkled with white politicians who have been involved in unethical and questionable behaviors. I have known some personally: Congressman Ed Mezvinsky of Iowa, Frank Thompson of New Jersey and Dan Rostenkowski of Illinois. Not only did some betray the public trust, they demonstrated a raw callousness, damaging their personal friendships and ruining relationships with their supporters.

Over the last half century, some voters and citizens as well as the staff of elected officials have treated them like deities, worshiping the very ground they walk on. Long terms in office may have exacerbated the problem. Despite, those inglorious stories, there remains much to celebrate about the work that I and others did to expand democracy and advance black political empowerment.

The back rooms of the political establishment, the places where the campaigns are designed and implemented, continue to be mostly populated by people who look like me, however. At the national level, there is a dearth of African American political operatives. Even in President Barack Obama's 2008 and 2012 campaigns there were only a few black political advisors, like Jim Hudson, for example. Perhaps this could be attributed to the notion that few people see the behind-the-scenes work as glamorous. It is tough, demanding and may offer little pay. Still, a more extensive and stronger network must be developed.

That fact becomes even more crucial for Hispanics, who are becoming the largest ethnic minority in the United States, shaping the political dynamics and augmenting the cultural narrative of the nation. Asians, to a lesser extent, also are expected to flex their political muscle. Interestingly, neither population has substantial political organizing experience—although there are nonprofit and special interest groups that have had an impact on their behalf at the state and local levels. Not many Hispanics have arrived on the national stage. Loretta Sanchez of California, Marco Rubio and Julian Castro, who became President Barack Obama's head of the U.S. Department of Housing and Urban Development, are among those that provide inspiration. But inspiration alone will not ensure the kind of political diversity we need and desire in America.

White folks, those with the deep political roots and skills, must continue to help achieve that goal. There has always been a cadre of whites doing that. I was not even aware until I conducted research for this book of the importance of people in my home state to the operation of the Underground Railroad. While not as treacherous as that experienced by slaves who sought to escape, my life's narrative clearly involves its own efforts to break away from the status quo and attendant discriminatory patterns of behavior and thought. I threw off shackles, went against the grain, learning about the obligations that came with freedom—not just for my group but for everyone.

Those who believe in a diverse America must do as I and my team of operatives did: train a new generation of leaders of color—not just those who hope to stand for office, but those working the precincts, designing and implementing the ground games, raising the money, and developing the message to galvanize American voters, dare I say all Americans.

The challenges faced today and in the coming years are immense. The huge inflow of money into our political system is overwhelming and dangerous to democratic society. It especially could have an adverse affect on people of color, whose resources do not, for example, rival that of many whites in the country's political or economic system. Worthwhile minority candidates must surmount huge barriers to gain a seat in office. That means that whites and those seeking to advance candidates of color must teach the art of political fundraising.

In addition, the science of political campaigns must be transmitted. More African American, Hispanic and Asian operatives must learn the basics of voter targeting and statistical analysis based on past precinct-by-precinct turnout in locales. While it's true that times have changed with the introduction of computers, the Internet and social media, the organizational cells remains unchanged. More trained experts, more political scientists are critical, if the Third Wave in the political development of people of color in America is to be as successful as the first two.

Electioneering is a noble cause, one in which I see many young whites participating. My hope is that they will respond to the call of this book to share with others what they know, to build coalitions, to assure the continuity of political progress across a diverse nation.

Without the help of whites such as myself, I doubt that African Americans would have experienced the swift and decisive political influence they gained. In telling my story, however, I may have ignored my late friend Bill Simpson's dictum: "The perfect consultant is one who can walk across freshly poured concrete and leave no footprints."